MW01056794

Sara Miller McCune founded SAGE Publishing in 1965 to support the dissemination of usable knowledge and educate a global community. SAGE publishes more than 1000 journals and over 800 new books each year, spanning a wide range of subject areas. Our growing selection of library products includes archives, data, case studies, and video. SAGE remains majority owned by our founder and after her lifetime will become owned by a charitable trust that secures the company's continued independence.

Los Angeles | London | New Delhi | Singapore | Washington DC | Melbourne

California Politics

For my sisters: Elise, Natasha, Juleann, Magdalena, and Simona

California Politics

A Primer

Seventh Edition

Renée B. Van Vechten

University of Redlands

FOR INFORMATION:

CQ Press
An imprint of SAGE Publications, Inc.
2455 Teller Road
Thousand Oaks, California 91320
E-mail: order@sagepub.com

SAGE Publications Ltd.
1 Oliver's Yard
55 City Road
London, EC1Y 1SP
United Kingdom

SAGE Publications India Pvt. Ltd.
Unit No 323-333, Third Floor, F-Block
International Trade Tower Nehru Place
New Delhi – 110 019
India

SAGE Publications Asia-Pacific Pte. Ltd.
18 Cross Street #10-10/11/12
China Square Central
Singapore 048423

Printed in the United States of America

ISBN: 978-1-0718-7544-5

This book is printed on acid-free paper.

Acquisitions Editor: Anna Villarruel

Editorial Assistant: Avren Keating

Production Editor: Vijayakumar

Copy Editors: Benny Willy Stephen

Typesetter: TNQ Technologies

Indexer: TNQ Technologies

Cover Designer: Candice Harman

23 24 25 26 27 10 9 8 7 6 5 4 3 2 1

BRIEF CONTENTS

DETAILED CONTENTS

ABOUT THE AUTHOR

Renée B. Van Vechten holds the Fletcher Jones Endowed Chair in American Politics and Policy at the University of Redlands where she is a professor of political science and chair of the public policy undergraduate program. She earned a BA in political science from the University of San Diego and a PhD from the University of California, Irvine. Van Vechten's political science research examines legislative processes and behavior, including the impacts of political reforms such as term limits. In addition to teaching about California politics, her courses concentrate on American institutions such as Congress, as well as the politics of food, the environment, and political reform. Her expertise on state-level politics and policy is evident in her textbook, *California Politics: A Primer*, and her scholarship on pedagogy and instructional practices has extended to curricular planning, research methods, online discussion forums, simulations, and internships. She was the lead editor of and contributor to the open-source book and resource collection, *Political Science Internships: Towards Best Practices* (APSA 2021: https://apsanet.org /internshipbook). Van Vechten has served as an executive board member for Pi Sigma Alpha, the national political science honors society, and on the American Political Science Association (APSA) Council and Executive Board as chair of the Teaching and Learning Policy Committee and as chair of the APSA Political Science Education organized member section. She has been a track moderator for the APSA Teaching and Learning Conference (TLC) several times, and was a founding co-chair for the first TLC at APSA in 2018. Service to APSA includes membership on awards committees, working groups, and two Presidential Task Forces (on Technology, 2015–16; on New Partnerships, 2017–20) that helped establish APSA's online teaching library, EDUCATE. Van Vechten is also active in the Western Political Science Association, having several times co-chaired a conference-within-a-conference on teaching and learning. She has received several teaching awards, including the Rowman and Littlefield Award for Innovative Teaching in Political Science (via APSA) in 2008, APSA's only national teaching award at that time. A resident of San Diego County, she is frequently consulted by local media for commentary about state and national politics.

PREFACE

Seduction has been California's superpower. The Golden State beckons immigrants, coaxes the optimistic to rebuild after wildfires ravage their neighborhoods, conjures new neighborhoods into being, and she entices struggling middle class families, college students, and DREAMers to envision a better life. The appeal of undiscovered riches still arouses hopes, dreams, and plans. But the California that dazzles the imagination remains elusive and her gilted robes have lost much of their allure.

As home values have reached highs never imagined even a few years ago, many residents have been priced out of local markets, and others are cashing out and heading for locations where the cost of living is manageable. Drought, fires, and floods have traumatized communities. For the first time since California became a state, the population has declined. Others are considering moving out of state for the first time in their lives. Although a mass exodus has not yet occurred, state representatives are eyeing a possible "brain drain" with concern, and tinkering with policies to stem the tide by refunding taxes, helping homebuyers, creating new infrastructure and construction jobs, investing in drought resistance, and establishing benefits for women seeking reproductive care, among other things.

A booming state economy made these measures possible in mid-2022, but economic expansion concentrates among those at the top. Growing inequality has bruised Californians in ways not unlike the rest of the states. Yet the state's economy continues to buoy the nation's fortunes, and new laws have enriched its reputation as an extraordinary place where "big things happen." Policy makers aim to shift all new vehicle sales to zero-emission models by 2035 and reduce waste by outlawing noncompostable single-use plastic, and new requirements and restrictions target law enforcement's dealings with the public—communities of color, particularly. After having fought Trump administration policies tooth and nail, Democrats at the state level have reasserted their support for immigrants, regardless of their status, extending limited assistance to them in the form of basic health care access, legal aid, and in past years, coronavirus relief aid. California has also implemented a "right to sue" over gun violence that mimics Texas's abortion law. Racial and ethnic justice continue to motivate policy making and policing reforms, which extends to the nation's first task force to study reparations for descendants of enslaved people.

Exceptionalism seems to run in California's political blood, and these developments reinforce the view that California occupies a class of its own. But how extraordinary are California's politics, really? This short text, *California Politics: A Primer*, attempts to outline this puzzle, providing readers with analytical tools to piece together an answer to this broad question. By emphasizing how history, political culture, rules, and institutions influence choices that lie at the heart of governing, the text moves beyond mere recitation of facts, pressing the reader to think about how these forces conspire to shape politics today and how they will help determine the state of affairs tomorrow. It asks the reader to consider what exceptional politics are and aren't, and what might be accomplished through government.

Because this book is intended to provide the essentials of California politics, brevity and breadth eclipse detail and depth. The following pages form a tidy snapshot of how the state is governed and how its politics work. Timely examples succinctly clarify trends and concepts, but to limit the book's length, some developments are given only brief attention or a passing mention. Instructors should consult the endnotes for additional data, resources, and details they can use to embellish their lectures and class discussions. Strong visuals in the form of cartograms, figures, charts, graphs, maps, and photos also allow readers to discern the basics quickly, but readers should also take time to uncover the clues to understanding politics and tease out the rich stories and patterns contained in these illustrations and in the accompanying captions.

WHAT'S NEW TO THE SEVENTH EDITION

Scholarly research and the most current government reports available inform this scrupulously updated text, which covers policy developments and elections through mid-2022. With COVID-19 no longer dominating the economy or political conversations, this edition focuses on policy developments that have been brought about by an unbalanced economic recovery that has enabled the moneyed few to thrive, most of the rest to struggle paying the bills, and Democratic state officials' efforts to spread the wealth; readers will also note that almost all monetary references (budget allocations) are now in the "b's" (billions). Notable revisions include a discussion of the 2021 gubernatorial recall (events discussed in Chapter 2 and mechanics in Chapter 3). How the courts are addressing inequities is covered in Chapter 6. The treatment of budget surpluses is described in Chapter 8, where infrastructure plans and the State Appropriations Limit (SAL, or Gann Limit) are taken up. In Chapter 9, particular attention is given to the dominance of Democrats and both the mechanics and effects of universal vote-by-mail and other electoral reforms. Summoning the importance of political geography, which is manifest in racial and ethnic divides and human development, profiles of the "Five Californias" (a product of the Measure of America program series produced by the Social Science Research Council and advanced in *A Portrait of California* by Kristen Lewis) have been renewed in Chapter 10. Racial and ethnic politics are addressed throughout the text, and public policies relating to the environment, housing and homelessness, incarceration, and infrastructure, among others, provide measures of the state's exceptionalism and exemplify California's status as either a leader or an outlier.

Further, informative visuals have been added or revised: one cartogram depicts recent protest activity in the U.S., and the other compares major spending on three ballot measures. Charts, maps, and graphs incorporate the most recent data releases by the secretary of state, the Legislative Analyst's Office, public affairs research organizations, and other state agencies.

Key terms are indicated with bold lettering in the text and are listed, with definitions and page numbers for reference, at the end of each chapter. Terms that may be considered secondary in importance are italicized.

TEACHING RESOURCES

This text includes an array of instructor teaching materials designed to save you time and to help you keep students engaged. To learn more, visit **sagepub.com** or contact your SAGE representative at **sagepub.com/findmyrep**.

ACKNOWLEDGMENTS

The clean and vigorous style in which this book is written is meant to prime the reader for engaging conversations about California politics. An expert crew at CQ Press launched this text, namely Charisse Kiino and former editor Nancy Matuszak, who skillfully shepherded the project through the first four editions. I couldn't have found a better development editor than in Avren Keating, whom I thank for their publishing prowess, incisiveness, responsiveness, and also extreme patience (during what seemed an endless writing process!). Many thanks also go to the smart acquisition, production, and marketing team that included acquisitions editor Anna Villarruel, marketing manager Jennifer Haldeman, production editor Vijayakumar, and copyeditor Benny Willy Stephen, whose premium work earns my admiration. I'm also honored that three editorial cartoons executed by my talented daughter, Ava, are included. With much appreciation for those colleagues who have taken the time to provide essential feedback on previous editions.

There are not enough thanks for the many extraordinary public employees of California who have helped provide critical source material for the book, from the responsive staff of the Legislative Analyst's Office to the legislative standouts such as Alison Dinmore Hughes of the Senate Housing Committee and Brian Ebbert of the Speaker's Office, on whose sharp insights and institutional memory I have come to rely. Molly Wiltshire and Mark Tollefson of the governor's office extended invaluable assistance, and yet more thanks go to photographers Jeff Walters and Lorie Shelley, Mark Stivers, Senator Anthony Portantino, the staffs of (and) Assembly members James Ramos and Rosilicie Ochoa-Bogh, and many (other) University of Redlands alums whose political insights continue to shape my theorizing, research, writing, and learning about California politics. The world needs more people like Redlands alum Matt Rafeedie, who provided impeccable research support when I needed it most. I stand in awe of the Measure of America research team led by Kristin Lewis and data experts Rebecca Gluskin and Laura Laderman, who dove deeper into their Portrait of California 2021–22 files and graciously provided exactly what we needed, and Alex Powers at SSRC who made that connection possible. Many thanks to Bill Higgins at CalCOG and the meticulous researchers at the Public Policy Institute of California, especially Dean Bonner, for their assistance and feedback provided. I'm indebted to my Irish cousin, Bill Stokes, who can be counted on for a filling serving of sagacity and neighborliness any time of year. A devoted community of teacher–scholars at the University of Redlands and in the teaching and learning mafia, from Oregon to New Jersey, remind me about what's worth working for and towards. My friends and family give life meaning: Charlie, my other half, is my perfect life partner, inspiring me to do good, to be better, and actually take vacations. He is the best dad to our Ava and Zachary (not to mention Remo), both of whom continue to wow me as they engage two different California institutions of higher ed on their terms (Fight on and Go Ags!). I also thank my late mom, Ann, and dad, Joe, faith-filled and selfless exemplars who taught me to live fully each day and find happiness in small things; Suzanne, who has gifted St. Joey of Vista with a renaissance; and my late in-laws, Pete and Ruth, for their moxie and legacy of generosity.

1 INTRODUCTION

As if the State of California weren't exceptional enough, it could be considered one of the largest countries in the world. Only four other nations had a larger gross domestic product than California in 2021, and its $3.36 trillion economy outrivaled those of India and all European countries except Germany.[1] With nearly 40 million residents, the state's population is on par with that of Canada.[2] In 2022, California was home to 186 billionaires, more than in Hong Kong and Russia combined.[3] Its territorial spread includes breathtaking coastlines, fertile farmland both natural and human made, one of the globe's hottest deserts, the highest and lowest points in the continental United States, dense urban zones, twenty-one mountain ranges, and ancient redwood forests—a resource-rich expanse with 1,100 miles of coastline and an area that could accommodate a dozen East Coast states.

Through good times and bad, California's reputation for being the "great exception" among the American states has intensified since the political journalist Carey McWilliams characterized it that way in 1949. The state is an exaggeration; it sparks global trends, and national and world issues permeate the state's politics. California is a state of extremes: climate change, cost of living, immigration, civil rights, public health crises, economic tides, and waves of social unrest push and pull on those who make policy decisions for one of the world's most diverse political communities.

Unlike elected officials in most democratic governments, however, California's representatives share responsibility for policymaking with ordinary Californians, who make laws through the initiative process at the state and local levels. This **hybrid political system** (a combination of direct and representative democracy) provides an outlet for voters' general distrust of politicians and dissatisfaction with representative government and enables the electorate to reshape it over time. If **politics** is a process through which people with differing goals and ideals try to manage their conflicts by working together to allocate values (valued things) for society—which requires bargaining and compromise—then California's system is especially susceptible to repeated attempts to fix what's perceived as broken, and parts of it may be periodically upended. For more than 100 years, the initiative process has permitted voters, wealthy corporations, and interest groups to experiment with the state's political system, from rebooting elections to

1

retuning taxation rates to reworking the lawmaking rules. Some of these reforms, which are discussed throughout this book, are celebrated as triumphs. Proposition 13 in 1978, for example, deflated ballooning property tax rates for homeowners (limited to 1 percent of the property's sale price) and arrested rate increases. On the other hand, direct democracy tends to promote all-or-nothing solutions that have been contrived without bargaining and compromise, two hallmarks of democratic lawmaking.

Despite people's faith in their own abilities to govern themselves, California's bulging population ensures that public policy issues exist on a massive scale, absorbing the attention of tens of thousands of policymakers at the local and state levels. More than one of every eight U.S. residents lives in majority-minority California, and 26.6 percent of Californians are foreign-born—the largest proportion among the states, with most immigrants today arriving from Asia as opposed to Latin America in recent years.[4] Among the entire population are approximately 2.6 million undocumented immigrants.[5] In 2010, just over 10 percent of the population was over age 65; by 2030, it will be one out of four people—a demographic group that saturates health-care systems.[6] California's criminal population is second only to that of Texas in size; about 140,000 remain in custody or are under some form of correctional control. Over half of the nation's unsheltered persons live in California, their futures complicated by a severe affordable housing shortage.[7]

These days, high inflation rates and sharply rising costs of living and doing business are squeezing most Californians: combined bills from groceries, gasoline, housing, energy, and other basic necessities have contributed to the out-migration of companies and people to states that are more affordable overall.[8] More homeowners are cashing out and moving out as rapidly rising home values have created record-high home equity, wealth that concentrates among older residents. California's population has *declined* for the first time in its history. In response to these developments, and thanks to a $308 billion budget (2022–23) that places California on a scale with small nations, Governor Gavin Newsom and Democratic legislators have allocated $17 billion for broad-based relief in the form of tax refunds; grants and assistance programs for renters, homeowners, and small businesses; accelerated the minimum wage increase to $15.50 for all employers as of January 1, 2023 (it's even higher in some cities); and raised aid payments to low-income residents. The state manages an unusually strong set of resources and aims to spread them widely, barring an economic recession.

Californians have found plenty of ways to distinguish themselves politically from the rest of the country, although they resemble most Americans in their general aversion to politics and feeling overtaxed.[9] The state votes Democratic: fully 63.5 percent of Californians voted for presidential nominee Joe Biden in 2020, repudiating Republican President Trump (only the percentages from Hawai'i, Maryland, and Vermont were higher) in the 2020 race.[10] California was among the first states to legally recognize a third gender option, enabling persons who do not identify as either female or male to mark "X" instead on official documents, and since 2003 has legally protected persons from discrimination based on sexual orientation and gender identity expression. The state is poised to manufacture its own low-cost insulin supply for diabetics. The nation's first consumer privacy law, now over five years old, gives individuals more control over their personal information. Following the U.S. Supreme Court's decision to overturn *Roe v. Wade*, California voters also added reproductive rights to the state constitution in 2022.

Senate President Pro Tem Toni Atkins (2018–present) plays a role in authoring landmark bills such as SCA 10, a Senate Constitutional Amendment to include reproductive rights in the state constitution. The legislature voted to place it on the November 2022 ballot and voters approved it by a large margin.

Source: California Senate Democrats via YouTube.

California has also tested the boundaries of federal versus state power in recent years. In defiance of Donald Trump administration policies that elected Democrats perceived to be antienvironment, the state doubled down on combating climate change through investments in green energy and tougher greenhouse gas emissions standards that it had been the first to establish in state law (Assembly Bill (AB) 32). California was the first state to legalize marijuana use for medical purposes in 1996 but behind several states in approving its recreational use in 2016. The state also successfully defended DACA (the federal Deferred Action for Childhood Arrivals program) in court on behalf of California's 183,000 "DREAMers" (children who were brought to the United States without documentation and have grown up in the country without formal legal status), and the state's longstanding DREAM Act (AB 540) extends in-state tuition and financial aid eligibility to approximately 75,000 students in California's public universities and community colleges.[11] Controversially, with Senate Bill (SB) 54 in 2017, the state became a "sanctuary" for nonviolent, noncriminal undocumented immigrants. As a **sanctuary state**, local and state law enforcement officials are prohibited from expending their resources to help federal agents enforce deportations, with exceptions for public safety considerations: local police have discretion to hold violent felons for federal authorities, immigration agents may interview jailed individuals, and database information may be shared about convicted criminals. Otherwise, state officials will not aid the Department of Homeland Security in targeting undocumented persons for removal from the United States. State Republican lawmakers have not succeeded in repealing these rights, and federal courts have affirmed that states have no obligation to enforce federal law.[12] The state also has ensured that state and local governments cannot use personal information to create religious registries of any kind.

Extreme weather events and their effects amplify California's distinctiveness, yet as former Governor Jerry Brown warned, it's "the new normal."[13] Extended drought and a bark beetle infestation have stricken forests, killing 172 million trees since 2010 and placing the rest in "mortal peril," elevating the risk of both wildfires and erosion that can transform whole regions into catastrophic infernos.[14] Of the twenty largest fires recorded in the past 90 years, all but two occurred in the last two decades.[15] The continued overpumping of groundwater due to lack of rain has caused land to sink faster than ever, a phenomenon called *subsidence* that buckles roads, irrigation canals, bridges, and pipes, costing state and local governments millions to fix. Climate extremes also include sudden deluges carried by atmospheric rivers, as in 2023, that can devastate infrastructure—although California is hardly alone in its vulnerability to such events.[16]

CalFIRE (Department of Forestry and Fire Protection) operates over 530 facilities statewide and will add new firefighter crews, infrastructure such as helicopter bases, and equipment in the next few years to help prevent and fight drought-fueled wildfires.

Source: Luis Sinco via Getty Images.

Water shortages have choked farmland, fisheries, and towns; they've forced steep cutbacks on water use and starved hydroelectric power plants—only to be replaced by floods. Typically, Central Valley Farmers jockey for the same water that helps feed Southern California, and they are pitted against environmentalists over how much flow should be diverted to replenish the failing Delta ecosystem, the complex Sacramento–San Joaquin River Delta estuary located east of San Francisco. A plan to pipe Sacramento River water underneath the imperiled Delta through a giant tunnel is the latest in a sixty-year saga of proposals that contains more drama than a Netflix series.[17] The current proposition, which would likely take at least ten years to realize and whose price tag would surpass the size of many states' entire annual budgets, illustrates the magnitude of issues in California, and also demonstrates the hazards of shifting from the status quo when big money and high-powered interests are at stake.

The availability, cost, distribution, storage, and cleanliness of fresh water represent a fraction of the complex, interrelated issues that state and local elected officials deal with year-round, a "must-do" list that grows perpetually. Climate change is altering delicate ecosystems, spawning invasive pests that carry infectious diseases, and it affects whether California can supply the fresh produce, craft beer, and wines that the world enjoys. Sustainability challenges loom while deteriorating bridges, roads, storm drains, water mains and storage, sewage treatment facilities, schools, and jails compete for the public's limited attention and money. New and affordable housing and expanding broadband access are also among the state's public **infrastructure** needs, systems that earn mostly C- and D grades for being in mediocre condition overall and requiring attention.[18] These needs range into the hundreds of billions of dollars, a deep hole that the state continues to fill—currently through an ambitious (but realistic) multiyear $52 billion infrastructure plan that builds on significant prior year investments and budget surpluses, as well as substantial federal commitments that will add billions more (Figure 1.1).[19]

Whether the goal is greater police accountability, lowering college fees, or restricting offshore oil drilling, different interests compete through the political process to get what they want. From small cities to Sacramento, governing officials weigh private against public interests, and generally they work hard to fix problems experienced by their constituents—a job that also requires them to balance the needs of their own districts against those of their city, county, or the entire state. This grand balancing act is but one reason politics often appears irrational and complex, but like the U.S. government, California's system was designed that way, mostly through deliberate choice but also in response to the unintended consequences of prior decisions. California's puzzle of governing institutions reflects repeated attempts to manage conflicts that result from millions of people putting demands on a system that creates both winners

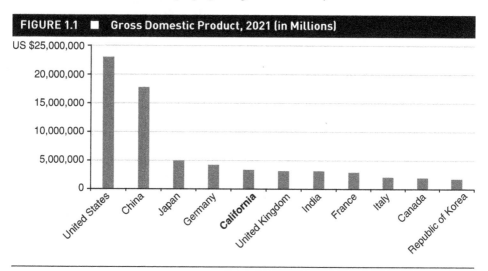

FIGURE 1.1 ■ Gross Domestic Product, 2021 (in Millions)

Sources: "Gross Domestic Product 2022," World Bank, July 1, 2022, https://databankfiles.worldbank.org/data/download/GDP.pdf; "GDP by State, 2021," Bureau of Economic Analysis, Interactive Tools, updated March 31, 2022.

and losers—not all of whom give up quietly when they lose. Like their federal counterparts, state officials tend to respond to the most persistent, organized, and well-funded members of society; on the other hand, some losers in California can reverse their fortunes by skillfully employing the tools of direct democracy to sidestep elected representatives altogether.

PRINCIPLES FOR UNDERSTANDING CALIFORNIA POLITICS

It may seem counterintuitive given the complexity of the state's problems, but California's politics can be explained and understood logically—although political outcomes are just as often frustrating and irresponsible as they are praiseworthy and necessary. In short, six fundamental concepts—choice, political culture, institutions, collective action, rules, and history—can help us understand state politics just as they help us understand national or even local democratic politics. These concepts are employed throughout this book to explain how Californians and their representatives make governing decisions and to provide a starting point for evaluating California's political system: does it work as intended? Do citizens have realistic expectations about what problems government can solve, the services or values it provides, and how efficiently it can do so? How does California's political system compare to others?

Source: Ava Van Vechten.

Choices: At the Heart of Politics. Our starting point is the premise that *choices* are at the core of politics. Citizens make *explicit* political choices when they decide not to participate in an election or when they cast a vote, but they also make *implicit* political choices when they send their children to private instead of public schools or refill a water bottle instead of buying a new one. Legislators' jobs consist of a series of choices regarding what to say, which issues to ignore, whose recommendations to take, which phone calls to return, and how to cast a vote. Choices are shaped by not only personal, "micro-level" factors such as values, beliefs, and background but also larger, "macro-level" forces in society, politics, the economy, and the immediate setting where rules, bargaining, and compromise come into play (Figure 1.2).

BOX 1.1
COMPARATIVE FAST FACTS ON CALIFORNIA

	California	Texas	United States
Capital	**Sacramento**	**Austin**	**Washington, D.C.**
Statehood	September 9, 1850 (31st state)	December 29, 1845 (28th state)	Declared independence from Great Britain July 4, 1776
Number of US House Members	52 (one less after 2020)	38 (two more after 2020)	435
Number of Counties	58	254	50 states
Largest City by Population*	Los Angeles, 3,849,297	Houston, 2,288,250	New York, 8,467,513
Total Population*	39,237,836	29,527,941	331,893,745
Percentage of Foreign-Born Persons, 2021*	26.6%	16.8%	13.5%
Median Annual Household Income (2020 Dollars)*	$78,672	$63,826	$64,994
Percentage of Persons Living below Poverty Level*	11.5%	13.4%	11.4%

*Population/demographic figures are based on the U.S. 2020 Census; estimates were current as of July 1, 2021 ("Quickfacts," U.S. Census Bureau, July 1, 2021, https://www.census.gov/quickfacts/fact/table/CA,US/PST045221). California's Department of Finance (DOF) estimated the state population at 39,185,606 (on January 1, 2022), or 117,552 fewer than in the previous year. "Slowing State Population Decline Puts Latest Population at 39,185,000," DOF, State of California, May 2, 2022.

Source: "QuickFacts: Population Estimates, July 1, 2021," U.S. Census Bureau, accessed July 31, 2022, https://www.census.gov/quickfacts/CA.

FIGURE 1.2 ■ Racial and Ethnic Makeup of California

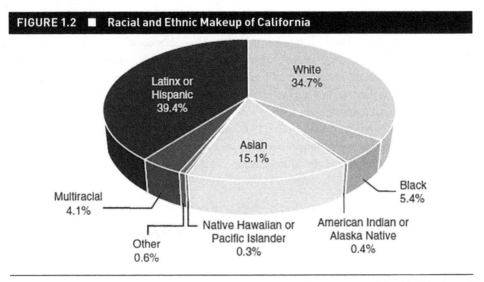

Latinx or
Hispanic
39.4%

White
34.7%

Asian
15.1%

Multiracial
4.1%

Black
5.4%

Other
0.6%

Native Hawaiian or
Pacific Islander
0.3%

American Indian or
Alaska Native
0.4%

Source: "QuickFacts: Population Estimates, July 1, 2021," U.S. Census Bureau, accessed July 31, 2022, https://www.census.gov/quickfacts/CA.

Political Culture*: Collective Attitudes and Beliefs About the Role of Government.* In large, heterogeneous societies crammed with people motivated by different goals, interests, and values, a successful political system provides a process for narrowing choices to a manageable number and allows many participants to reconcile their differences as they make choices together. The decisions and customs that emerge from this process generally express the attitudes, beliefs, norms, and values about government that a political majority holds, and give their governing system a distinct culture—a **political culture** that varies from state to state. Compared to Texans or Nevadans, Californians tend to focus on equity and are more willing to regulate businesses in favor of workers and the environment and to offer public programs that address those at the margins of society. Three other features that define California's political culture are a historical fondness for reforming government through ballot measures, a preference for Democratic officials but general detachment from political parties, and a willingness to use state regulatory power—themes that will resurface throughout this book as we examine California's exceptionalism.

Institutions*: Organizations and Systems That Help People Solve Collective Action Problems.* Political systems also facilitate compromises, trade-offs, and bargains that lead to acceptable solutions or alternatives. Institutions help organize this kind of action. Political **institutions** are organizations built to manage conflict by defining particular roles and rules for those who participate in them. In short, they bring people together to solve problems on behalf of a community or society, enabling the authoritative, or official, use of power. Election systems are a good example: there are rules about who can vote and who can run for office, how the process will be controlled, and how disputes resulting from them will be resolved. Through institutions like elections, **collective action**—working together for mutual benefit—can take place. The same can be said of other institutions such as traffic courts and political parties; in each setting, people work together to solve their problems and allocate goods for a society. It should be noted, however, that the use of power and authority through political institutions can benefit some and harm others; fair and equal outcomes are not automatically ensured through democratic institutions.

Rules: Codes or Regulations Defining How Governing Power May Be Used. Rules also matter. Rules are authoritative statements, codes, or regulations that define who possesses the power to help govern and how they may legitimately use it, and rules create incentives for action or inaction. Rules are framed in constitutions; they may be expressed as laws or in administrative rules, executive orders, or court opinions, for example. For instance, if one party reaches supermajority status in the state legislature (as has been the case with Democrats since 2016), the minority party is rendered virtually powerless because their votes are not needed to pass special bills or taxes that require approval by two-thirds of the membership. Unwritten rules, also known as **norms**, also guide behavior, and daily interactions help enforce what is expected and acceptable, as reflected in the degree of civility among politicians.

History: The Past Helps Set the Terms of the Present. Rules are also the results of choices made throughout history, and over time, a body of rules will change and grow in response to cultural shifts, influential leaders, uprisings, natural disasters, scandals, economic trends, and other forces—some gradual, some sudden—creating further opportunities and incentives for political action. Enormous economic tides that define eras (think the Great Recession or the Great Depression) exert especially disruptive forces in politics because behemoth governments are not designed to respond nimbly to rapid and unanticipated changes; budgets and programs are planned months and years in advance, with history providing clues to decision makers about probable developments. Sudden readjustments, particularly those made in hard times, will reverberate far into the future.

Thus, recognizing that both choices and the rules that condition them are made within a given historical context goes a long way toward explaining each state's distinctive political system. A state's political culture also contributes to that distinctiveness. These are the elements that make New York's state government so different from the governments of Idaho, Tennessee, and every other state, and we should keep them in mind as we consider how California's governing institutions developed—and whether California belongs in a class of its own. In essence, a unique set of rules, its culture, and its history are key to understanding California politics. They help explain the relationship between Californians and their government, how competing expectations and values propel change, and why elected officials can have a hard time running the state, even when times are good—and especially when they're not.

Many influencers, from *New York Times* editors to business leaders, have at one point or another declared California to be teetering on the brink of collapse, "ungovernable," or a lost paradise. That chatter is being revived as economic conditions push a greater number of people to leave or consider leaving the state for more affordable places. Among those who either cannot leave or can afford to stay, the sentiment that things can and should be better motivates many to pursue change through politics at the local and state levels. And, like the journalist Carey McWilliams, they believe that "nothing is quite yet what it should be in California."[20]

The Golden State remains a land of mythical proportions, set apart from the rest by its commanding economy, geography, and population. And as with fairy-tale giants, it falls hard when calamity hits, and recovery takes an agonizingly long time. On the other hand, a pumping economic engine has led to record budgets and reserves, and recently that largesse has translated into targeted state spending on infrastructure and broad-based relief in ways that reflect the majority party Democrats' vision of social justice. This book explores the reasons for the current state of affairs and evaluates how history, culture, institutions, and rules contribute to the sense that California is exceptional. Diverse generations have brought its distinctiveness to life, and collectively they have created a political system that at first glance seems incomparable in all its complexity, experimentation, and breadth. In this book we ask whether California is a justifiable outlier, a state whose politics defy simple categorization. Along the way, we also consider what it will take for California to achieve the foundational aim of a democracy: for government to serve the people's welfare and interests effectively, comprehensively, and sensibly over the long term.

The California state capitol building in Sacramento serves as a stage for public demonstrations and events.

Source: Renée B. Van Vechten.

KEY TERMS

Collective action: working together for mutual benefit.

Hybrid political system: a political system that combines elements of direct and representative democracy.

Infrastructure: physical facilities, structures, installations, or systems providing essential services to societies, such as roads, airports, water treatment plants, or internet connectivity.

Institutions: systems and organizations that help people solve their collective action problems by defining particular roles and rules for those who participate in them and by managing conflict.

Norms: unwritten rules that guide acceptable or expected behavior, enforced through daily interactions.

Political culture: the attitudes, beliefs, and values about government that a majority in a state hold, as expressed in their customs and the political choices its citizens and leaders make.

Politics: a process of bargaining and compromise through which people with differing goals and ideals try to manage their conflicts by working together to allocate values for society.

Sanctuary state: a term referring to a state that adopts policies or laws shielding undocumented immigrants from federal arrest or deportation, through one or more measures; California law prohibits state law enforcement from cooperating with federal authorities in facilitating the apprehension or deportation of persons with unauthorized status.

2 CRITICAL JUNCTURES
California's Political History in Brief

EARLY CALIFORNIA

The contours of California's contemporary political landscape began to take shape in 1542, when Spanish explorer Juan Cabrillo claimed the Native American lands now known as San Diego for a distant monarchy, thereby paving the way for European settlements along the West Coast. Assisted by Spanish troops, colonization followed the founding of Catholic missions throughout Latin America and spread to Alta (then "northern") California with Mission San Diego de Alcalá in 1769. These missions, as well as fortified military presidios (army posts), were constructed along what became known as El Camino Real, or the King's Highway, a path that roughly followed a line of major tribal establishments. Native peoples were systematically subordinated and decimated by foreign diseases, soldiers, and ways of life that were unnatural to them, and the huge mission complexes and ranches, or rancheros, that transformed their lands became the focal points for food production, social activity, and economic industry in the region.

The western realm containing California became part of Mexico when that country gained independence from Spain in 1821, and for the next 25 years, Mexicans governed the region, constructing presidios and installing military leaders to protect the towns taking shape up and down the coast. In 1846, a rebellious band of American settlers, declaring California a republic, raised the hastily patched Grizzly Bear Flag at Sonoma. Within weeks, the U.S. Navy lay claim to California, and for the next two years, an uncomfortable mix of American military rule and locally elected "alcaldes" (mayors who acted both as lawmakers and judges) prevailed.

Following the Mexican-American War of 1848 that ended with the Treaty of Guadalupe Hidalgo, California became the new U.S. frontier astride a new international border. The simultaneous discovery of gold near Sacramento provoked an onslaught of settlers in what would be the first of several significant population waves to flood the West Coast during the next 125 years. The rush to the Golden State was on.

MAP 2.1 ■ California's Missions

THE RISE OF THE SOUTHERN PACIFIC RAILROAD

The tumult that lawless gold-seekers stirred up convinced many that civil government was needed. Spurning slavery and embracing self-governance, a group of mostly pre-gold-rush settlers and Mexican-American War veterans convened to write a state constitution in 1849 (replaced by a major revision in 1879); a year later, the U.S. Congress granted statehood, bypassing the usual compulsory territorial stage, and shortly thereafter Sacramento became the state's permanent capital. Although gold had already lured nearly 100,000 adventurers to the state in less than two years, the region was considered a mostly untamed and distant outpost, separated from the East Coast by treacherous terrain and thousands of miles of ocean travel. Growing demand for more reliable linkages to the rest of the country led to the building of the transcontinental railroad in 1869, an undertaking that resulted in the recruitment of thousands of Chinese laborers and millions of acres of federal land grants to a few railroad companies. Eleven million acres in California were granted to the Southern Pacific Railroad alone.[1]

The wildly successful rail enterprise not only opened the West to rapid development near the turn of the century but also consolidated economic and political power in the Central Pacific Railroad, later renamed the Southern Pacific Railroad. Owned by barons Collis Huntington, Mark Hopkins, Leland Stanford, and Charles Crocker—the **Big Four**—the Southern Pacific extended its reach to virtually all forms of shipping and transportation. Their monopoly had direct impacts on all major commercial activity within the state, from wheat prices to land

Enduring persistent racial discrimination, punishing conditions, and a lack of labor and safety protections, Chinese immigrants laid thousands of miles of railroad tracks during the late 1800s and early 1900s.

Source: © Everett Collection Historical/Alamy.

values and from bank lending to the availability of lumber. The railroad tycoons' landholdings enabled them to control the prosperity or demise of entire towns that depended on rail stops throughout the West. Power didn't come cheap, however, and they fostered "friendships" in the White House, Congress, courts, and local and state governments by finding every influential person's "price." As famously depicted in the (1882) editorial cartoon, "The Curse of California," the "S.P." (Southern Pacific Railroad) dominated every major sector of the state's economy—and politics—like a relentless octopus.

PROGRESSIVISM

The Southern Pacific's hold over California government during the late 1800s cannot be overestimated. According to one historian, a generation of Californians believed that the influence of the railroad extended from the governor's mansion in Sacramento to their own town halls, and that the political machine determined "who should sit in city councils and on boards of supervisors; who should be sent to the House of Representatives and to the Senate in Washington; what laws should be enacted by the legislature, and what decisions should be rendered from the bench."[2]

The Southern Pacific's grip over California industry and politics was smashed, bit by bit, by muckraking journalists whose stories were pivotal in the creation of federal regulations aimed at breaking monopolies; by the prosecution of San Francisco's corrupt political boss, Abe Ruef; and by the rise of a national movement called "**Progressivism**." Governor Hiram Johnson (1911–17) personified the idealistic Progressive spirit through his efforts to eliminate every private interest from government and restore power to the people.

Governor Johnson spearheaded an ambitious reform agenda that addressed a wide range of social, political, and economic issues targeted by Progressives in other U.S. states. His agenda was not only grounded in a fundamental distrust of political parties, which had been hijacked by the Southern Pacific in California, but also built on an emerging philosophy that government could be run efficiently, like a business. Workers' rights, municipal ownership of utility companies, conservation, morals laws, and the assurance of fair political representation topped the list of items Hiram Johnson tackled with the help of the California legislature after he entered office in 1911.

New laws directly targeted the ties political parties had to both the railroads and potential voters. Although *secret voting* had become state law in 1896, the practice was reinforced as a means to protect elections and ensure fairness. The ability of political party bosses to "select and elect" candidates for political offices was undercut with *direct primary elections*, whereby any party member could become a candidate without obtaining permission from any higher-ups, and regular party members could choose their nominees freely. The legislature also reclassified local elected offices as "**nonpartisan**," meaning that the political party labels of candidates did not appear on the ballot if they were running for municipal offices, including city councils, local school boards, and judgeships. Efficiency, the Progressives believed, demanded that voters and officials be blind to partisanship, because petty divisions wasted valuable time and resources. They felt the important concern was the *best person* for the position, not the candidate's political party identification; after all, they argued, there was no partisan way to pave a street. This principle extended to government employees, who would now be part of a **civil service** system based on merit (*what* one knew about a position and *how well* one knew it), rather than the former system based on **patronage** (*who* one knew and party loyalty). All of these practices continue today.

A more ingenious method of limiting political party power was accomplished through **cross-filing**, which meant that candidates' names could appear on *any* party's primary election ballot without their party label indicated. In effect, Republicans could be listed on Democrats' ballots and vice versa, thereby allowing candidates to become the official nominees for more than one party. This rule, which remained on the books until 1959, initially helped Progressives but later allowed Republicans to dominate the legislature despite a Democratic Party majority of voters after 1934.

Progressives transformed the relationship between citizens and government. They accomplished this first by *guaranteeing women the right to vote* in 1911 and then by adopting the tools of *direct democracy*: the *recall*, the *referendum*, and the *initiative* process (discussed in Chapter 3), arguably the most significant of all their reforms. By vesting the people with the power to change the constitution or make laws directly—even new laws that could override those already in place—Progressives redistributed political power and essentially redesigned the basic structure of government. No longer was California a purely representative democracy; it now had a *hybrid government* that combined direct and representative forms of democracy. Elected officials would now compete with the people and special interests to make law. The Progressives had triggered the state's first giant political earthquake.

It should be noted that the Progressives' efforts to widen access to political power did not extend to everyone, and some of the laws they passed were specifically designed to exclude certain groups from popular decision-making and civic life. Some of the most egregious examples reflected the White majority's racial hostility toward Chinese- and other Asian-born residents and descendants, which took the form of "Alien Land Laws" denying landownership, the right to self-defense in court, and other basic civil rights to anyone of Asian descent—laws that would not be removed from the state's books for another half century.

THE POWER OF ORGANIZED INTERESTS

Ironically, the Progressives' attacks on political parties and the Southern Pacific created new opportunities for other kinds of special interests to influence state government. Cross-filing produced lawmakers with weak party allegiances, and by the 1940s, they depended heavily on lobbyists for policy-relevant information as well as "amusements" to supplement their meager $3,000 annual salary. The legendary Artie Samish, head of the liquor and racetrack lobbies from the 1920s to the 1950s, personified the power of the "third house" (organized interests represented in the lobbying corps) in his ability to control election outcomes and tax rates for industries he represented. "I am the governor of the legislature," he brazenly boasted to a journalist in the 1940s. "To hell with the governor of California."[3] He was convicted and jailed for corruption not long after making this statement, but his personal downfall hardly disturbed the thriving, cozy relationships between lobbyists and legislators that continued to taint California state politics (Figure 2.1).

The Curse of California

Source: George Frederick Keller/Public domain/Wikimedia Commons.

GROWTH AND INDUSTRIALIZATION IN THE GOLDEN STATE

To outsiders, the image of California as a land of undiscovered riches and mythical possibility persisted even as the Great Depression took hold in the 1930s. As depicted in John Steinbeck's *The Grapes of Wrath*, hundreds of thousands of unskilled American migrants from the mid- and south-western Dust Bowl ("Okies" and "Arkies," as they were pejoratively called by Californians) flooded the state, provoking a stinging social backlash that lasted at least until war production created new labor demands. The Depression also helped breathe life into the socialist political movement of Upton Sinclair, an outspoken, unconventional writer who easily won the 1934 Democratic nomination for governor by waging an "End Poverty in California" (EPIC) campaign, which promised relief for lower- and middle-class Californians through

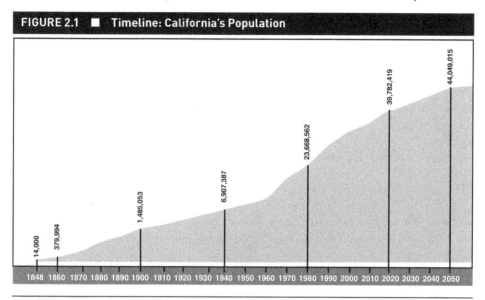

FIGURE 2.1 ■ Timeline: California's Population

Sources: Population estimates 1848–50 from Andrew Rolle, *California: A History* (Wheeling, IL: Harlan Davidson, 2003). Population estimates 1860–2015 from U.S. Census Bureau. Population estimates 2020–50 from California Department of Finance, Demographic Research Unit, "Report P-1: Population Projections by Race/Ethnicity, 2010–60 (Baseline 2019)," http://dof.ca.gov/Forecasting/Demographics/Projections/.

Note: Population estimates from 1848 to 1880 are for non-native populations. Native populations were not included in the U.S. Census prior to 1890.

a radical tax plan. His near-win inspired left-wing Democrats to fortify social programs and mobilized his opponents, whose furious anti-EPIC counteroffensive places it among the first modern media-driven smear campaigns.[4]

Rapid urban and industrial development during the first decades of the twentieth century accompanied the invention of the automobile and the step-up in oil production preceding World War II. Industrialization during World War II restored the state's golden image, bringing defense-related jobs, federal funds, manufacturing, construction, and dazzling prosperity that accelerated postwar. Ribbons of roads and highways tied new towns to swelling cities and delivered newcomers to California at spectacular rates. The building sector boomed while orange trees blossomed. To address labor shortages, in 1942, the federal "Bracero" program created a new agricultural labor force by facilitating the entry of Mexican laborers into the United States, beckoning millions of men and their families to the country. Their efforts laid the foundations for California's thriving modern agribusiness sector.

Tract-housing developments materialized at an unprecedented rate, spawning demand for roads, water, schools, and other critical infrastructure. In 1947, the state fanned the spread of "car culture" with an ambitious ten-year highway plan that cost $1 million per working day. Flood control and colossal irrigation projects begun in the 1860s had transformed the San Francisco Bay and the Sacramento–San Joaquin River Delta region from wetlands filled with wildlife into a labyrinth of levees, tunnels, canals, and dams that enabled midcentury farmers to feed expanding populations. Los Angeles continued to invent itself by sprawling across semiarid southlands, adding manufacturing plants and neighborhoods that survived on water imported from the north, thereby triggering "water wars" that continue to this day. Infrastructure spending was concentrated on moving water to the thirsty south via the State Water Project (SWP), the building of schools, establishing a first-class university system, and keeping freeways flowing—priorities that governors Earl Warren and Edmund "Pat" Brown (Jerry Brown's father) advanced through the mid-1960s.

UNLEASHING THE INITIATIVE

The political landscape was also changing dramatically midcentury. Cross-filing, which had severely disadvantaged the Democrats for forty years, was effectively eliminated through a 1952 initiative that required candidates' party affiliations to be printed on primary election ballots. With this important change, Democrats finally realized majority status in 1958 with Pat Brown in the governor's office and control of both legislative houses.

Several U.S. Supreme Court cases also necessitated fundamental changes in the way that Californians were represented in both the state and national legislatures. Between 1928 and 1965, the state had employed the "federal plan," modeling its legislature on the U.S. Congress, with an upper house based on geographic areas (counties rather than states) and a lower house based on population. Many attempts had been made to dismantle the federal plan because it produced gross overrepresentation of northern and inland rural interests and severe underrepresentation of southern metropolitan residents in the state Senate (three-fourths of sitting senators represented low-density rural areas), but it remained in place until the U.S. Supreme Court established the "one person–one vote" principle in *Reynolds v. Sims* (1964) and California's system was judged to be in clear violation of it.[5] After 1965, political influence passed from legislators representing the north to those representing the south and also from rural "cow counties" to urban interests.

The revival of parties in the legislature during the 1960s was greatly assisted by the Democratic Speaker of the California State Assembly, "Big Daddy" Jesse Unruh, who understood how to influence the reelection of loyal partisans by controlling the flow of campaign donations, what he referred to as the "mother's milk of politics."[6] Unruh also helped orchestrate an overhaul of the legislature through Proposition 1A, a measure designed to "Update the State!" via constitutional cleanup in 1966. Prop 1A *professionalized* the lawmaking body by endowing it with the "three S's": higher *salary*, many more *staff*, and year-round *session*. The intent was to free the legislative body from the grip of lobbyists and endow it with essential resources to compete on more equal footing with the executive branch. Lawmakers' annual pay doubled to $16,000 to reflect their new full-time status, and staff members were hired to write and analyze bills.

Professionalization transformed the legislature into a highly paid, well-staffed institution that quickly gained a reputation for policy innovation. Within five years, the legislature was described as having "proved itself capable of leading the nation in the development of legislation to deal with some of our most critical problems."[7] The applause didn't last long.

Propelled by anger over skyrocketing property taxes while the state accumulated a multibillion-dollar budget surplus, voters revolted against "spendthrift politicians" who "continue to tax us into poverty."[8] Fully realizing the energizing power of a grassroots political movement through the initiative process, citizens overwhelmingly approved **Proposition 13**, which limited property owners' tax to 1 percent of a property's purchase price and limited increases to 2 percent a year.[9] Prop 13 also forever changed the rules regarding general taxation by requiring a two-thirds vote to raise any taxes in the state, a **supermajority** rule that can empower a minority determined to block tax increases and by extension can jeopardize the legislature's ability to balance the annual budget. Prop 13 triggered the dramatic use of the initiative process that continues today.

The faith in self-governance and mistrust of politicians that spurred Progressives into action and citizens to approve Prop 13 continued to cause political tremors in California politics. The view that citizens were more trustworthy than their representatives only intensified during the 1980s after three legislators were convicted of bribery in an FBI sting labeled "Shrimpscam" (a fictitious shrimp company "paid" legislators to introduce bills favoring the company), reinforcing the perception that Sacramento was full of corrupt politicians. State lawmakers' reputation for being "arrogant and unresponsive" grew along with the power of *incumbency* (being an elected official) and as membership turnover in the legislature stagnated. In 1990, lawmakers were targeted again, this time by Proposition 140 (discussed in Chapter 4), which imposed term limits on all elected state officials, eliminating the chance to develop a long career in a single office. By 2004, lifelong legislative careers were over.

The passage of Proposition 13 in June 1978 opened a new chapter in California history, demonstrating the power of the initiative. Here the young Governor Jerry Brown meets with one of the initiative's authors, Howard Jarvis (right), to acknowledge the voters' message that government spending must be kept in check. Prop 13 inspired similar tax revolts across the U.S.

Source: Robbins/AP Photos.

Parties and elections continue to be targeted through ballot initiatives. Echoing the old cross-filing law, in 2010 Californians enacted the "Top-Two primary" (Prop 14), a "voter preference primary" system that allows *all* candidates for an office to be listed on one ballot but with their political party affiliation indicated. *All* registered voters, including independents, may cast a vote for whomever they prefer, not just their own party's candidates. For each state or Congressional office (but not the presidency), the two candidates who receive the most votes move to a runoff in the November general election.[10] Through Prop 11, voters transferred the authority to redraw electoral district lines (boundaries defining the geographic areas that legislators represent) from state lawmakers to an independent body, the Citizens Redistricting Commission, a group *prohibited* from manipulating district boundaries to advantage or disadvantage a party, person, or group, a practice known as gerrymandering. As a group that is reconstituted every ten years, they redrew district maps after the 2010 and 2020 U.S Censuses.

Voters have also altered policymaking processes by controlling decision-making rules. Proposition 98, enacted in 1988, significantly constrains the legislature by mandating that public schools (grades K–12) and community colleges receive an amount equal to roughly 40 percent of the state's general fund budget each year. In 2000, voters eased the passage of school bonds by lowering the supermajority vote requirement to 55 percent (from two-thirds).[11] Prop 26 recategorizes most "fees and charges" as taxes, subjecting them to a two-thirds supermajority approval, and Proposition 25 allows legislators to pass the state budget with a simple majority vote (lowered from a two-thirds supermajority). Voters also recently mandated that all bills must be in print at least 72 hours before a legislative vote and for audiovisual recordings of all public proceedings to be posted online within 24 hours.[12] This sampling of initiatives reveals a firmly established reform tradition that will continue to reshape California's government and how it operates.

HYPERDIVERSITY IN A MODERN STATE

Hybrid government reinforces California's distinctiveness, but probably no condition defines politics in California more than the state's great human diversity, which is as much a source of rich heritage and culture as it is a divisive force that drives competition for political, economic, and social influence. Differences stemming from ethnicity, race, gender, religion, age, sexuality, ideology, socioeconomic class, and street address (to name but a few sources) do not inevitably breed conflict; however, these differences often are the source of intense clashes in the state. The political realm is where these differences are expressed as divergent goals and ideals in the search for power, group recognition, or public benefits, and the vital challenge for California's political representatives and institutions is to aggregate interests rather than aggravate them.

A post–World War II baby boom inflated the state's population, and waves of immigration and migration throughout the mid-to late-twentieth century produced minor political tremors.[13] A marked national population shift from the northern, formerly industrial "Rust Belt" to the southern Sun Belt boosted California's economy and population over the latter half of the twentieth century. Another wave of people from Southeast Asia arrived during the late 1960s and 1970s following the Vietnam War, and the most recent influx of immigrants occurred during the 1980s and 1990s with large-scale migration from Mexico and other Latin and Central American countries. California is home to the largest Asian population in the United States, including Southeast Asians, who constitute the fastest-growing ethnic group in the state (about 15.1 percent overall); Chinatown in San Francisco remains the oldest enclave of its kind in North America.[14] Latinxs, having displaced Whites in 2016 as the state's largest ethnic group, now constitute 40 percent of the state's population.[15]

Immigration, legal and illegal, as well as natural population growth have produced a hyperdiverse state in which a multitude of groups vie for public goods, services, recognition, power, and influence, and yet they don't share equal access to conditions that will help them thrive. California's history is littered with examples of civil rights starkly deprived, beginning with the state-sanctioned extermination and enslavement of Native Americans in the 1850s,[16] the internment of Japanese Americans in camps during WWII, and midcentury discriminatory housing and employment laws that enshrined generational inequality and injustice, to name a few. Although Governor Pat Brown signed a fair housing law in 1964 ending discrimination by property owners who refused to rent or sell to non-White persons, voters retaliated with Proposition 14, a constitutional amendment enabling private discrimination and housing segregation. Black people, in particular, were excluded from living in the most desirable neighborhoods and relegated to areas where property values scarcely appreciated in comparison. The U.S. Supreme Court invalidated so-called "**redlining**" arrangements in 1967 as a violation of the Fourteenth Amendment's equal protection guarantee, but inequitable residential housing patterns have persisted.

Prop 14 helped set the stage for the 1965 Watts Riots (or Watts Rebellion or Uprising) in Los Angeles, where police officers' violent interactions with a Black motorist ignited a six-day episode resulting in 32 deaths and the destruction of 1,000 buildings. The same despair and anger over police brutality echoed in 1992 after four White police officers were acquitted of having severely beaten speeding suspect Rodney King; once again the city erupted into flames, ending in similar property damage and 50 deaths. In late May 2020, after George Floyd gasped that he couldn't breathe and died while pinned under the knee of a Minnesota policeman, the nation exploded in turmoil. National Guard troops patrolled California cities to restore order after rioting and looting of businesses, and masses of peaceful protesters demanded racial justice and reform. Governor Gavin Newsom responded with pledges to repair policing through enforcement of SB 392, a curb on the use of deadly force by law enforcers, and SB 230, which requires implementation of implicit bias and de-escalation training; to continue a moratorium on the death penalty; and to pursue greater social equity through investments in education and health care, among other efforts.

Race and ethnicity continue to stir debates over what it means to be a citizen and who is "deserving" of state benefits. Undocumented immigrants number approximately 2.6 million in California,[17] and impassioned campaigns have been waged over how to treat this shadow population who, despite the state's sanctuary laws, live in fear of federal deportation. Ballot measures concerning immigration-related issues have included denying public benefits to undocumented persons (Prop 187 in 1994, much of which was judged unenforceable), making English the state's official language (1986), and teaching children only in English (passed in 1998) and then restoring non-English language instruction almost twenty years later (in 2016).[18] Recently, state lawmakers have granted undocumented immigrants legal aid to fight deportation; Cal Grants and in-state tuition rates for "DREAMers" (the California Development, Relief, and Education for Alien Minors Act, known as the DREAM Act, was signed into law in 2011, benefiting about 75,000 college and university students who have undocumented status[19]), rendering California one of twenty-four states or education systems to do so[20]; health care for low-income undocumented persons[21]; and noncommercial driver's licenses through AB 60,[22] which some oppose for symbolic and practical reasons even though evidence shows that licensing undocumented individuals helps reduce hit-and-run accidents,[23] and this right exists in sixteen other states and the District of Columbia.[24] California will also replace all references to "aliens" with the term "non-citizen" in state statutes (laws).

Residential patterns also raise questions about the relative values of cultural assimilation and cultural preservation. Also known to representatives as "communities of interest," certain neighborhoods, barrios, "Little Saigons," or "Chinatowns" have performed the historical role of absorbing foreign laborers and refugees, among them approximately 50,000 Vietnamese who arrived after the Vietnam War and approximately 3 million Latinxs who joined family members in the United States as part of a 1986 federal amnesty program. The trends of "balkanization" (communities separated by race or ethnicity) and **gentrification** (the movement of affluent residents into renovated city zones from which poorer residents have been displaced) have become more pronounced during recent decades, reflecting widening income inequality. These patterns are also manifest in five radically different community types identified by political geographers, who call them the "Five Californias."[25] Indicated mainly by income and education levels, health, and related opportunities, the realities that these five different social classes experience translate into divergent sociopolitical needs and demands. As the majority struggle fiercely to make ends meet, the top One Percent thrive while they both disproportionately fund state government and influence policy (see Chapter 9).

The sheer volume of basic human and special needs created by this hyperdiversity has tended to outstrip government capacity in the areas of health care, housing, public education, legal aid and correctional services, infrastructure development, environmental protection, and public welfare. Population growth will continue to drive taxation, budget, and policy debates, providing plenty of fissures that will test the foundations of state government, especially during economic downturns when people's needs multiply.

RECALLING A GOVERNOR, TAKE ONE

The constant hum of gradual population change contrasts sharply with the sudden jolts that unexpected events can send through a political system. The most significant political earthquake of the new millennium in California hit in 2003 with the recall of Governor Gray Davis, a dizzying, circus-like event that solidified the state's image as a national outlier. The mild-mannered Governor Davis had gained a reputation as a "pay-to-play" politician who rewarded friendly public employee unions with generous contracts and was blamed for tripling the car tax, sky-high electricity bills, and overdue budgets that contained accounting gimmicks.[26] For the first time ever, enough signatures were gathered to trigger a special recall election, and a few months later, Californians would use direct democracy to replace their governor and simultaneously choose a successor.[27] More than half (55.4 percent) of voters decided to shake up government and selected "yes" on the recall question, and almost half of them (48.7 percent) chose actor Arnold Schwarzenegger to replace Davis.

Having overpowered 134 competitors, Republican Governor Schwarzenegger positioned himself as a political outsider and assumed centrist positions, championing the environment

Schoolchildren in Escondido are among the state's plurality (40 percent) Latinx population. In 2020–21 they represented more than half (55 percent) of all students enrolled in California K–12 public schools, whereas non-Hispanic Whites were 22 percent, Asian and Pacific Islanders were 10 percent, and African Americans were 5 percent.

Source: Sandy Huffaker/Corbis via Getty Images.

and government reform, and earning the label of "RINO" (Republican in Name Only) from his detractors because he worked closely with Democratic leaders. His climate-friendly legacy includes having signed AB 32, the nation's first law to regulate greenhouse gas emissions, which provides a foundation for the state's carbon emissions cap-and-trade system and greenhouse gas-related mandates (see Chapter 4 for more about AB 32).[28] Schwarzenegger may also be remembered for a jaw-dropping $27 billion budget deficit that mushroomed near the end of his term.

Closing the monumental budget gap topped Democratic Governor Jerry Brown's agenda when he took office—for the second time in his life—during the "Great Recession" in 2011. Extensive public service informed Brown's approach the second time around: he had held a variety of state, party, and local offices including state attorney general and Oakland mayor after having served two terms as one of the youngest governors in state history (1975–80).[29] Now Edmund G. "Jerry" Brown addressed budget deficits by obtaining voters' approval of new taxes to fund public education (Prop 30) and he sliced health care and education funding that fellow Democrats considered sacred. California's "green economy" flourished under Brown, and the state emerged as a major engine in the nation's economic recovery and acceleration. In his final term as the oldest governor in California history, his "progressive Democratic" values collided with those of the conservative-minded President Trump. When federal rollbacks of environmental protections intensified, Brown called the Trump administration's approach "a miasma of nonsense,"[30] and with the attorney general's help, the state sued the Trump administration (usually successfully) more than 100 times over weaker water and air pollution standards, immigration, oil and gas extraction, pesticide regulations, and more.[31]

Under federal court orders to reduce rampant overcrowding in state prisons, Brown also aggressively pursued prison reform. Through shifting nonserious, nonviolent, nonsexual inmates (known as "triple-nons") to county jails and parole, the incarcerated population was reduced to levels at or below federal court mandates in a process called "**realignment**." Brown also resisted creating new crimes, reversed automatic sentencing enhancements through new laws, granted a record number of pardons and commutations, and endorsed the popular initiative revising the state's "three-strikes" law to impose life sentences only for violent and serious felonies.[32]

If California had appeared "ungovernable" when Brown took office, the four-term governor helped restore the state's reputation for being "exceptional" in both positive and negative ways. Flush with four straight years of budget surpluses and an economic engine that had revved California's GDP into the world's top five, the state was also bursting with homelessness and astronomically high housing costs; wrestling with drought, wildfires, and the Trump administration; and nursing an ever-expanding inequality gap. Brown's replacement, Gavin Newsom, had his work cut out for him when he took office in 2019.

On any given night, approximately 69,000 people experience homelessness in Los Angeles County. In 2023, Mayor Karen Bass stepped up efforts to clear out homeless encampments and help move residents into temporary and permanent housing.
Source: Ted Soqui/AP Photos.

PANDEMIC POLITICS AND SURVIVING A RECALL

Fresh from the 2018 elections that returned a Democratic supermajority to the legislature and all but one executive office, former San Francisco mayor and Lieutenant Governor Gavin Newsom assumed office during a time of relative prosperity. However, with earth-shaking power, almost overnight the coronavirus pandemic scrambled life as most people knew it. In March 2020, anticipating a surge in COVID-19 cases, Newsom became the first U.S. governor to declare a state of emergency and ordered all residents to shelter in place, a shutdown that extended to all schools and nonessential business and government operations. Over seemingly endless months, social unrest grew: first among those who wanted the economy to reopen faster and then by multitudes pushing for racial justice and changes to policing policies. Mass protests, demonstrations, marches, and uprisings marked the summer of 2020.[33]

Newsom's exercise of emergency powers affected all aspects of life, from mandatory mask-wearing to business closures, actions that prompted relief among supporters and outrage among opponents, some of whom were determined to oust the governor through a recall election. After a judge extended the deadline for collecting signatures (due to COVID restrictions), the signature threshold was met in March 2021 and Newsom would become the fourth governor in U.S. history to defend his seat before the end of his term.[34]

Despite public commotion over COVID restrictions and Newsom's personal missteps (namely, attending an unmasked dinner party at a posh restaurant after warning citizens to avoid indoor gatherings),[35] ultimately the governor's popularity among most Democrats and independents proved stronger than the contempt of his foes, particularly as the field of 46 potential replacements took shape. Newsom successfully dissuaded strong Democratic competitors from entering the race as a Republican frontrunner emerged: Black conservative radio talk show host Larry Elder, whose provocative style echoed that of President Trump. In an all-mail ballot election held October 2021, Newsom survived the recall attempt by attracting the same vote percentage with which he had been initially elected (61.9 percent), essentially sealing his reelection in 2022 and prompting calls to reform the recall process (see Chapter 3).

As COVID restrictions loosened, most Californians continued to be stung by the global pandemic's lingering effects which local and state governments could do little to ease. Even as the state banked billions more tax revenues than projected—a sign that the top one percenters were thriving—unreliable supply chains and skyrocketing prices of everything from gas to rents and food thwarted Newsom's aim to build "a more inclusive and equitable future for all."[36] In that vein, his priorities have included making affordable housing more accessible through tax refunds and emergency rental assistance, and his budgets have dedicated billions to address homelessness such as through Project Roomkey (also Homekey), a grant program for converting motels and hotels into safe, transitional housing for people who are homeless. Newsom has endorsed accelerated minimum wage increases (rising to $15.50 per hour on January 1, 2023 compared to $7.25 at the federal level), and devised low-carbon climate change initiatives such as requiring new construction to use clean energy and all new cars sold in California to be electric by 2035. Also, in response to the U.S. Supreme Court's reversal of *Roe v. Wade*, a judgment granting states the right to decide whether abortion should be legal within their boundaries, Newsom sought to expand reproductive rights and abortion access through state grants and supported a state constitutional amendment to enshrine abortion rights.

Efforts such as these have not stemmed the flow of outmigration, and California has been losing residents to other states since 2001.[37] For the first time in history, during the pandemic, the state's population actually declined: births did not offset the number of people moving out of the state, and because other states' populations have been rising faster, California lost a seat in the House of Representatives in 2020 (now at 52 seats, still the most by far). Despite a historic budget surplus driven by the top income earners, for the majority of Californians, unaffordable housing, water shortages, soaring living costs, and the hazards of extreme weather events have made *simply getting by* the new "California dream."

A viral video of George Floyd's last words, "I can't breathe," and death at the hands of Minneapolis police provoked outrage, unprecedented demonstrations for racial justice, and an outcry against police brutality, including this uprising in Los Angeles on May 30, 2020.

Source: Warrick Page via Getty Images.

CONCLUSION: POLITICAL EARTHQUAKES AND EVOLVING INSTITUTIONS

Like real seismic events, political earthquakes are difficult to predict. Some of the tensions that produce them are ever present, such as in the demographic fault lines that underlie inequalities or define the uneasy alliance between representative and direct democracy. Periodic ruptures that take the form of ballot measures, recall elections, landmark legislation, or even uprisings release some of that tension. Although political earthquakes may be triggered by conditions or events that can't be controlled—such as a pandemic, a weak global economy, a new federal administration, or Supreme Court decisions—the shock waves these events produce have the potential to bring about transformations both large and small. Throughout California's history, political earthquakes have reconfigured relationships between the elected and the governed, between citizens and their governing institutions, and among citizens. Each of these upheavals has involved choices about who may use power and how they may do so legitimately. Rules have also mattered: in some cases, the shake-ups were about whether to change the rules themselves, whereas in other cases the rules shaped the alternatives available and determined who could choose among them, be they voters, legislators, or other leaders such as governors. Often, policy decisions provoke supercharged emotional reactions because they raise questions about shared values and have the potential to shape the social, economic, and political culture in which people will live. Finally, history also plays a role in creating opportunities for action or in creating conditions that shape alternatives. As this historical review demonstrates, California's past pulses in the political institutions, culture, rules, and choices of today, which in turn will provide keys to unlocking the Golden State's political future.

KEY TERMS

Big Four: Collis Huntington, Mark Hopkins, Leland Stanford, and Charles Crocker, four railroad tycoons who wielded disproportionate influence over California politics, having owned the Central (later Southern) Pacific Railroad that built the western length of the transcontinental railroad (1863–69).

Civil service: government employment that is not based on political party loyalty alone but rather on merit that is usually earned through professional training and experience. Endorsed by Progressives.

Cross-filing: an early form of an open primary election, in which the name of any candidate (minus political party affiliation) could appear on any political party's primary election ballot. Officially in effect in California from 1913 to 1959.

Gentrification: the movement of affluent residents into renovated city zones from which poorer residents have been displaced.

Nonpartisan: elections in which names of candidates (usually for local offices) appear on ballots without party labels. Established by Progressives.

Patronage: the awarding of government jobs to political party loyalists.

Professionalization: Proposition 1A in 1966 made the state legislature a full-time operation resembling the U.S. Congress; professional legislators have high salaries,

many full-time staff members, and year-round sessions.

Progressivism: members of a national political movement that took root in state-based political parties of that name in the early 1900s; they tried to reform government to rid it of special interests and return it to "the people." Notable actions in California included electoral reforms such as the establishment of direct democracy.

Proposition 13: a landmark proposition in 1978 that limited property taxes to 1 percent of the purchase price of a property and imposed a two-thirds vote threshold for raising taxes. Rekindled Californians' usage of the initiative process.

Realignment: the process of shifting state prison inmates to county jails and parole in order to reduce prison overcrowding.

Redlining: a residential zoning practice whereby certain (more desirable) areas are declared "off-limits" to members of minority groups, indicated by red lines on city maps; until 1967 this was employed as a means of keeping Black people and other minorities from settling in "White" neighborhoods.

Supermajority: a majority rule that requires reaching a threshold above 50 percent plus one. The threshold is commonly two-thirds in California for raising taxes and passing urgency measures.

3 DIRECT DEMOCRACY

As a "Schedule I" drug under U.S. law, marijuana is still illegal. Growing, possessing, selling, and using it are federal criminal offenses. Not so at the state level. In the November 1996 general election, Californians voted on several proposed laws or **ballot measures**, including Proposition 215, a law that legalized the medical use of cannabis within California's borders. Twenty years after decriminalizing medical marijuana, California became the fifth state to legalize marijuana for recreational purposes through Proposition 64, another law that citizens—not legislators—proposed. Although federal drug enforcement agents can still arrest people for the sale and use of cannabis, California's government has responded to these voter-approved laws by setting up regulations for all manner of marijuana activity and only allows law enforcement to enforce the *state's* rules created under Prop 64.

Direct democracy was intended to supplement the regular lawmaking process, to be a safe-guard for when the legislature "either viciously or negligently fails or refuses" to act.[1] Yet, on mundane and complex matters alike, whether they have considered them on the merits or not, and being accountable to no one but themselves, "on election day every voting Californian is a lawmaker."[2] Indeed, the U.S. Supreme Court confirmed in 2015 that the people are in fact a legislature when they exercise their power to make laws.[3] For more than a century, California has had a *hybrid government* that is part representative, part direct democracy, a design that the nation's founders carefully avoided.[4]

At first, like most U.S. states, California's government reflected the U.S. founders' belief that elected representatives working in separate branches—the executive and legislative—would check each other with overlapping powers, filter the passions of their constituents through a deliberative process, find compromises, and create good public policy. Lawmakers and presidents would compete for power, and these arrangements would safely allow ambition to counteract ambition, as James Madison noted in the *Federalist Papers*. Abandoning this logic, in 1911, California Progressive reformers removed those checks by establishing the initiative, referendum, and recall, thereby creating a hybrid government in which the people can create and vote on laws without their representatives' involvement. What we might call the first branch of California government is the people's power to govern themselves through the instruments of direct democracy. Article II of the state constitution affirms this view: "All political power is inherent in the people … and they have the right to alter or reform it when the public good may require."

THE STATEWIDE INITIATIVE PROCESS

At the state level, the **direct initiative** gives Californians the power to propose constitutional amendments and laws (also called "statutes") that fellow citizens will vote on in November general elections without the participation of either the legislature or the governor. Variants of the initiative process exist in 23 other states, including the **indirect initiative**, in which lawmakers must consider and sometimes amend citizen-initiated proposals before they are presented to the public for a vote. Although California legislators may consider any proposed law, generally they are barred from making changes of any kind to citizens' actual ballot **propositions** either before or after an election. However, they hold the power to propose constitutional amendments, bond measures, and changes to existing laws that voters approved as ballot measures, all of which can appear as propositions in either primary or general elections that are subject to popular vote—so-called **legislatively referred measures**.

Prior to the "Prop 13 revolution" that emboldened Californians to use the initiative process, Oregon led the states with the most citizen initiatives. Since then, Californians have produced more than any other state.[5] Considering all types of measures, including bonds, referenda, and legislatively referred initiatives, California holds the record with 557 measures having been put to voters 1979–2022.[6] Voters reject most citizen initiatives, however. From 1912 to 2021, they only approved 35 percent of them.[7] Proposed laws typically fail long before they make it to the ballot because their sponsors fail to gather enough signatures in time or too many submitted signatures are invalidated; in fact, 74.5 percent of proposed initiatives fail to qualify.[8]

Initiatives cover all manner of subjects. Issues that frequently surface include taxation, welfare, public morality, immigration, education, criminal justice, and civil rights. Most prevalent are measures that focus on government and the political process—reforms targeting the rules for political participation or the behavior of elected officials—and it's no coincidence that term limits for statewide officials exist almost exclusively in states with the initiative process

(Louisiana is the only exception). Without a doubt, initiatives have fundamentally altered California government and politics (Table 3.1 and Figure 3.1).

Unfortunately, reforms are forced on government incoherently and are not based on a process that involves compromise. They also cannot be amended or changed once approved, except by the people through the initiative process.[9] For example, voters approved changes to the juvenile justice system in 2000, requiring that minors aged 14–18 who committed certain violent offenses be tried as adults, among other intricate provisions relating to gangs

TABLE 3.1 ■ Selected Landmark Initiatives in California, 1966–Present		
Number	**Description**	**Year**
Proposition 1A	Constitutional reform, legislative professionalization	1966
Proposition 9	"Political Reform Act" (campaign finance reform)	1974
Proposition 13	Property tax limitation	1978
Proposition 98	Minimum annual funding levels for education	1988
Propositions 140 and 28	Term limits for state officeholders; 12 years total in either house for lawmakers	1990; 2012
Propositions 184 and 36	Three-strikes law; applies to violent/serious crimes only	1994; 2012
Proposition 187	Ineligibility of undocumented persons for public services (note: mostly invalidated by courts)	1994
Propositions 215 and 64	Medical use of marijuana; recreational use of marijuana	1996; 2016
Proposition 5	Tribal state gaming compacts, tribal casinos	1998
Propositions 227 and 58	Elimination of bilingual education; restoration of bilingual (multilingual) instruction	1998; 2016
Propositions 11 and 20	Citizens redistricting commission to redraw state and congressional districts	2008; 2010
Proposition 8	Definition of marriage (invalidated by U.S. Supreme Court in 2015)	2008
Proposition 14	Open primary elections (Top-Two Primary)	2010

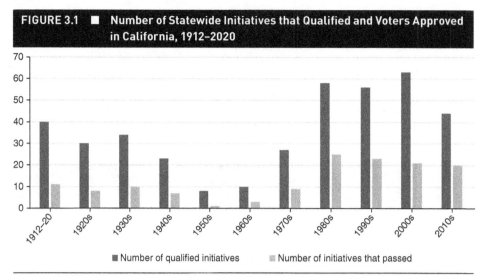

FIGURE 3.1 ■ **Number of Statewide Initiatives that Qualified and Voters Approved in California, 1912–2020**

■ Number of qualified initiatives   ■ Number of initiatives that passed

Source: "Initiative Totals by Summary Year, 1912–2022," Office of the Secretary of State, State of California, https://elections.cdn.sos.ca.gov//ballot-measures/pdf/initiative-totals-summary-year.pdf.

Notes: Each decade begins with the odd numbered year (e.g., 1921). Excludes referenda and measures referred by the legislature.

and parole. Unable to address some of the injustices that arose from the law, and desiring to reduce costs and promote rehabilitation, former Governor Jerry Brown pushed Proposition 57 to the voters in 2016, and they ultimately agreed that the law should require judges— not district attorneys—to determine whether minors should be tried as adults under certain circumstances.

The initiative process both directly and indirectly conditions the actions of all California elected officials, as intended. Yet some initiative measures exacerbate divisions, eroding representatives' ability to act collectively for the common good. For instance, Proposition 26 reclassifies almost all regulatory fees and charges as taxes so that they are subject to the same two-thirds vote threshold that Prop 13 imposed. While this change may seem fairer because it requires both sides to come together in agreement, in fact it privileges the "super-minority" (a few people) over the simple majority (that is, the most people) because absolutely no revenue-raising measures can succeed without the minority's consent (unless one party forms a supermajority, as the Democrats have on-and-off since 2012; see Chapter 4). Historically, supermajority rules like these have driven Democratic majority lawmakers and Republican minority lawmakers into long standoffs over how to balance the state budget, regulate businesses, address public health issues, and clean up the environment. In other words, direct democracy conditions the way representative democracy works.

Citizens can propose laws or money-raising measures at the city, county, and state levels in California. Any registered voter may propose a state law (an *initiative statute*) or a change to the state constitution (a *constitutional amendment*), and both types pass with simple majority approval. However, because the average person lacks the money and time to gather hundreds of thousands of valid voter signatures for statewide propositions, well-funded interest groups now dominate a system that was intended to *reduce* their influence. In practice, nearly anyone who can spend between $3 million and $7 million to hire a signature-gathering firm can qualify a measure for the ballot, and the average cost typically exceeds $7 per valid signature because so many names are disqualified.[10] Special interest groups, corporations, wealthy individuals, political parties, and even elected officials (playing the role of "concerned citizens") use the initiative process to circumvent regular lawmaking channels because it "is the only way for [them] to get the policy they want."[11] Large donors practically monopolize the system: a mere 48 entities, from businesses to individuals to unions, contributed *half* of the approximately $2.3 billion spent on initiative campaigns from 2000 to 2012, while "small donors" who gave $1,000 or less accounted for just over *2 percent* of that total.[12] Although the process remains primarily a check against government unresponsiveness and corruption, Hiram Johnson's Progressives would probably be surprised at how the process works today.

Preparation Stage: Drafting, Public Review, and Titling

The first step in bringing an idea to the ballot is drafting, or writing, the text of the proposed law. Measures are worded carefully to fit the needs and goals of their sponsors, and it is their responsibility to correct errors or ambiguities that may later provide opponents with a convenient excuse to challenge them in court. A proposed initiative must be submitted with $2,000 to the attorney general's office (note: *not* the secretary of state's office), where it will be posted online for a 30-day public review period. Up to 5 days after the review period concludes, authors may change the wording before the *attorney general* assigns a title and summary of 100 words or fewer, which will be printed on the petitions circulated for signatures.[13] From that point on, the wording of the proposed law cannot be changed. The state also prepares a fiscal analysis of the proposed law if the attorney general requests one.

Qualification Stage: Circulating Petitions for Signatures and Signature Verification

During the qualification stage, the initiative's proponents must circulate formal petitions containing the official title and summary and gather enough valid voter signatures to qualify the measure for the ballot. "Official Top Funders" must also be disclosed and their donations will be posted on the secretary of state's website. Signatures can come from anywhere in California, but everyone who signs must be a registered voter in the county where the petition is signed. Signature requirements are based on a percentage of all votes cast for governor during the previous election: until 2026, the requirement is 5 percent for an initiative (546,651 signatures) and 8 percent for a constitutional amendment (874,641 signatures). Because voter turnout determines the signature requirements, it can be easier or harder, or more or less expensive, to qualify an initiative within a four-year period.

Proponents have 180 days (6 months) to collect signatures on their petitions in person.[14] Normally a signature collection firm is hired to run the statewide effort, and the rule of thumb is to gather almost twice as many signatures as required because up to 40 percent or so will likely be invalidated.[15] In practice, this means collecting well over 1 million signatures with costs ranging from about $3.50 to almost $13 per valid signature, depending on urgency and company fees.[16] Means of collecting signatures include *in person* in public places, such as grocery stores or churches, using the "clipboard method" (by one person) or "table method" (one person sits at a table while a companion approaches passersby); *direct mail* (generally not cost-effective); and *door-to-door* (rare). Online signature gathering is not allowed.

After 25 percent of the required number of signatures have been gathered, the initiative's proponents must notify the secretary of state, who will then relay the measure to the legislature. Although the language can't be changed at this point, the Assembly and Senate must hold public hearings that are intended to heighten awareness and enhance the public record about the proposed law.

Only authorized proponents may submit signed petitions to the appropriate elections official, typically the *county clerk* or registrar of voters in the county where each petition was filled out. The county clerks will count and verify the signatures by using a random sampling technique to determine how many signatures qualify. If, at least 131 days before the next general election, the *secretary of state* concludes that enough registered voters signed the filed petitions in total, they certify the measure and give it a number, and it becomes known as "Proposition [number]." Proponents may withdraw their measure at any time before it qualifies, meaning at least 131 days before the election. Occasionally the threat of an initiative will prompt the legislature to address the issue. Legislators sprang into action to devise California's new consumer privacy law as the authors of an initiative dangled a stronger version that had already qualified for the ballot. The authors pulled it just hours before the deadline, only after the legislature unanimously approved it and Governor Brown signed it into law.

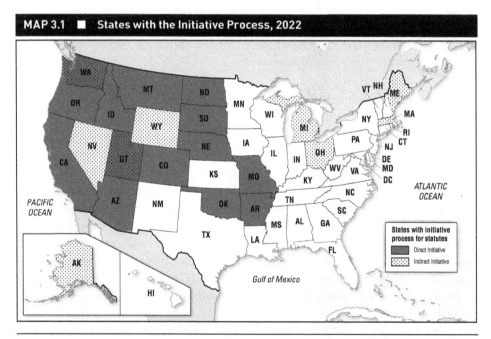

MAP 3.1 ■ States with the Initiative Process, 2022

Source: National Conference of State Legislatures, "Initiative and Referendum States," http://www.ncsl.org/legislatures-elections/elections/chart-of-the-initiative-states.aspx.

Campaign Stage: Persuading Potential Voters

Most initiative attempts fail during the qualification stage because insufficient signatures were gathered or because too many were found to be invalid, but for successful proponents, the campaign stage begins the moment the secretary of state certifies their measure. In the coming months, they will usually raise and spend millions of dollars to mobilize or sway voters. A thriving political consulting industry has grown around the need to manage fundraising, social media campaigns, television and radio advertising, and mass mailings. The price of initiative campaigns has become supersized, and the most expensive in U.S. history have taken place in California. Unlimited donations to ballot measure campaigns are legal—in fact, courts consider them an expression of free speech—and it is not uncommon for supporters and opponents to spend more than $100 million alone or combined on highly controversial measures (Map 3.2). About $381.5 million was contributed to eight ballot measure campaigns in 2018, and spending shot up to $767 million in 2020 for the same number of initiatives.[17] In 2020, app-based companies, including Uber, Lyft, DoorDash, and Instacart, set an astonishing new record by spending over $205 million to exempt themselves from a law that forced them to treat drivers as employees (Prop 22).[18] This example illustrates that big companies or industries directly affected by new taxes or regulations tend to spend wildly to defeat threats. In addition to tracking campaign finance activity, the secretary of state meanwhile prepares the official ballot guide that will be sent to all registered voters (available online), which includes an analysis of every measure's purpose, effects, and fiscal impacts, along with arguments and rebuttals.

MAP 3.2 ■ Relative Spending on Three Ballot Measures

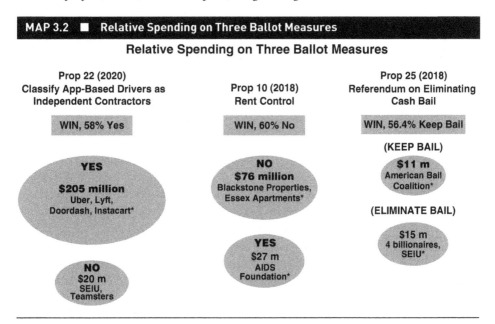

*Top contributors are indicated.

Sources: Powersearch, Office of the Secretary of State, State of California, accessed June 20, 2022, http://powersearch.sos.ca.gov/.

Notes: All figures are reported in real 2020 and 2018 dollars (without adjustments) and rounded. Figures do not include independent expenditures.

Postelection Stage: Court Challenges and Implementation

Only a *simple majority* is needed to pass an initiative, to recall an elected official, or approve a state bond. Initiative laws generally take effect within five days of being certified, unlike regular bills, which normally go into effect on January 1 the following year.[19] Election results don't always settle issues, however. Opponents often file lawsuits as soon as the votes are counted, triggering expensive court battles over a measure's constitutionality, meaning, or validity. These battles can last years and may result in partial or total invalidation of the measure. A legal challenge to Proposition 8, a constitutional amendment defining marriage as between a man and a woman, was initiated shortly after the proposition's passage in 2008. The case twisted through the state courts, where it was eventually upheld by the California Supreme Court. It was then pushed into the federal court system, where it was struck down by a district court as unconstitutional. The U.S. Supreme Court declined to hear the case in 2013, allowing the appellate court's ruling to stand, so same-sex marriages in California became legal that year. In June 2015, the U.S. Supreme Court settled the issue by ruling that the Fourteenth Amendment requires all states to issue marriage licenses to same-sex couples and to recognize same-sex marriages performed in other states, thus invalidating Prop 8.

Public officials may also search for ways to get around laws they find objectionable, and there is always the likelihood that a contentious issue will be revisited in a future proposition, because new laws often have unintended consequences and because losers always have another chance to prevail.

The Power of the Initiative Process

Initiative use is robust for other reasons. Corporations and special interest groups find initiatives appealing because they know that successful measures can translate into financial gain or friendlier regulations. Aspiring politicians and lawmakers build their reputations by sponsoring propositions that can't get traction in the legislature. Competition also plays a role: adversaries can take their fights to the ballot with dueling, "rival" measures that propose very different solutions to a problem. If *both* rival measures receive enough votes to pass, the one attracting *more* votes goes into effect. Constitutional amendments must be listed on the ballot first, a rule that ensured Governor Brown's tax-raising measure, Prop 30, would appear at the top of the 2012 ballot, well ahead of his opponent's measure, Prop 38 (Figure 3.2).[20]

Today, the power of the average voter has been eclipsed by industry initiative activity and special interest group imperatives. Millionaires and billionaires, not average citizens, can afford to qualify their pet projects or big ideas. There are no limits on contributions to ballot campaigns, and two-thirds of all donations are in amounts of $1 million or more.[21] The result: voters endure fanatical campaigns waged by organizations and corporations with deep pockets, their strategies packaged in media barrages containing oversimplified messages. Usually armed only with these biased accounts, voters must decide on complex policies frequently crafted without the benefit of compromise, and these policies may set rules that are difficult to amend later. Not surprisingly, voters confronted with thick ballot guides often look for shortcuts such as endorsements on which to base their decisions, and confused voters tend to vote "no," especially when the ramifications of voting "yes" are unclear.

FIGURE 3.2 ■ Sample Ballot with Initiatives

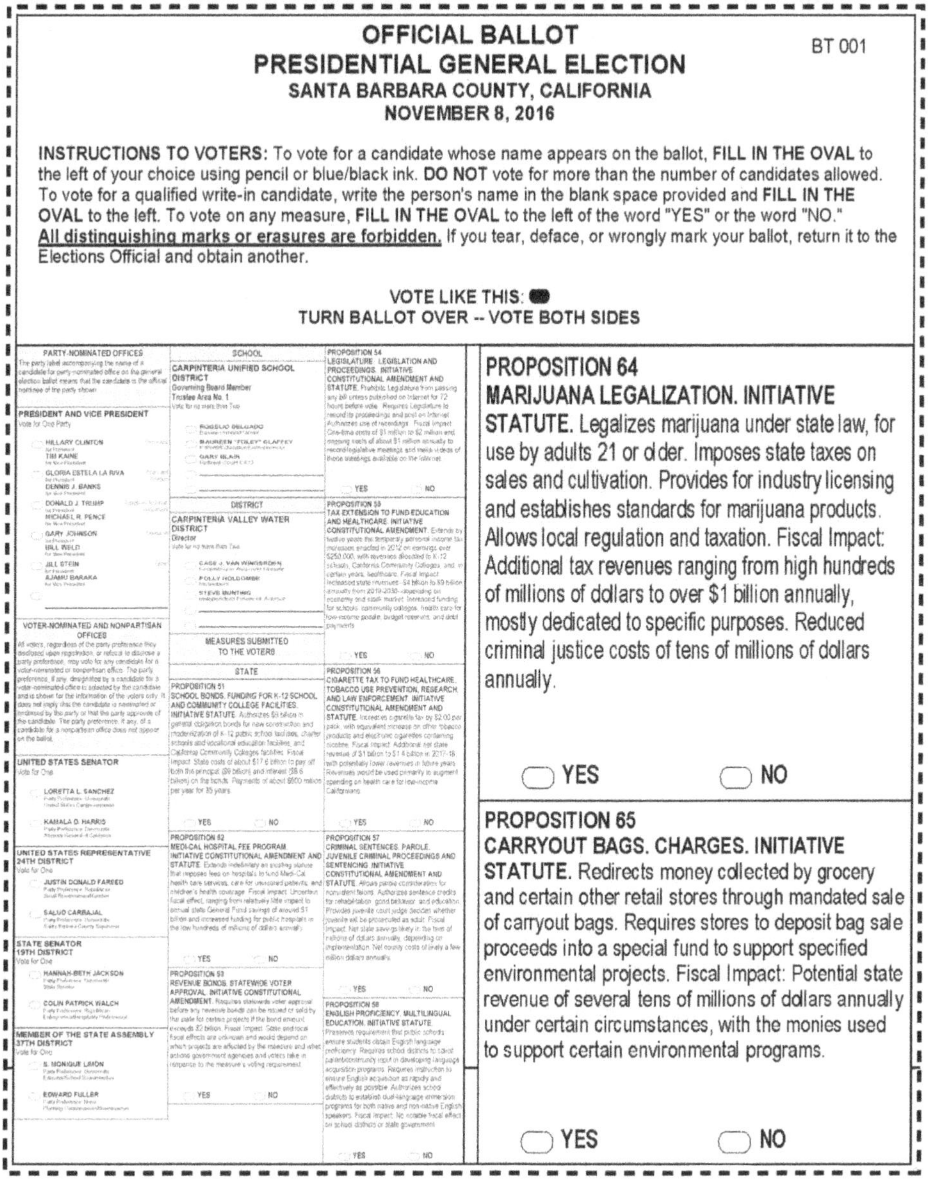

OFFICIAL BALLOT
PRESIDENTIAL GENERAL ELECTION
SANTA BARBARA COUNTY, CALIFORNIA
NOVEMBER 8, 2016

BT 001

INSTRUCTIONS TO VOTERS: To vote for a candidate whose name appears on the ballot, **FILL IN THE OVAL** to the left of your choice using pencil or blue/black ink. **DO NOT** vote for more than the number of candidates allowed. To vote for a qualified write-in candidate, write the person's name in the blank space provided and **FILL IN THE OVAL** to the left. To vote on any measure, **FILL IN THE OVAL** to the left of the word "YES" or the word "NO." <u>All distinguishing marks or erasures are forbidden.</u> If you tear, deface, or wrongly mark your ballot, return it to the Elections Official and obtain another.

VOTE LIKE THIS: ●
TURN BALLOT OVER -- VOTE BOTH SIDES

PROPOSITION 64
MARIJUANA LEGALIZATION. INITIATIVE STATUTE. Legalizes marijuana under state law, for use by adults 21 or older. Imposes state taxes on sales and cultivation. Provides for industry licensing and establishes standards for marijuana products. Allows local regulation and taxation. Fiscal Impact: Additional tax revenues ranging from high hundreds of millions of dollars to over $1 billion annually, mostly dedicated to specific purposes. Reduced criminal justice costs of tens of millions of dollars annually.

○ YES   ○ NO

PROPOSITION 65
CARRYOUT BAGS. CHARGES. INITIATIVE STATUTE. Redirects money collected by grocery and certain other retail stores through mandated sale of carryout bags. Requires stores to deposit bag sale proceeds into a special fund to support specified environmental projects. Fiscal Impact: Potential state revenue of several tens of millions of dollars annually under certain circumstances, with the monies used to support certain environmental programs.

○ YES   ○ NO

Source: Courtesy of Santa Barbara County, California.

Still, Californians of all types (about 67 percent) like the system and think it's a "good thing that a majority of voters can make laws and change public policies."[22] That said, only 15 percent of adults think that the system is fine the way it is; over 80 percent feel that major or minor changes are needed, from reducing the number of propositions to making the system less complicated and confusing.[23] Given California's history, it is only a matter of time before citizens further reform the process (see Box 3.1). Representatives may also enact reforms through regular lawmaking channels: recently they voted to require publicizing the top donors to ballot measure campaigns (SB 47), and changed the rules so that citizen-generated initiatives may appear only in general elections or special elections called by the governor. However, the legislature may still place initiatives, constitutional amendments, or bonds on any state election ballot.

BOX 3.1
REFORMING THE INITIATIVE PROCESS

Is the initiative process ripe for reform? Californians overwhelmingly support their right to make laws alongside the state legislature, but many acknowledge the process isn't perfect. Its built-in biases have long been recognized, and resource-rich special interests have advantages over average citizens at every stage, a situation that contradicts the original intent of empowering the many at the expense of the few. Fixing these problems and others will require rebalancing individual power and free-speech rights. Opinion is sharply divided over whether and how to address these complex issues and how effective any solutions would be.

Problems and Suggested Remedies

Problem: Paid circulators can collect valid signatures more easily than volunteer-based groups can; virtually anyone can qualify an initiative by paying a professional signature-gathering firm about $3 to $7 million (depending on number of signatures needed and proximity to deadlines).

Remedy: Ban paid signature gathering or require that a certain percentage of signatures be gathered by volunteers. Extend the deadline to a year, enabling grassroots volunteer movements more time to organize.

Problem: Big money dominates the initiative process.

Remedy: Because capping campaign donations violates free speech protections, improve disclosure laws instead.

Problem: Ballot measures are confusing and complex.

Remedy: As in Oregon, establish an independent citizens' commission to hold hearings, evaluate propositions, and make recommendations. Use more social media to help voters find reliable, comprehensive election resources and information. If two conflicting measures are being considered in the same election, place them together in the ballot pamphlet and explain which will prevail if both pass. Publicize legislative hearings to generate more substantive discussion about a measure's probable impacts.

Problem: There are too many initiatives.

Remedy: Require the legislature to vote on proposed laws first. After a public hearing on a measure, the legislature could vote on passing it, with or without any changes that the initiative's authors may approve or reject. Courts could help verify that the legislature's version is consistent with the authors' intentions. Also, if a measure requires a supermajority vote of the legislature, require the same threshold for the ballot measure.

Problem: It is too difficult to revise initiatives once they become law. They cannot be changed except through future ballot measures, even if flaws are discovered.

Remedy: Require initiatives to allow the legislature to amend measures after a certain amount of time, holding lawmakers to strict guidelines, special conditions (such as a supermajority vote), or further review.

Problem: The process clutters the state constitution with redundant and contradictory amendments.

Remedy: Require a constitutional revision commission to help find obsolete, unnecessary, or contradictory language and to make recommendations that voters or lawmakers may act on.

Problem: Too many initiatives are declared unconstitutional.

Remedy: Empower the attorney general or a panel of active or retired judges to review proposed measures for problematic legal issues and to inform the voters. Give authors more time to fix or withdraw their measures.

REFERENDUM

Citizens can try to repeal or replace laws through an initiative, but they also can challenge recently signed laws, parts of laws, or redistricting maps through a **referendum** (referenda, plural). To trigger a statewide vote to reconsider a law, petitioners must collect the same number of valid signatures required for an initiative (546,651, until the next election in 2026) within 90 days after the targeted law goes into effect. If the referendum qualifies for the ballot—and since 2011, referenda may appear only on general election ballots—voters must choose to vote "yes" if they want to retain the law in question or "no" if they want to nullify it. Referendum by petition happens rarely: only 53 have qualified for the ballot since 1912, and voters have historically been more likely to repeal existing laws than to retain them (58 percent of targeted laws were rejected through referenda; 42 percent were retained).[24] Gaming compacts negotiated between Native American tribes and the governor usually are presented to voters as referenda, and the people have approved all but one (rejected in 2014). In 2022, voters participated in a referendum on prohibiting flavored tobacco products, ultimately upholding the law that had been adopted in 2020.

A far more common type of referendum is a *bond measure*, first approved by two-thirds of the legislature and then passed along to voters for simple majority approval (the thresholds for <u>local</u> general obligation bonds are different). The constitution requires that voters approve state borrowing above $300,000. Bond measures authorize the state treasurer to sell bonds on the open market, which essentially are promises to pay back with interest any amounts loaned to the state. Bonds are typically used to finance gigantic infrastructure projects ranging from water restoration to library renovation, and since 2000, bonds approved by voters average over $5 billion, with the largest being a $19.925 billion water bond in 2006. Most bond measures have passed with minimal controversy.[25] Importantly, financing state government projects with billion-dollar bonds involves substantial financial penalties and hidden costs: a sizable share of the state's annual budget each year is dedicated to paying interest, or "servicing the debt," and *taxpayers end up paying nearly twice the face amount of what is borrowed* after the interest and capital are repaid. Few voters realize that a $15 billion bond will actually cost around $26 billion to pay off, although the final price tag depends on interest rates and inflation, which brings the actual, amortized costs closer to $1.40 per dollar borrowed.[26]

Source: Ava Van Vechten.

RECALL

California is one of 19 states allowing voters to remove and replace *state* elected officials between regular elections, meaning that they can **recall** lawmakers, justices, and anyone serving in an elected executive capacity, such as the governor or attorney general. It is also one of at least 30 states permitting the recall of *local* officials, including any person elected in a city or county, or to a court, school or community college board, or special district board.[27] Citizens do *not* have the right to recall federal representatives, meaning U.S. House and Senate members.

A state-level recall election contains two parts: first, voters answer "yes" or "no" as to whether the representative in question should be removed from office; second, they may choose a replacement from any candidate listed on the ballot, regardless of whether they voted to remove the official. This process of removing politicians before their term ends differs categorically from impeachment, whereby charges of misconduct in office are leveled, a trial is held by the state Senate with a two-thirds vote required to convict, and the Assembly votes to impeach (a deed that hasn't occurred in California since the mid-1800s).[28]

Low recall success rates are partly ensured through fairly high signature requirements and relatively short deadlines for all types of offices. Signature thresholds vary with the office and size of the jurisdiction, meaning the area represented by the targeted official. For lawmakers and appeals court judges in California, for instance, petitioners have 160 days to meet the signature threshold, which is equal to 20 percent of the votes cast in the last election for the official being recalled. For mayors and other local officials, the number is based on registered voters, which varies with city size.[29] For statewide officials, signatures must be obtained from voters in at least five different counties, with minimums in each jurisdiction tied to the prior election results. These rules also apply to recalling the governor, and proponents have just over five months to submit valid signatures equal to 12 percent of the votes cast during the previous gubernatorial election (over 1.3 million signatures), a low percentage compared to other states. In Kansas, the signature threshold to prompt the recall of a governor is 40 percent of votes most recently cast for that office.

Signature gathering to qualify initiative petitions typically peaks before important deadlines. Unlike legislatively-referred measures that can be voted on in primary or general elections, citizen-initiated measures may appear only on general election ballots.

Source: Renée B. Van Vechten.

No specific grounds for removal are needed to launch a recall in California—officials can be recalled for any reason or cause—but proponents must state their reasons on the petitions they circulate. Since 1913, 179 recalls have been launched against state elected officials in California, but of the *eleven* that ultimately qualified for the ballot, only *six* succeeded.[30] By far, the most dramatic examples have been gubernatorial (relating to governor) recalls in 2003 and 2021, as discussed in Chapter 2.

Rules favor short election seasons in which voters have little time to vet the candidates, and although it takes a simple majority to recall an incumbent, the replacement wins by plurality vote (the most votes of all cast). This process can have serious consequences, as the 2021 recall against Newsom exposed: a replacement could be voted into office by a tiny, unrepresentative segment of participating voters. Relatively low signature thresholds also incentivize opponents to pursue expensive special elections (the election in 2021 cost over $200 million) that may simply validate the majority's preferences (Newsom scored the same percentage he had won in 2018 and more actual votes in the recall). The episode prompted the legislature to adopt a limited number of reforms addressing local level recalls, but they sidestepped more fundamental reforms at the state level.

DIRECT DEMOCRACY AT THE LOCAL LEVEL

It shouldn't be surprising that the three forms of direct democracy—the initiative, referendum, and recall—are available in every California county, city, and school district and are used more frequently at the local level than at the state level. Voters are regularly invited to weigh in on changes to their city constitutions (charter amendments), local laws, bonds, citizen initiatives, and recalls of local officials. Local measures are adopted more often than state propositions, but seldom spark a sensation unless they stem from a local scandal or endanger profits (such as land use changes affecting developers), or public morality is at issue (sex and drugs).

Recalls of local officials—meaning a county supervisor, city council member, mayor, school or community college board member, or special district official—are still uncommon, but because officials can be recalled for any reason with a high success rate (about three out of four succeed), strategic-minded, well-funded groups threaten and use recalls both as a political weapon and to keep representatives accountable.[31] A new change to local recall law requires a separate subsequent election of a replacement if an official is recalled. Local **referenda** also remain rare occurrences. On the other hand, Californians "lead the nation" in their use of local **initiative** processes to generate new laws.[32] Success rates are high: from 2001 to 2020, two out of three local measures passed—virtually the opposite of what happens at the state level.[33] Most local initiatives relate to matters of growth and development, also known as *land use* or zoning (approve new housing developments or protect open space); governance or political *reforms* (impose term limits or conduct elections differently such as by allowing Saturday voting); public *morality* (porn actors in Los Angeles County must wear condoms during filming thanks to a county initiative); local *taxes* (typically to place high rates on marijuana sales or hotel stays to pay for homelessness programs or fund 911 and other emergency services). Special taxes "earmarked" or designated for specific purposes require two-thirds approval, whereas all-purpose tax increases need only a simple majority.[34]

Parcel tax proposals appear frequently on local ballots as well; these are additional taxes or assessments based on square footage of a property, number of units, or a house's or building's value that voters can impose on themselves to pay for local infrastructure projects, such as renovating local schools or hospitals. Typically these "piggyback" taxes are attached to a property tax bill. These are similar to local general obligation bonds which must be approved by a *supermajority* (two-thirds vote), but most school bonds have a lower threshold (55 percent).

When wealthy interests have a stake in the outcome, especially large corporations or unions, campaign spending can quickly accelerate far beyond locals' means. In 2022, oil driller Aera Energy, aided by Chevron, pumped over $8.2 million to defeat local Measures A and B which would have required current environmental reviews to apply to old wells, overpowering environmentalists' $1.1 million effort in support (Patagonia was the largest donor).[35] Usually when the spending disparity nears 10-to-1, "The voters are hearing from only one side. Your voice is drowned out (Figure 3.3)."[36]

With two exceptions, the procedures for circulating a petition for a city or county initiative are similar to those at the state level and are spelled out in the state's election codes: signature requirements, strict circulation guidelines, signature verification carried out by the county registrar of voters, and certification either by the registrar or the city clerk. One exception is that signature requirements vary among cities because they are based either on prior turnout for a general election (such as votes

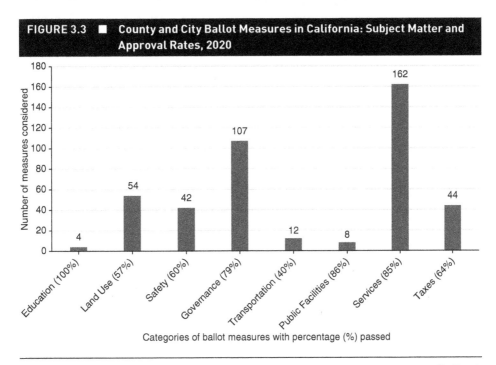

FIGURE 3.3 ■ County and City Ballot Measures in California: Subject Matter and Approval Rates, 2020

Categories of ballot measures with percentage (%) passed

Source: Leonor Ehling, Shannon Williams, Valory Messier, Fleur Marfori, and Sebastian Cambrey, "California County, City, and School District Election Outcomes: Candidates and Ballot Measures, 2020 Elections (Trend Table B)," Institute for Social Research, Center for California Studies, CSU Sacramento, 2021, https://csu-csus.esploro. exlibrisgroup.com/esploro/outputs/dataset/California-Elections-Data-Archive-CEDA/99257830890201671.

Note: Of 454 city and county measures, 68.5 percent passed overall. Numbers in parentheses represent the percentage of measures that passed (and have been rounded).

cast for mayor) or voter registration; thus, in 2022, it took 17,958 valid signatures to qualify an initiative ordinance or charter amendment in San Francisco but 24,770 in the City of San Diego.[37]

The second glaring difference lies in local use of the *indirect initiative*. Unlike the state process, citizens must first file a notice of intent to circulate a petition, and depending on the number of valid signatures gathered, the local governing board (either the city council or county supervisors) may first consider and adopt a proposed measure without alteration before it is submitted to voters. If the local governing body approves the measure, then it becomes a local law.

Los Angeles requires nearly 300,000 valid signatures (not less than 10 percent of all votes cast for governor within the county) for the Board of Supervisors either to adopt the ordinance at their next regular meeting or to call a special election for voters to consider it.[38] Local initiatives are placed on ballots as "Measure [letter]," such as "Measure U," unlike state propositions, which are assigned numbers. In 2020, all California voters encountered at least one kind of local ballot measure, 722 in all.[39]

CONCLUSION: THE PERILS AND PROMISES OF HYBRID DEMOCRACY

The tools of direct democracy—the initiative, referendum, and recall—render California's government a hybrid type in which citizens possess the power to make or reject laws and elect or eject representatives, one of only 11 states that permit all three.[40] Yet even among this minority, California's uncommon brand of direct citizen empowerment sets it apart. From being the first state to legalize medical marijuana to having staged the only modern recall of a governor, California politics stand apart not only because of its hybrid form but also because of the policies and outcomes it has produced.

California's blend of representative and direct democracy gives the people tremendous power to govern themselves, but, ironically, citizens generally do not feel as if they are in control. In an immense and sprawling state, money is a megaphone, and the initiative process favors the well-funded. Because of the money they can spend to spread their messages across major media markets, resource-rich special interests overshadow a process that was established to give voice to the powerless. If short of cash, groups can capitalize on social media and email to spread messages strategically and mobilize citizens to vote, but they compete to be heard.

The initiative process creates winners who use public authority to establish their version of reform and their vision of "better" policy that reflects their values and interests. It also produces losers who have the right to overcome their opponents by imposing their vision of good government through future ballots should enough voters agree with them. This give-and-take over time is the essence of political struggle, but in a purely representative democracy, conflicts are harnessed by elected officials and saddled to a lawmaking institution where they are tamed through deliberation and compromise. Because initiatives offer one-size-fits-all solutions and are not open to amendment, direct democracy precludes bargaining and compromise. Unlike bills, which pass through many hands and multiple points where they can be challenged, tweaked, reconsidered, or adjusted to accommodate concerns, the referendum, recall, and initiative take *one* unchanging form that demands merely a "yes" or "no" response from voters at *one* point in time. The initiative process in California also unleashes political conflicts to a diverse population where deafening, one-sided arguments circulate via social media and paid political advertising. Simple messages and emotional appeals are easier to broadcast across the expanse of California than the nuances and complexities normally associated with lawmaking and policycraft. Most people lack the time to sort through complex issues thoroughly.

Furthermore, the initiative and referendum processes tend to breed irregular systems of laws and rules. Thus, new reforms are layered on prior reforms in California, and newer laws are imperfectly fitted to existing statutes, an incremental process that tends to yield a disordered system of governing. This is a key reason the Golden State's government appears illogical. In fact, state building through the ballot box has proceeded incoherently for decades, often in response to scandals and crises, but often because of voters' hopeful desire for better government.

Even though voters make far fewer decisions at the ballot box than legislators make in a typical morning in the Capitol, the political, fiscal, and social impacts of initiatives and referenda can profoundly upset the status quo—frequently with unintended consequences. Yet direct democracy is sacred in California. Despite the systemic flaws that people see in the initiative process, a majority of citizens believe they make better public policy decisions than elected officials do,[41] and voters continually reshape their government with the goal of "making things work." California's hybrid democracy doesn't ensure that things will get better or that government will work more efficiently, but direct democracy feeds citizens' hopes that it will. For better or worse, Californians will continue to use direct democracy to restructure their relationships with their government and with each other.

KEY TERMS

Ballot measure: a proposed law or amendment to the state constitution or local charter that appears on an election ballot for the voters' consideration, usually labeled as "Proposition [#]" or "Measure [letter]."

Direct initiative: a citizen-proposed law that requires a vote of the people instead of the legislature to become law.

Indirect initiative: a citizen-proposed law that must be first considered by the legislature, which then may adopt it; if not adopted, it will appear on the next election ballot. In California, only *local* initiatives may be enacted through this method.

Legislatively referred measure: a proposed state law (statute), constitutional amendment, or bond (ballot measure) that

the legislature has passed and that requires voter approval to take effect.

Parcel tax: a method of raising local revenues by assessing a characteristic of a property, such as square footage or number of units.

Propositions: a proposed state law or constitutional amendment that appears on an election ballot for the voters' consideration; another word for "ballot measure."

Recall: an election in which the people may decide to remove a sitting elected official from office and replace that person with a new representative.

Referendum: in California, a statewide vote held to allow the people to reject or retain a law recently passed by the legislature and signed into law by the governor.

4 THE STATE LEGISLATURE

Should all schoolchildren be vaccinated against COVID-19? Should alcoholic drinks be available for take-out and delivery? What should be done with a blockbuster budget surplus of nearly $100 billion? Legislators grapple with questions like these through the lawmaking process. They are obligated to express the will of the citizens they represent, and they make decisions that touch almost every aspect of people's lives.

DESIGN, PURPOSE, AND FUNCTION OF THE LEGISLATURE

In California's system of separated powers, the legislature makes law or policy, the executive branch enforces or implements it, and the judicial branch interprets the other branches' actions and the laws they make. Chapters 2 and 3 discussed how the people also dabble in lawmaking through the initiative process, but it's legislators who are responsible for solving the state's thorny problems. California's full-time lawmakers are far better suited to the task than are average citizens. They directly confront complex issues year-round and are assisted by professional staff members who help anticipate outcomes of the bills they create, research the history of similar attempts, evaluate alternatives, and estimate costs of proposed laws.

California's legislature resembles the U.S. Congress in both structure and function. Like its federal counterpart, it is bicameral, meaning that it's divided into two houses that check each other. Legislators in both the state's 80-member lower house, called the *Assembly*, and the 40-member upper house, the *Senate*, represent districts that are among the most populous in the nation: based on current population estimates, 80 Assembly districts contain just under a half-million **constituents**, a term referring to all residents who are represented by an elected official within a defined area, and with nearly 1 million constituents, the 40 Senate districts are larger than U.S. House districts (now numbering 52).[1] As with Congress, lower house elections are more frequent: Assembly members serve two-year terms, whereas Senators serve four years at a time.

Candidates for the state legislature submit to grueling, expensive campaigns that mirror those of Congress. Well-paid and heavily staffed, legislators also meet year-round like Congress members do; their "professionalized" status puts them in a small class of states that equip the legislature to counterbalance the administrative branch. Only the legislatures of Michigan, New York, and Pennsylvania are comparable to California's, and excepting six states that *approach* professionalized status, the remaining "citizen" legislatures are on a sliding scale of short sessions, low pay, and few staff.[2] Unlike members of the U.S. Congress, however, California legislators have **term limits**, meaning that representatives may only be reelected a specified number of times and cannot build long careers in office. Voters started the term limit clocks for lawmakers in 1990 with Proposition 140 and then altered the rules with Prop 28 (in 2012) so that Assembly members and state Senators may now serve a total of twelve years in a single house or can split their time between the two chambers. A *lifetime ban* means that lawmakers are prohibited from serving in either office once they've reached the twelve-year limit.[3] The newer term limits law has helped steady a legislature that for years was agitated by consistently high membership turnover as legislators anxiously searched for their next job and left either before their six-year limit in the Assembly was exhausted or before they met their eight-year limit in the Senate; in 2012, almost half the institution (47.5 percent) was new. Turnover stabilized before 2022 brought a torrent of resignations, mostly due to redistricting, Congressional ambitions, and term limits.[4] Observers note that legislators now tend to stay and build expertise, wait longer to scout their next jobs, are once again tackling "big picture" issues and long-term projects, and the Senate is again attracting first-time legislators (rather than former Assembly members, primarily) which helps equalize the chambers. Overall, term limits have profoundly influenced individual representatives' perspectives and the way the legislature operates, a point revisited later in this chapter (and see Box 4.2).

BOX 4.1
FAST FACTS ON THE CALIFORNIA LEGISLATURE

Lower house: Assembly, 80 members

Upper house: Senate, 40 members

Term length: Assembly, 2 years; Senate, 4 years

Term limits: 12 years (combined) in the Assembly and/or Senate, lifetime ban

Majority party in Assembly and Senate: Democratic

Leaders: Speaker of the Assembly, president pro tem of the Senate, minority leaders of the Assembly and Senate

Leaders' salaries: $141,097* annually plus a per diem of $214/day**

Legislators' salaries: $122,694* annually plus a per diem of $214/day**

Source: "Salaries of Elected Officials," California Citizens Compensation Commission, effective December 1, 2022, https://www.calhr.ca.gov/cccc/pages/cccc-salaries.aspx.

Note: On June 22, 2022, commissioners voted to increase elected officials' salaries (effective December 5, 2022).

*Legislators also receive a car allowance of $300 per month, which replaced the state-paid vehicle and gas card in 2011.

**The nine-month in-session rate of $214 per day is based on the 2022 federal government reimbursement rate for daily expenses associated with working away from home ($145 for lodging and $69 for food). Total amounts vary annually with the number of days in session and by chamber. Legislators must be physically present in the capitol, and a few legislators refuse per diems. On average, each Assembly member collects over $40,000 in per diem payments annually.

BOX 4.2

TERM LIMITS: POLITICAL EARTHQUAKE

Have term limits for legislators been good or bad? Both supporters and detractors can find ammunition in the findings. One thing neither side can deny, however, is that the reform has dramatically shaped representation and the environment in which legislators work. As of 2012 (with Prop 28), legislators can serve twelve years "in the Assembly, Senate, or both, in any combination of terms," and their experiences help illuminate the law's effects.

Prior to the passage of Prop 140 in 1990, state legislators were belittled as out-of-touch careerists who had developed cozy relationships with lobbyists and whose reelection seemed guaranteed. The legislature's reputation sank further after a Federal Bureau of Investigation (FBI) sting in 1988 netted 14 state officials who were charged with bribery, including three legislators who went to prison.

The electorate was ready for change when an initiative modeled on one passed shortly before in Oklahoma qualified for the ballot. It restricted senators to two terms (a total of eight years) and Assembly members to three terms (six years) during their lifetimes. Echoes of the early California Progressives were heard in proponents' sweeping promises to restore a "government of citizens representing their fellow citizens."* The measure quickly gained momentum and passed. Although twenty other states subsequently adopted term limits, the laws were invalidated or repealed in six of them, bringing the total number of states with term limits to fifteen currently. Californians revised their term limits law in 2012 after being persuaded that lawmakers would stop "campaigning for their next office" and "develop the expertise to get things done" if those officials were permitted to stay up to twelve years in one chamber.** Sixty-one percent of voters approved the change through Prop 28.

Term limits rattled capital politics. New faces began replacing the familiar ones as veteran legislators sought different offices, and as experienced staff members were driven into private lobbying firms after Prop 140 slashed legislative budgets. Within a few years, longstanding Assembly Speaker Willie Brown was mayor of San Francisco and many other legislative careers were ending for good. Overall, the wide-ranging effects of term limits have touched virtually every aspect of legislative life, and they have ranged from positive to negative.

Willie Brown, Speaker of the California state Assembly from 1980 to 1995, was an easy target of term limits supporters for his perceived abuses of power and flashy style.

Source: AP Photo/Susan Ragan.

Electoral Effects

- Competition for political offices at *all* levels, from city councils and county boards of supervisors to U.S. Congress, remains robust as more termed-out legislators seek opportunities to stay in politics.
- Open-seat primary elections created through term limits are ferociously competitive, usually attracting millions of dollars in donations and independent spending.
- Incumbents are almost always reelected (about 95 percent of them are), thereby reducing electoral competition. Many face no serious challengers, and some run unopposed. In the 2022 primaries, 11 percent of incumbents had no major party opponent.
- Most legislators seek reelection to the same seat, staying put until their twelve-year limit is exhausted.
- Whereas the Senate used to be a logical step-up for Assembly members, many brand-new Senators lack Assembly experience (seven of eight freshmen elected in 2022).

Membership Effects

- **Open seats** have hastened the diversification of membership. Those identifying as persons of color and LGBTQ+ are elected at higher rates than might be expected through redistricting or population change. In 2023, half of the entire body were Latinx,

Black, Asian American or Pacific Islander, tribal members (one), or Middle Eastern (two). The first Muslim woman (Senator Aisha Wahab, an Afghan American) was elected in 2022.

- Although more women have been *candidates* since the adoption of term limits, the total percentage of women legislators follows a longer historical (generally upward) trend *predating* term limits: finally, at 42.5 percent in 2023, they have reached a new high.
- In 2023, Democratic women far outnumber Republican women (43 to 8). Women occupy more leadership roles than ever before.

Institutional Effects

- The relative power of Assembly members and Senators and their leaders is equalizing once again. Prior to Prop 28, the average senator had about two-and-a-half times as much legislative experience as the average Assembly member.
- Newer legislators have experienced the effects of recent state laws and have fresh ideas about how to address problems arising from them.
- "Institutional memory" is shallower than before term limits, meaning the members are relatively less expert across a range of policy areas and less knowledgeable about policy history or how state systems interrelate. Longer terms in a single chamber are helping lawmakers build expertise and long-term perspectives.
- Experienced lobbyists representing powerful special interests can exert undue influence over legislators, but lobbyists must work harder to establish relationships with legislators, who are likely to regard lobbyists with skepticism.

Behavioral Effects

- "Lame duck" legislators (those in their last terms) lack electoral accountability to their current districts and can vote based on their own conscience without fear of reprisal.
- Legislators in their last terms may try to please their next possible constituency when voting, but some feel less obligated to lobbyists or donors.
- Longer tenures under Prop 28 seem to be spurring more complex, long-range bills; previously this suffered, as legislators often lacked the time and incentive to tackle big projects or issues that would outlast their short time in office.
- Most lawmakers seek other offices (about two-thirds do so within two years of being termed-out) or continue to work in the public sector, but institutional turnover is slowing as they "play it safe" by staying in the same office until their clocks run out.

Sources: Author's data; Devin Lavelle, "Demographics in the California Legislature: 2021–22 Session," California State Library, November 2020; Elizabeth Castillo, et al., "How Diverse is the California Legislature?" CalMatters, updated May 5, 2022; Eric McGhee," "New Term Limits Add Stability to the Legislature," PPIC, November 12, 2018, https://www.ppic.org/blog/new-term-limits-add-stability-to-the-state-legislature/; Thad Kousser, Bruce Cain, and Karl Kurtz, "The Legislature: Life under Term Limits," in *Governing California: Politics, Government, and Public Policy in the Golden State*, 3rd ed., ed. Ethan Rarick (Berkeley, CA: Public Policy Press, Institute of Governmental Studies, 2013).

*Peter Schabarum, Lewis Uhler, and J. G. Ford, Jr., "Argument in Favor of Proposition 140," in *Voter Information Guide for 1990*, Office of the Secretary of State, State of California.

**Jennifer A. Waggoner, Kathay Feng, and Hank Lacayo, "Argument in Favor of Proposition 28," in *Voter Information Guide for June 2012*, Office of the Secretary of State, State of California.

Legislators are elected from districts resembling jigsaw puzzle pieces that are redrawn once per decade based on U.S. Census data. The California state legislature commanded this **redistricting** process until voters—weary of mapping tricks to keep the same representatives in office—passed Proposition 11, the Voters FIRST Act (in 2008), transferring the mapmaking power to an independent citizens' commission—making California one of 15 states to relocate this pivotal power outside the regular lawmaking body.[5] Their authority to redesign California's U.S. House districts, enabled in 2010 through Prop 20, was indirectly tested in a federal court case against Arizona's citizen redistricting commission, and the U.S. Supreme Court upheld the principle that a citizen commission may help determine the "time, manner, and place" of Congressional elections through redistricting, just as it does for state government.[6]

Reconstituted once a decade through a multistage process, the politically balanced and demographically diverse 14-member **Citizens Redistricting Commission** is charged with drawing Assembly, Senate, Board of Equalization (see Chapter 5), and U.S. House districts based on "strict, nonpartisan rules designed to ensure fair representation."[7] The rules mandate equal population, adherence to the federal Voting Rights Act, contiguous (all parts touching) and compact districts that aim to keep "**communities of interest**" intact (neighborhoods as well as cities and counties), and eliminate protection for **incumbents** (current officeholders) and political partisanship from consideration.[8] These rules are designed to prevent **gerrymandering**, or the manipulation of district boundaries to help or harm a political party, incumbent, or community. Commissioners note that virtually every aspect of the process is open and participatory.[9] After U.S. Census reporting delays due to COVID-19, the 2021 commission undertook extensive public education outreach through social media, held 196 public meetings around the state, received over 36,000 comments about communities and boundary lines, and "held long and difficult debates" over where to draw the lines.[10] While redistricting remains inherently "messy" because the mapmakers are citizens and they create winners and losers, the district maps reflect a nonpartisan approach and have survived court challenges.[11] Democrats dominate most districts due to their higher state party registration numbers as well as natural "sorting," meaning that people tend to settle near others like themselves. The resulting district maps reflect these realities, not gerrymandering.

Although a few high-profile criminal cases have been brought against California lawmakers over the past century, hundreds of public-spirited men and women have served and are serving resolutely and honorably as California state legislators. Yet, a fervent antipolitician, antigovernment sentiment prevails among Californians, and the individuals whose job it is to sustain representative democracy are scorned rather than appreciated for the challenging work they do. As this chapter shows, lawmakers work hard to fulfill the expectations of their constituents and to meet the relentless demands of almost 40 million people (Figure 4.1).

CALIFORNIA REPRESENTATIVES AT WORK

California's legislature has come a long way from the days when allegiances to the Southern Pacific Railroad earned it the nicknames "the legislature of a thousand steals" and "the legislature of a thousand drinks." Today its full-time, professional members are the highest paid in the nation, earning more than $122,000 per year, plus per diem payments intended to cover living costs when

FIGURE 4.1 ■ California Party Control, 1994–2022														
Year	94	95	96	97	98	99	00	01	02	03	04	05	06	07	08
Governor	R	R	R	R	R	D	D	D	D	D	R	R	R	R	R
Senate	D	D	D	D	D	D	D	D	D	D	D	D	D	D	D
Assembly	D	S	R	D	D	D	D	D	D	D	D	D	D	D	D

Year	09	10	11	12	13	14	15	16	17	18	19	20	21	22
Governor	R	R	D	D	D	D	D	D	D	D	D	D	D	D
Senate	D	D	D	D*	D*	D	D*	D*	D*	D*	D*	D*	D*	D*
Assembly	D	D	D	D*	D*	D*	D	D*	D*	D*	D*	D*	D*	D*

Source: "California Party Control: 1992–2022," Ballotpedia, https://ballotpedia.org/Party_control_of_California_state_government.

*An asterisk denotes Democratic supermajority status (2/3 or above) for at least part of the year. Between 2012 and 2014, Democrats briefly lost and regained supermajority status through member resignations, a recall election, and special elections.

they're working away from home. Special interests and their lobbyists still permeate Sacramento politics with their information, favors, and money, but legislators' loyalties these days are conditioned by partisanship and splintered by the demands of 120 districts that they must balance against the perceived needs of one titanic state. Nowadays, about a dozen freshmen are climbing the steepest part of the learning curve.[12] Their crammed schedules are split between their home districts and Sacramento (see Table 4.1, "Schedule for Assembly member James Ramos, May 17, 2022"). Much of their work takes place in a brand-new office building one block from the old Capitol, the "Swing Space" as it is known, because it will house all legislators and their staff until a new annex building to replace the old one is built (estimated time to completion is six to eight years). One block away, the Assembly and Senate chambers and a few committee hearing rooms in the domed Capitol building continue to operate during the construction process.

Democratic **supermajorities** in both chambers—meaning the majority party comprises at least two-thirds or more of the membership—have brought about a different kind of politics since 2012, the first year in modern times that Democratic membership reached this critical threshold. Rather than needing to find a few Republican votes when supermajority votes are taken, now Democratic leaders manage factions *within* the Democratic majority (they held 62 out of 80 Assembly seats and 32 of 40 Senate seats in 2023), as they usually need to persuade moderate, business-friendly Democrats to support the party's agenda. They also have the power to overcome a governor's veto (last used in 1980). Adding to this the fact that only a simple majority is needed to pass the budget, Republican representatives' objections do not change the outcomes of most policy debates. However, it may be surprising that day-to-day, legislators from both political parties work together in committees, socialize outside the legislature, and often agree on fixes for local and state problems, many of which aren't partisan. Every term, hundreds of bills pass "on consent," or unanimously. Partisans may disagree on fundamentals, and their core differences are exacerbated during economic downturns and magnified by controversial issues such as providing health care

TABLE 4.1 ■ Schedule for Assembly Member James Ramos, May 17, 2022	
8:00 a.m.:	Check-In Session, Assembly. State Capitol.
9:00–10:30 a.m.:*	Inland Empire Caucus Labor Meeting (breakfast). Vallejo's Restaurant.
10:15–11:00 a.m.:*	In Office. Swing Space Office.
11:00 a.m.:	Public Service Announcement for Memorial Day recording. Democratic Caucus Office.
12:00–1:30 p.m.:	Democratic Caucus Meeting, lunch provided. Capitol Members Lounge.
1:30–3:30 p.m.:*	Budget Subcommittee 1, May Revision on Health Depts. Swing Space 1100.
3:00 p.m.:*	Meet Governor Newsom's Chief of Staff about AB 1314 (Feather Alert).
3:30 p.m.:*	Meet & Greet with university students from district.
4:15–5:15 p.m.:	Interview with Spectrum News for Memorial Day re: legislation that would impact veterans.
5:15–6:30 p.m.:	California State Sheriff's Assn Reception. Cafeteria 15 L.

Source: Office of Assembly Member James Ramos.

*Note schedule overlaps.

for undocumented immigrants—yet *members of the two parties work together often*, rather than rarely. **Bipartisanship** plays an essential role in California politics.

In many ways, the legislature is a microcosm of California (see Figure 4.2), increasingly reflecting its diversity. For the first time ever, in 2016–17, over half of all Assembly members identified as racial or ethnic minorities, rendering it a majority-minority chamber (55 percent persons of color as of 2023).[13] The Senate remains mostly White (60 percent). The number of women began rising in the mid-1970s long before term limits, but their numbers have fluctuated in recent years; the 2022 elections set a new record of 51 women legislators (42.5 percent). As of 2023, with twelve members of the LGBTQ caucus—the first of its kind to be officially recognized by a state legislature—California is the first state to reach 10 percent LGBTQ representation in its lawmaking body. The extent to which a legislature is, as U.S. founder John Adams put it, "an exact portrait, in miniature, of the people at large,"[14] is a measure of *descriptive representation*. The extent to which members translate their values, backgrounds, and preferences into meaningful policies is *substantive representation*. Their work as representatives falls into several large categories: *lawmaking and policymaking, annual budgeting, constituency service,* and *oversight* of the executive branch.

Lawmaking and Policymaking

Assembly members and senators fulfill their representative functions chiefly through performing various aspects of **lawmaking**, or codifying rules of conduct, and **policymaking**, defined loosely as, "what government decides to do or not to do." To deal with approximately 5,000 bills and measures introduced in a two-year session, they rely on legislative staffers to gather information, listen to their colleagues, hear arguments from hundreds of people—mostly lobbyists—about proposed laws, and visit sites such as schools and businesses where they interact with community leaders and citizens to get a better sense of their districts. They introduce bills addressing problems that lobbyists or constituents bring to their attention; bills that could become new **statutes**, or official laws, are variously referred to as "legislative proposals," "proposed legislation," "pieces of legislation," or simply "**legislation**" as they move through the lawmaking process. As members of committees (where the bulk of policymaking occurs), they help shape or amend legislation after hearing from government employees, experts, and other witnesses who will potentially be affected by proposed changes. They deliberate and vote on bills, first in committee, and later on the Assembly or Senate floor, where every member has a chance to vote on every piece of legislation that is voted out of committee. Because all bills must be passed in identical form by both houses before they can be sent to the governor for a signature or veto, members also build support for, or opposition to, measures that are moving through the other house.

As in Congress, much of a legislator's workload is derived from membership on committees, the institution's powerhouses. The bulk of lawmaking is done through 33 Assembly and 22 Senate policy and fiscal committees known as **standing committees**—enough for eligible members of the majority

The Assembly floor is normally a beehive of activity when in session. From the Speaker's view at the polished wood desk, the Democrats are seated to the left and Republicans to the right, reflecting their traditional ideological placement (Democrats appear on the right in the photo). Members cast votes by pressing buttons on their desks, and votes are registered on digital display boards at the front of the chamber.

Source: AP Photo/Rich Pedroncelli.

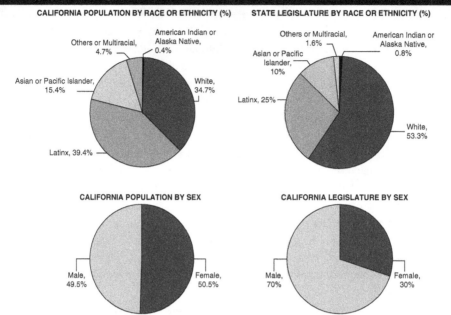

FIGURE 4.2 ■ Profile of California's Population versus California State Legislature, mid-2022

CALIFORNIA POPULATION BY RACE OR ETHNICITY (%)

American Indian or Alaska Native, 0.4%
Others or Multiracial, 4.7%
White, 34.7%
Asian or Pacific Islander, 15.4%
Latinx, 39.4%

STATE LEGISLATURE BY RACE OR ETHNICITY (%)

Others or Multiracial, 1.6%
American Indian or Alaska Native, 0.8%
Asian or Pacific Islander, 10%
Latinx, 25%
White, 53.3%

CALIFORNIA POPULATION BY SEX

Male, 49.5%
Female, 50.5%

CALIFORNIA LEGISLATURE BY SEX

Male, 70%
Female, 30%

Sources: "Table H-2: Population and Percent Change by Race: 2010 and 2020," 2020 Redistricting Data (Demographics), Department of Finance Demographics Unit, State of California, August 2021, https://dof.ca.gov/forecasting/demographics/redistricting-data/#hist; "QuickFacts California," U.S. Census Bureau, accessed June 30, 2022, https://www.census.gov/quickfacts/fact/table/US/PST045221.

Note: Assemblyman Adrin Nazarian (born in Iran) is included as a person of color.

party to become a chair if desired. In both chambers, all standing committees meet regularly and are permanently staffed by policy specialists whose intimate knowledge of past and present policy solutions allows them to play key roles in analyzing and shaping the bills referred to their committee.[15]

After a bill is referred to a policy committee, the chair usually schedules a public hearing for it, at which point the author, lobbyists, government officials, and others may provide information and arguments for and against it.[16] Bills also may be heard in committee to create an opportunity for debate and discussion, even if those bills are unlikely to succeed. Bills that are problematic may be "held," or set aside (to die), either at the author's request or the chair's request. Lobbyists often suggest changes to bills during hearings to accommodate their clients' concerns. After the language is finalized and the committee members vote, the next steps for a bill involve either further policy hearings or being moved to specialized committees that either consider costs (Appropriations) or apply rules for debate (Rules); the last step is being sent to the floor for debate and a full vote by all members of that chamber. The process repeats in the other house (Figure 4.3). After any differences are resolved, both chambers vote on the bill and send it to the governor for a signature or veto. With the governor's autograph (or without it after ten days), it becomes a state law and is officially **chaptered**.

FIGURE 4.3   ■   How a Bill Becomes a Law

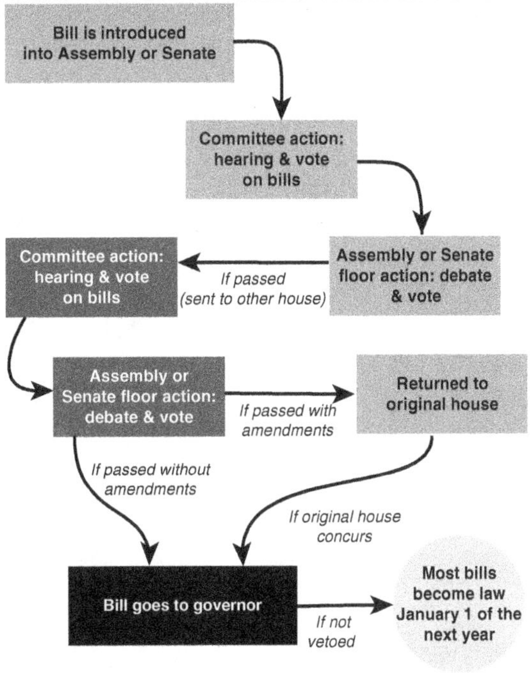

In bygone eras, committee chairmen would rule over their fiefdoms for decades, protecting pet projects, crushing ideas at a whim, and blessing other bills before releasing them for final consideration by all members. Power is no longer highly concentrated in a few leaders and chairs as it once was, because steeper turnover leads to relatively less expert members. In fact, many freshmen without legislative experience have chaired committees under term limits; their perspective is informed chiefly by recent personal experiences outside Sacramento.

Today, each bill bears the imprint of a unique set of players, is shaped by the rules, and is affected by timing. Throughout the bill passage process, **"stakeholders"**—individuals and groups either directly or indirectly affected by a law or policy, meaning those who have a stake in the outcome—voice their concerns, demanding or pleading for accommodation. Observers are often surprised at the overt influence that special interests wield in the process. Legislators listen and respond to objections by amending (changing) the details or by killing bills entirely. Lawmakers tend to be extra sensitive to the fears and threats expressed by well-financed, vocal, influential, and entities that support their political party or are active in their districts—or as some say, "The squeaky wheels get the grease." If a bill is being considered that would force large companies to disclose their greenhouse gas (GHG) emissions, then lobbyists for agribusinesses, railroads, and oil and gas companies will likely be arguing that it is an unnecessary and costly regulation in face-to-face meetings with lawmakers or their staff and will be forcefully presenting their cases in committee hearings, just as environmental lobbyists will be vigorously arguing that it will help the state better address climate change. Lawmakers weigh this type of input when deciding how to vote.

Relationships also matter. Partisans tend to support fellow partisans, but legislators who share specific interests or characteristics might become allies, even "across the aisle." Apart from the all-important political **party caucuses** in both houses, which are formal groups that help legislators coordinate their work and strategize together, other **caucuses** enable bipartisan collaboration on related issues. Several are based on demographics (Latino, Black, Women's, or LGBTQ, for example), others are based on mutual policy interests (outdoor sporting, environmental, etc.), and a couple are region-based (Bay Area, rural, etc.). There is also an influential "Mod Caucus" (some say the "Mod Squad"), an informal association of Democratic legislators who consider themselves to be ideologically moderate and probusiness. Over time, representatives tend to develop what is commonly referred to as "social capital": a shared sense of norms, interpersonal networks, and trust among colleagues. Because, in the final analysis, compromise and bargaining are key, relationships among the players—from legislative staff to legislators to lobbyists to the governor's staff—help facilitate the necessary give-and-take to co-construct workable policy solutions.

Bills vary in scope, cost, urgency, and significance and cover every imaginable topic. Regular bills that are first introduced into the Assembly will be given the designation "AB" (Assembly Bill) and a number, or if first introduced into the Senate, "SB" and a number.

The Assembly continues to diversify. By 2023, women in the Assembly held 33 of 80 seats (there were 18 women Senators), 42.5 percent of the legislature, a new record. Persons of color represented over half (55 percent) of the Assembly and 40 percent of the Senate.

Source: Photo by Ash Kalra via Instagram/Public Domain.

Of lowest significance but highly symbolic are simple *resolutions* passed to express the legislature's position on particular issues. For example, the Senate and Assembly approved a joint resolution urging the U.S. President to "protect student loan borrowers" by cancelling up to $50,000 of loan debt per person (SJR 1).

Inexpensive *district bills* that deal with a city's or county's local concerns may matter a lot to the people directly affected by the legislation but usually have only minor impacts on state government. Opening Bear Lake Reservoir to year-round recreation is one example.[17] Many bills relate to the administration of government and *make technical changes* or *amendments to existing state law*. Proposed statutes might *impose mandates*, or obligations, on local governments or agencies, or private businesses, such as requiring that public high schools start classes no earlier than 8:30 a.m. Recent laws have also mandated that organic waste must be composted, and severely limit police from using rubber bullets and tear gas on protesters. Other bills *create new programs, define crimes*, suggest *constitutional amendments* that could appear as a future ballot measure for the people's approval, or *create "pilot programs"* that allow policies to be tested before attempting to make them permanent.

Legislators also introduce bills that at first glance may appear to make modest changes, but when enacted into law, can have enormous effects on Californians and their local governments, especially over time. For instance, the **California Environmental Quality Act**, the state's preeminent environmental protection law known as **CEQA** (pronounced "see-kwa"), signed into

Assembly member Lori Wilson, surrounded by other state legislators, held a press conference to warn against the disproportionate effects on women of color that the U.S. Supreme Court's decision to overturn *Roe v. Wade* would have. The Court delivered their opinion in June 2022.

Source: Office of Assembly member Lori Wilson/Jeff Walters.

law by Governor Ronald Reagan in 1970, was developed to supplement new federal regulations regarding land use and pollution and foster public disclosure. It "requires state and local agencies to identify the significant environmental impacts of their actions and to avoid or mitigate those impacts, if feasible."[18] An environmental review must be completed for any public works project or any commercial activity requiring a government permit, and if potentially damaging activities are detected in the plans, then alterations must be made. Having matured through statutes and court opinions over the years, CEQA codes have had profound impacts on infrastructure development, including the design, size, cost, location, and time to completion of projects such as apartment buildings, airport expansions, and water storage. CEQA is thus partly to blame for a growing housing shortage afflicting the state, because strict regulations have caused property development costs to rise, placed some areas off-limits to development, and can be abused to delay construction projects by tying them up in court. Lack of new construction is especially acute near the expensive coast, so that low-paid workers are forced to seek housing further inland, which in turn causes traffic and pollution to escalate. Home prices and rents vary statewide, but the average renter and homebuyer pay about *two-and-a-half times* the national average, and even the least expensive housing markets are more expensive than the national average.[19] A major update to CEQA regulations in 2019 helped streamline processes, enables some exemptions for housing developments near transit centers and mixed-use projects, and changes the way transportation impacts are measured.[20] The legislature has the power to exempt projects from CEQA as it recently did for state college and university student housing.[21]

CEQA amendments belong in a category of bills that have multimillion- or billion-dollar impacts, tend to demand intricate knowledge of existing law, affect many different groups, and usually require years of preparation, study, and compromise. Unraveling knotty problems takes several years and the input of many stakeholders. With "big bills" legislators try to comprehensively address issues such as homelessness, workers' compensation benefits, or water; reshaping the state health-care system to comply with federal regulations is another big-ticket item. Health insurance for millions of residents has been achieved through a state-run plan called "Covered California," or through low- or no-cost Medi-Cal, the state's version of universal health insurance for low-income and disabled people, including approximately 950,000 undocumented adults eligible for pregnancy and emergency services. The federal Affordable Care Act (ACA) expands coverage and supplies billions of dollars to support 14.6 million people who benefit from Medi-Cal, about 37 percent of the state's entire population, and full-scope coverage will extend to all low-income adults, regardless of immigration status, by 2024.[22]

Given the scope and complexity of policy issues, legislators need help. Knowledge is power in Sacramento, and although lobbyists are always ready and willing to share their information, legislators rely heavily on staff to help them understand problems and develop policy. Thousands of staff members work directly for legislators in the capitol, in district offices, or for committees, and only three states (New York, Pennsylvania, and Texas when it's in session) employ more.[23]

Inside each legislator's capitol and district offices are *personal staff*: individuals hired to prepare bills their bosses will introduce, analyze the thousands of other bills that cross a legislator's desk during a two-year term, assist with scheduling, and connect with constituents and lobbyists. Professional *committee staff members*, or consultants, work for a specific Assembly or Senate committee, and manage all aspects of shepherding bills through the process, from scheduling witnesses who will testify at committee hearings to writing detailed analyses of bills. In addition, staff work for both political parties' leadership and routinely provide their own bill analyses and vote recommendations to their party members.

Legislators also heavily depend on institutional housekeepers like the Assembly chief clerk or the Senate's secretary to ensure that legislators follow standing rules and parliamentary procedures. The nonpartisan *Legislative Analyst's Office (LAO)* has been the so-called conscience and eyes and ears of the legislature for 75 years, providing professional analysis of the annual budget as well as fiscal and policy advice based on in-depth research of statewide programs. With more than forty full-time analysts who cover all manner of policy issues, such as education, health, criminal justice, and infrastructure, the LAO remains one of the premier sources of information about state programs and the budget. Similarly, since 1913, the nonpartisan *Legislative Counsel* has acted as an in-house law firm, recrafting legislators' proposals into formal bills, rendering legal opinions, and making bill information available electronically (any bill can be accessed online at http://leginfo.legislature.ca.gov).

It should also be noted that the majority party controls the fate of nearly all bills because a **simple majority** vote (41 in the Assembly, 21 in the Senate) is all that's needed to pass most bills, although a good number of noncontroversial bills pass unanimously. With a simple majority also needed to pass the annual budget, the majority party can enact its agenda without being held hostage by a minority party trying to extract concessions in exchange for votes. The bottom line: today, minority-party Republicans are at the mercy of majority-party Democrats when it comes to lawmaking, and their bills rarely move out of committee. A majority party can safely ignore the minority unless votes are needed to pass urgency bills or fiscal measures such as new tax or fee hikes that require a two-thirds **supermajority** (54 in the Assembly, 27 in the Senate), and when the majority party holds a supermajority of seats, the minority occupies an even more discouraging position. The 2012 elections laid a new milestone when, for the first time since 1883, Democrats secured a supermajority in both houses, and they have reclaimed that high-water mark almost continuously since 2016.[24] With a "veto-proof" majority that has been as high as 61 members, the Democrats can raise taxes or fees, pass urgency measures, or even override a gubernatorial veto (although they haven't tried to do so since 1980) without any Republican votes. As Governor Jerry Brown once opined, "The Republicans appear to have no power. They aren't needed for any votes."[25] To be effective, Republicans contribute to the process in other ways. For instance, they keep the majority party accountable by raising pointed questions in committee hearings and voicing concerns during floor debates, by shaping their bills to attract consensus, by trying to amend the Democratic majority's bills to soften potential impacts on their constituents, and by publicly challenging the majority's decisions.

Annual Budgeting

It takes the legislature more than half the year to work out an annual budget for the **fiscal year** (FY) that starts July 1 and ends the following June 30, twelve months covered by the state budget. The process formally begins on or before January 10 when the governor submits a preliminary version to the legislature, and it should end by June 15, when the budget is officially due. Long-overdue budgets had been the norm for decades, but delays ceased after voters passed Prop

25 in 2010, an initiative that lowered the vote threshold needed to enact the budget to a simple majority and denies legislators' pay if late.

During the winter and spring, the budget committees and subcommittees in both houses divvy up the work of determining how much money is needed to keep government programs running in the next FY. They use the governor's budget as a benchmark for estimating costs and potential state revenues. Big-ticket items such as education are either automatically funded or, like basic health-care services and prisons, are permanent commitments, leaving a relatively smaller chunk of the budget pie for discretionary purposes; therefore, in a typical year, each legislator fights hard for the crumbs. An exceptional situation arose in 2022 as the budget surplus surged to a staggering $97.5 billion, half of which must be spent on schools and half refunded to citizens because of an upper limit on state spending, a cap known as the **"SAL" (State Appropriations Limit)** or **Gann Limit**. Passed by voters in 1979 (and amended in 1990), a ceiling on total spending is set by a complex formula that also applies to local governments.[26] Legislators and the governor sparred over wish lists and how to return money to citizens, ultimately opting to fund more childcare, emergency rental assistance, health care, and provide cash rebates to taxpayers.

The budget process becomes incendiary during economic downturns as painful cuts become necessary and lawmakers pivot to protect their favored programs and principles. Their anxiety is tempered by trust when there is a **trifecta**, meaning that both houses of the legislature and the governorship are controlled by one party (as has been the case in California since 2010, and also in 14 Democratic states and 23 Republican states as of mid-2022). The budget wraps up after the Assembly Speaker, the Senate president pro tem, the governor, and their staff negotiate over final numbers and the governor signs the budget into law (June 30th deadline).

Constituency Service and Outreach

Constituency service entails "helping constituents navigate through the government system,"[27] particularly when their troubles stem from bureaucratic "red tape." Legislators hire personal staff members to help them respond quickly to requests, and these caseworkers, who typically work in district offices, spend their days tracking down answers from administrators in state agencies like Caltrans and scheduling appointments at other state agencies for frustrated constituents, among other things. Representatives take constituency service seriously, although this part of the job is not mentioned in the state constitution. Many consider it "paramount to return every phone call, letter, and e-mail" and make government seem friendlier through personal contact.[28]

Through energetic outreach efforts, most legislators promote their problem-solving efforts to the residents of their districts (their constituents). They communicate their activities and accomplishments through multiple channels—social media, e-mail, official websites, in person—and weekends are usually spent at community events such as new business openings, 5K races, ground-breakings for public facilities, parades, and so forth. Through this kind of "face time," or public relations, as some members call it, representatives get to know their constituents better and what they care about, and reinforce their chances for reelection by enhancing their name recognition and reputation.

Executive Branch Oversight

Who monitors programs to ensure that a law is being carried out according to the legislature's intent? Ideally, Assembly members, Senators, and their staff members should be systematically reviewing programs and questioning administrators by having them appear before committees, but term-limited legislators often lack the time and staff resources to determine if the laws they have created are being faithfully executed. In practice, they rely on investigative reports in the media, lobbyists, citizens, and administrators to sound the alarm about needed fixes. Once a problem is identified, the Assembly and Senate can rescue legislative intent in a number of ways. For example, they might follow up with the offending administrator in person or write a bill to clear up confusion over an existing statute. On the rare occasion when an issue grabs the media's attention, lawmakers might respond more dramatically, by interrogating uncooperative administrators in a public forum, such as in a select committee hearing, and then threatening to audit their departments (possibly leading to further public embarrassment), yank authority away from them, or reduce their program funding (a governor can also fire irresponsible administrators). In addition, Senators influence programs through their power to confirm hundreds of gubernatorial appointees to the major executive departments and influential state boards and commissions, such as the seventeen-member California Community Colleges Board of Governors. Leaders in both houses also have the privilege of directly appointing some members to select state boards, such as the California Coastal Commission.

To make laws or create the annual budget, members of both the Assembly committees and Senate committees conduct "hearings" at which invited experts, government administrators and officials, lobbyists, and community members share their knowledge and answer questions about measures the committee is considering. Most meetings are both livestreamed and open to the public in person, subject to COVID-19 safety protocols.
Source: Senate Photographer Lorie Shelley.

LEADERS

Aside from the governor, the Speaker of the Assembly and the president pro tem of the Senate are among the most powerful figures in Sacramento. Along with the governor and the minority leaders of each house, these individuals form the "Big Five" of California government: the leaders who speak for all their fellow party members in their respective houses and are ultimately responsible for cobbling together last-minute political bargains that clinch the budget or guarantee the signing of big bills. These days, the "**Big Three**" Democratic leaders (the top two legislative leaders plus the governor) are most visible and central to the process; the Big Five are rarely convened because Republicans lack the power to change the outcomes.

A party leader's job is to keep his or her majority in power or to regain majority status. Clarifying rules and waiving them when necessary, fundraising, and policymaking all serve that overarching objective. Leaders oversee their party caucus and help shape the electorate's understanding of what it means to support a Democratic or Republican agenda. These elites help shape agendas but rarely impose them on their peers; broader party agendas tend to emerge as issues gain popular currency (abortion rights, racial equity, gun violence, or homelessness, for example), and as individual legislators develop their ideas into bills. However, the general rule is: what leadership wants, leadership gets. Leaders' ability to obtain desired outcomes rests on many factors, including their personal style and how aggressively they dispense perks and wield credible weapons, such as removing members from choice committees, killing bills, or distributing campaign funds. Leaders have been known to reduce office budgets midyear, endorse the opponent of an incumbent, and move members out of offices or parking spaces to new and undesirable locations for disloyalty. For instance, Assemblyman Evan Low was removed as chair of the Business and Professions Committee in 2017 after he cast the Assembly's only Democratic vote against the bill that raised gas taxes and imposed new car registration fees, and again in 2021 after allegedly challenging Rendon's speakership.

The Speaker is the most visible member of the Assembly and its spokesperson at-large. They negotiate budgets, bills, and policies on behalf of the entire membership; curry a high profile with the press; and cultivate a distinct culture of discipline and institutional independence through a unique and personal leadership style. Speaker Anthony Rendon was elected by his members to be a "hands-off" leader, unlike his predecessors who reigned with a heavier hand. Rendon has decentralized power by allowing committee chairs to use their own discretion in prioritizing bill hearings; initially he *asked* members, rather than instructed them, to reduce their bill loads during the COVID-19 pandemic.

The Senate's president pro tem plays these same roles, and Toni Atkins is a collegial leader who aims to cultivate consensus in her Democratic caucus. Under revised term limits, the two leaders possess roughly equal clout. The Speaker appoints chairs and members to all Assembly committees, as does the president pro tem in the Senate through chairing the all-powerful, five-member Rules Committee. The president pro tem also can use the Rules Committee's power over the governor's key administrative appointments as a bargaining chip in budget and bill negotiations—a tool the Speaker lacks.

Speaker Anthony Rendon held on as leader after a surprise challenge from fellow Democrat Robert Rivas in spring 2022. Rivas jumped ahead of potential rivals and fought to be the successor well before Rendon stepped down. The Democratic caucus later agreed to elect Rivas as Speaker in spring 2023.

Source: AP Photo/Rich Pedroncelli.

These days, neither the Speaker nor the Senate president pro tem regularly leads floor sessions. Visitors catch glimpses of these leaders as they crisscross the floor to speak privately with members in an effort to find support for bills and negotiate deals while normal business proceeds. More often than not, a colleague acting as an assistant "pro tem" guides floor proceedings. Although the lieutenant governor (LG) is given the title of "president" of the state Senate, no executive branch official ever presides; practically speaking, it would be considered a strange breach of protocol. The LG can, however, cast a tie-breaking vote if needed.

Leaders never forget that they are chosen by colleagues and stay in power only as long as they can maintain high levels of trust and confidence by meeting their colleagues' political needs. This was as true for the inimitable former Speaker Willie Brown (1980–95) as it is for Speakers today. No tyrants can survive, if only because potential replacements impatiently wait in the wings—and under term limits, opportunities arise with some regularity. Brown presided over the Assembly for almost fifteen years. In the span of fifteen years following his exit, there were *ten* Speakers. During the past 25 years, most have served for about two years apiece, but Rendon's seven-year stretch indicates that Speakers might serve for longer periods under the twelve-year term limit law. After fending off a challenge from rival Democrat Robert Rivas, who attempted to oust him in May 2022 by securing support from fellow caucus members, Rendon hung onto his post. Following the November election, the Democratic caucus voted to keep Rendon as Speaker until June 30, 2023 and made Rivas the Speaker-designee.

CONCLUSION: OF THE PEOPLE, FOR THE PEOPLE

California's professionalized legislature is geared to lead the largest state in the nation and has few peers. Only a handful of other state legislatures are similarly compensated, staffed, work year-round, and produce as much pathbreaking legislation. Yet in many respects, California's lawmaking body is not in a league of its own: it is not the only body with term limits, or a citizens' redistricting commission, or an unusual electoral process that produces expensive elections (see Chapter 9), or a veto-proof supermajority, or is subject to popular initiatives that can reshape the rules in any given year. Rather, it is both the imposing magnitude and bulk of progressive, often left-wing policies produced by its Democratic supermajority that make it seem exceptional, particularly because these are diametrically opposed by majorities in other, more conservative U.S. states. States' recent actions on access to abortion and guns are just two areas of stark differences: while 26 states moved to ban abortion, California leaders championed adding reproductive rights to the state constitution and making it possible for citizens to sue gunmakers and sellers for relief from harm caused by gun violence.

Although the legislature's basic framework has changed little since the constitutional revision of 1879 (the 40-member Senate and 80-member Assembly remain intact), major changes to redistricting, election laws, campaign finance rules, ethics laws, compensation levels, staffing, and session length, as well as term limitations, have molded and remolded California's legislative environment. Almost all of these changes have been thrust upon the institution through ballot measures, and while many have achieved their intended aims, some have had unintended consequences. Because of term limits, for instance, the relationship between the Assembly and Senate has shifted and changed remarkably since the 1970s when both houses were newly professionalized and held roughly equal power: after term limits were adopted in 1990, the Senate assumed the role of a discerning "upper" house and maintained that status for more than twenty years. However, the chambers have equalized once again thanks to the term limit modifications that voters approved through Proposition 28. Consequentially, this rebalancing of institutional power affects leaders' relative influence over which bills get passed and the form those laws ultimately take.

In addition to a set of rules that changes periodically, larger, uncontrollable forces also condition how the legislature operates. For example, the COVID-19 pandemic transformed the work environment through social distancing measures, radically altering legislators' daily interactions with each other, staff members, lobbyists, other government actors, and the public. Some of those adaptations have become more permanent features of the lawmaking process, such as the livestreaming of daily events (floor sessions and committee hearings) and allowing stakeholders who are remotely located to participate virtually in committee hearings.

Democratic and Republican representatives work hard to enact policies that reflect the people's will and needs as they understand them. And when it comes to the scope of issues with which it deals, the California legislature comes closer to the U.S. Congress than any other state legislature in the nation, so it leads by example—good, bad, or both, depending on one's perspective. It remains the best hope for each citizen to achieve a degree of representation that would be unimaginable under an unelected bureaucracy, a dictatorial governor, or even a part-time legislature responsible for helping to govern one of the largest "countries" on the globe. The lawmaking body is closer to the people than the other two branches could ever be: neither the elected executives nor judges can understand the needs and interests of California's communities as thoroughly as firmly anchored representatives can.

KEY TERMS

Big Three: Speaker of the Assembly, president pro tem of the Senate, and the governor. These three leaders usually confer and negotiate over big bills and the budget.

Bipartisanship: agreement or cooperation between members of two opposing political parties, such as when Republicans and Democrats work together.

California Environmental Quality Act (CEQA): (pronounced "see-kwa") Signed into law by Governor Ronald Reagan in 1970, this major environmental protection law supplements federal land use and pollution regulations. This complex law requires governments, builders, and developers to identify the significant environmental impacts of their actions and to avoid or mitigate those impacts.

Caucus: an organization through which like-minded legislators coordinate their policymaking efforts.

Chapter (or "chaptered"): a bill passed by the legislature and signed by the governor becomes law and the language is inserted into the state's official codes, or volume of law; the secretary of state officially assigns it a Chapter Number corresponding to the subject matter in the codes.

Citizens Redistricting Commission: a group of fourteen mapmakers, chosen through a rigorous process stipulated in Proposition 11 (the Voters First Act), who redraw the district boundaries that determine representation for the state Assembly and Senate, Board of Equalization, and U.S. House of Representatives. Chosen once every ten years, following the decennial census.

Community of interest: as defined in the California Constitution, a population that shares common social or economic interests that should be included within a single district for purposes of its effective and fair representation.

Constituency service: actions lawmakers take to address the particular needs of individuals in their district.

Constituent: a person who resides in a district that is represented by an elected official.

Fiscal year (FY): the twelve months for which a budget is effective; in California, July 1 to June 30 of the following year.

Gann limit: see "state appropriations limit"

Incumbent: a person who currently holds an elected seat; for example, a legislator.

Lawmaking: codifying rules of conduct, or formalizing the rules about what practices are acceptable in a society; also called "legislating."

Legislation: laws or proposed laws.

Open seat: an election in which no incumbent is attempting to be reelected.

Party caucus: a formal organization of all members of a political party; the Democratic Caucuses and Republican Caucuses of both the Senate and Assembly organize their members for legislative action through these groups.

Policymaking: what government chooses to do or not to do about an issue.

Redistricting: the process of redrawing the district lines for representation; a citizens' commission completes this task in California, designing single-member districts (one representative per district).

Simple majority vote: a winning vote threshold of 50 percent plus one (51 in the Assembly; 21 in the Senate), needed to pass most bills.

Stakeholder: an entity such as an individual, group, government agency, business, or organization that has an interest (a "stake") in the outcome of a government decision because it is (or they are) either directly or indirectly affected by the outcomes.

Standing committee: a fiscal or policy committee that meets regularly to process bills and is assisted by permanent staff (in 2022 there were 33 Assembly standing committees and 22 in the Senate).

State appropriations limit (SAL) or Gann Limit: Passed by voters in 1979 as Prop 4 (and amended in 1990 as Prop 111), a ceiling on total spending is set by a complex formula that also applies to local governments. The cap is anchored to total state spending in FY 1978–79 and adjusted for population and inflation. When tax revenues exceed this limit over a two-year period, half must be spent on schools and the balance must be returned to citizens as rebates (unspecified in the law).

Statute: a formal or written law.

Supermajority: a voting threshold above a simple majority, as in two-thirds (54 in the Assembly and 27 in the Senate), required for raising taxes and passing urgency measures; or a political party that has attained at least two-thirds of the membership.

Term limits: a restriction on the number of times a person can be elected to or serve in an elective office. In California, after elected officials have reached the limit of twelve years in the legislature (or eight years [two terms] in an executive office), they cannot serve in that office again (a lifetime ban).

Trifecta (also known as "unified" or "single party" government): one political party holds a majority in both chambers of the legislature and the governor's office.

5 THE EXECUTIVE BRANCH

"CALIFORNIA AND CANADA PARTNER TO ADVANCE BOLD CLIMATE ACTION"

(June 9, 2022). Consistent with a voluntary partnership established with New Zealand, Canadian Prime Minister Justin Trudeau and *Governor Gavin Newsom* announced an agreement to share information to reach zero-emission and carbon neutrality goals and conserve 30 percent of land and water by 2030, among other actions. The state is pressing ahead with ambitious climate goals after the U.S. Supreme Court limited the Environmental Protection Agency's (EPA's) regulatory authority and reach in *West Virginia v. U.S. EPA*.[1]

"GOVERNOR NEWSOM SIGNS LEGISLATION TO PROTECT WOMEN AND PROVIDERS IN CALIFORNIA FROM ABORTION BANS BY OTHER STATES"

(June 24, 2022). Following the U.S. Supreme Court's decision to overturn *Roe v. Wade*, a federal case that had enabled abortion rights nationwide, *Governor Gavin Newsom* signed a bill to protect patients and providers from civil liability imposed by other states. Declared state *Attorney*

General (AG) Rob Bonta at the bill signing ceremony, "We refuse to turn back the clock and let politicians exert control over a person's body."[2]

"ATTORNEY GENERAL BONTA AFFIRMS HIS SUPPORT FOR COMMONSENSE GUN LAWS IN RESPONSE TO U.S. SUPREME COURT DECISION"

(June 23, 2022). After the U.S. Supreme Court ruled in *New York State Rifle & Pistol Association, Inc. v Bruen* that citizens have a right to possess and carry firearms, *State AG Rob Bonta* reaffirmed that carrying a loaded and concealed weapon without a permit is illegal in California. He vowed to sponsor laws allowing victims to sue gunmakers, to seize weapons from prohibited persons, and to end sales of illegal untraceable ("ghost") guns.[3]

CALIFORNIA'S PLURAL EXECUTIVE

As the U.S. Supreme Court announced their momentous decisions in June 2022, including striking down a national right to abortion, cramping states' ability to deny concealed weapon permits, and curtailing the EPA's regulatory authority, the Court's conservative majority made it clear that they would forge a different balance of power between states and the federal government. As the above scenarios show, state executives jumped into action after hearing the news. AG Rob Bonta swore to curtail illegal firearm sales while Governor Newsom signed a law protecting all persons from civil liability for providing, aiding, or receiving abortion care in the state, and he expanded alliances globally to fight climate change.

The Founders of the United States rejected the notion that more than one person could effectively lead an executive branch. They argued that only a single individual, the president, could bring energy to an office that would otherwise be fractured by competing ambitions and differences of opinion. What then are we to make of California's plural executive, which comprises a whopping eight constitutional executive officers plus a five-member board—one of the biggest sets of leaders in the nation? In a state where Democrats attract the great majority of votes overall, administrative duties spread over a dozen constitutional officers are less challenging than one might expect, but success is often conditioned by partisan loyalties and personal relationships. Elected executives who are ideologically compatible largely support each other's decisions, and only one of twelve is a Republican. On the other hand, when offices are divided among Democrats and Republicans in top offices, as has been the case in some years, inconsistent governing decisions can cause confusion and create legal conundrums.

Term limits on each office—two four-year terms under Prop 140—also affect how executives behave. As ambitious colleagues, they can be potential or actual rivals for each other's seats, playing a game of political musical chairs. Usually members of the same party avoid challenging each other and wait for a seat to open; Controller Betty Yee, for example, was termed out in 2022 but has delayed a run for Treasurer until 2026, avoiding a match-up with incumbent Fiona Ma. To stay relevant, executives work on building their own name brand, but despite their towering responsibilities, they remain obscure to average residents. Relative anonymity is one reason why (U.S. Vice President) Kamala Harris announced her candidacy for U.S. Senate almost two years ahead of the 2016 election: even high-profile state executives need to create name recognition across a wide and largely

Attorney General (AG) Rob Bonta serves as the state's top lawyer and "top cop" who represents the people of California in court. Seizures of illegal weapons are just one tool the AG uses to enforce the state's strict gun control laws; bringing lawsuits against lawbreakers is another.

Source: California Department of Justice, Office of Rob Bonta.

inattentive electorate. The story behind her candidacy also demonstrates the important interplay of partisanship and personal relationships among state executives: as then-state AG she might have tried to run for the governorship, but then-Lieutenant Governor (LG) Gavin Newsom was aiming squarely for it in 2018, and between the two of them, Harris decided to run for U.S. Senate and Newsom for governor, a mutual agreement that benefited both.

The duty of an **executive** is to carry out laws and policies. Whereas federal administrators direct their departments and agencies to implement a coherent presidential agenda, in California, a wide assortment of departments, agencies, boards, and commissions serves different masters: the governor, other California executives, the legislature, the entities they are supposed to regulate, or a combination of these. Years of legislative and administrative turf battles, as well as governors' agendas and popular initiatives, have produced a thicket of state organizations, some of which retain independent regulatory power and many more of which follow the governor's lead. In theory, the dispersion of power across several top offices inoculates government against the worst effects of a single, inept leader, but fragmentation can obscure accountability. Who's responsible for paying out billions for fraudulent unemployment claims and endless backlogs at the Employment Development Department (EDD), or long lines at the Department of Motor Vehicles (DMV), for instance?

The tangled, bureaucratic nature of state government is probably nowhere more apparent than in the realm of education. Although the *governor* influences education through annual budgetary choices, it is the elected *state superintendent of public instruction* who heads the system by constitutional mandate, overseeing the *Department of Education*, the agency through which the public school system is regulated and controlled as required by law, taking cues from the administration's powerful *State Board of Education*, also appointed by the governor but technically administered by the superintendent, who in turn implements the educational regulations of the state board—not to mention the *Assembly* and *Senate education committees* that steer education bills into law, or the *local school district boards* that actually operate schools day to day(!). This sort of confusion exists because not only are educational policy issues complex but also because the governor, the superintendent, legislators, local officials, and the people want to influence one of the state's most important public resources.

BOX 5.1
FAST FACTS ON CALIFORNIA'S PLURAL EXECUTIVE

Elected executive offices:
    Governor

    Lieutenant governor (LG)

    Attorney general (AG)

    Secretary of state

    Controller

    Treasurer

    Superintendent of public instruction

    Insurance commissioner

    Board of Equalization (4 of 5 elected to the board)

Number of executives: 8, plus the Board of Equalization (12 persons)

Balance of political parties: 10 Democrats, 1 Republican, 1 nonpartisan (2022 elections)

Governor's salary: $224,020

Salary for AG and superintendent: $194,587

Salary for controller, treasurer, and insurance commissioner: $179,215

Salary for secretary of state, LG, and Board of Equalization members: $168,015

Terms of office: Four years

Term limits: Two terms (lifetime ban)**

Source: "Salaries of Elected Officials," California Citizens Compensation Commission, effective December 5, 2022, http://www.calhr.ca.gov/cccc/pages/cccc-salaries.aspx.

Note: On June 22, 2022, commissioners voted to increase elected officials' salaries.

*Once an executive has served two terms in a particular office, that person may not run for the same office again. Term limits took effect with Prop 140 in 1990 but did not apply to anyone who served prior to 1990, including Jerry Brown, who served four terms total as governor: from 1975 to 1982, and from 2011 to 2018.

Since taking office, Governor Newsom has added various commissions and task forces to the bureaucratic mix. Former Governor Jerry Brown sought to do the opposite and trimmed the administrative branch, proving that greater efficiency can be achieved through reorganization. For example, after a negative audit of the state's major tax collection agency, the Board of Equalization (BOE), he and legislators seized the opportunity to gut the state agency and, at a breakneck pace rarely reached by state government, created the new Department of Tax and Fee Administration and transferred almost all of BOE's tax-related responsibilities to it (Figure 5.1).

CALIFORNIA'S GOVERNOR

According to the state constitution, "The supreme executive power of this State is vested in the Governor," which places them *first among equals*. None of the eleven other elected executive officers—not even the LG—take direction from the governor, although the governor can require those peers to produce information relevant to their jobs. The most widely recognized and most powerful figure in California's state government possesses constitutional duties mirroring those of most other state governors; what distinguishes the office is both the size and hyperdiversity of the constituency, which is the entire state population, as well as the resulting volume of conflicts to be addressed.

The usual route to office is through a battering, expensive election process. Only former Governor Arnold Schwarzenegger initially escaped primary and general election contests, as well as an extended campaign, by winning office through a recall election in 2003, replacing the unpopular Governor Gray Davis, who was only one year into his second term. Those with prior elected experience, strong partisans, and prodigious fundraisers tend to survive the regular winnowing process—qualities that helped Newsom, former LG and mayor of San Francisco, win the seat in 2018. Newsom's triumph in a 2021 recall election almost guaranteed his reelection to the office in 2022 by scaring off strong challengers.

Head of State

A governor has responsibilities both formal and informal. As *head of state*, the governor appears at official ceremonies and public events, summarizes California's outlook and their agenda in an annual "State of the State" address, receives and entertains foreign dignitaries, and speaks for Californians on both national and international political stages. They also function as the state's official liaison to federal officials in Washington, D.C. and work with other state governors to advance causes nationally. They may sign "memoranda of understanding" (MOU) or "cooperation" (MOC) with other heads of state, voluntary agreements to share information or technology that are not legally binding because the U.S. Constitution bars state officials from making foreign treaties.

Chief Executive

The power to execute or carry out California law rests with the governor. Putting the law into practice is not something the governor can do alone, however. Newsom employs about 150

FIGURE 5.1 ■ **California Executives and Musical Chairs, 2022**

Under term limits that took effect in 1990, an individual may be elected to the same seat only twice. Elected officials are usually looking for their next jobs long before eight years are up, and open statewide offices are attractive options to those who have campaigned statewide and have run other aspects of state government. In a term-limited era, it's all about the "next" office. Note: A dotted line and attached box indicate that the executive served as an elected legislator in the Assembly, the state Senate, or both.

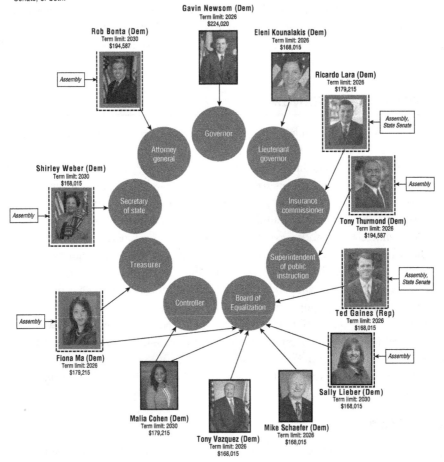

Sources: State of California/Public domain/Wikimedia Commons; California Commission on the Status of Women and Girls/Public Domain; California Board of Equalization, District 4/Public Domain; Florence Low/Public domain/Wikimeida Commons; California Board of Equalization; US State Department official photographers/Public domain/Wikimedia Commons; State of California/Public domain/Wikimedia Commons; LightSlash/CC BY-SA (https://creativecommons.org/licenses/by-sa/4.0)/Wikimedia Commons; California State Senate/Public domain/Wikimedia Commons; Mountain View City Council/Public Domain; MCStaff/Public domain/Wikimedia Commons.

key "personal" staff to provide advice and assistance with research and communication (Jerry Brown's staff hovered around 90; Schwarzenegger employed about 200). Agency secretaries, who oversee major departments containing multiple agencies, help implement laws, rules, and programs throughout the state consistent with the governor's vision. They are among the 800 top-level appointees placed throughout the administration to direct state programs. Collectively, these appointees put into practice the governor's version of good governance through the daily decisions they make about thousands of issues.

The governor also appoints members to about 320 state boards and commissions with more than 2,000 slots to be filled, most of them volunteer positions. Examples include boards that manage county fairs, professional licensing bureaus, and specialized councils that deal with everything from marine fisheries to the arts to sex offenders. Some appointments require Senate approval, and only a fraction of appointees serve at the governor's pleasure, meaning that only a few can be let go for almost any reason. Civil service laws protect virtually all state employees, and roughly 99 percent are hired based on merit rather than nepotism, favoritism, or patronage.[4] Outside of this, on rare occasion the governor may name a replacement to an open U.S. Senate seat or constitutional executive office, but never the U.S. House or state legislature. The governor also has the power to fill vacancies throughout the judiciary (superior, appellate, and supreme courts), although his appointees to appellate and supreme courts must first be reviewed and confirmed by two different judicial commissions and are later subject to voter approval at retention elections (see Chapter 6).

Whereas the governor may also issue proclamations (formal declarations) and **executive orders** instructing state employees in how to implement a law or policy, the governor's power falls short of forcing his constitutional partners, such as the controller or AG, to act. Emboldened by emergency powers during the pandemic, Newsom legally used executive orders to make binding decisions without the legislature, such as closing in-person schooling (Table 5.1).

Legislative Powers

Legislatively, the governor plays a significant role by *setting policy priorities* for California not only through proposed laws but also through the budget. Governors may *call special elections* and *extraordinary legislative sessions* to deal with pressing matters; Governor Brown called two extra legislative sessions in 2015–16 to address funding for roads and highways and also health care. The expertise of long-term, dedicated, permanent employees in the executive branch tends to give the governor significant institutional advantages over the legislature.

Governors *propose laws* and signal to legislators what kinds of bills they would or wouldn't sign—usually by cueing each other through informal interactions in the workplace, which ceased when Sacramento shut down in 2020–21 during the pandemic. Normally, the governor's key staff and agency heads *build relationships and coalitions* with lawmakers, interest groups, and other stakeholders, *monitor bills* at all stages of the legislative process, and *testify* before Assembly or Senate committees about pending measures. Staff also participate in critical final negotiations over a bill's wording and price tag. The governor's legislative secretary advises the governor to *veto* or *sign* legislation, because a bill submitted to the governor by the legislature becomes law after twelve days without **gubernatorial** action. In 2021–22, Newsom signed 997 bills into law; he has tended to veto

TABLE 5.1 ■ Modern-Era California Governors by Party Affiliation		
1943–54 (12)	Earl Warren	Republican*
1955–58 (4)	Goodwin Knight	Republican
1959–66 (8)	Edmund "Pat" Brown	Democratic
1967–74 (8)	Ronald Reagan	Republican
1975–82 (8)	Edmund "Jerry" Brown Jr.	Democratic
1983–90 (8)	George Deukmejian	Republican
1991–98 (8)	Pete Wilson	Republican
1999–2003 (5)	Gray Davis	Democratic
2003–10 (8)	Arnold Schwarzenegger	Republican
2011–18 (8 + 8 earlier)	Edmund "Jerry" Brown Jr.	Democratic
2019–present	Gavin Newsom	Democratic

Note: All were elected in November of the previous even-numbered year.
*Warren also received the nomination of the Democratic Party.

bills at a rate similar to Brown's (roughly 13–16 percent overall).[5] Like governors in four out of five states, the governor of California wields the **line-item veto**, the power to reduce or eliminate dollar amounts in bills or the budget. This is also called "blue pencil" authority, because in the 1960s, governors actually used an editor's blue pencil to cross out items in print. Newsom deleted only $5.3 million through the line-item veto power for his first budget, as compared to Brown whose range was zero dollars (2016–18) to $195 million (in 2012, a tough budget year). Veto overrides of line-item vetoes or any bill passed by the legislature are rarely attempted or successful; legislators generally regard them as a tool to embarrass the governor and they are wary of retaliation. In fact, the last recorded successful override occurred in response to one of "young" Governor Jerry Brown's budget-related line-item vetoes in early 1980.[6]

Budgeting Power

Budgeting power arguably gives the administration a powerful advantage over the Assembly and Senate. By January 10 of each year, the governor submits to the legislature a proposed annual state budget for the upcoming fiscal year. The muscular **Department of Finance (DOF)**, a permanent clearinghouse for state financial and demographic information, works in tandem with the governor, executive departments, and agencies to specify the initial budget based on projections and revises it in May based on actual tax receipts. By law, the *director of finance* serves as the governor's chief fiscal policy advisor, employing over 500 professionals who work year-round to prepare the following year's budget and enact the previous year's financial plan. Like the legislative analyst

According to the U.S. Department of Housing and Urban Development, over half (51 percent) of the nation's homeless unsheltered population lives in California. To address soaring homelessness, Gov. Newsom has dedicated billions of dollars to new programs such as "Project Roomkey" and now "Project Homekey," a grant program enabling cities, counties, and tribes to turn motels and hotels into housing for those in need.

Source: Noah Berger/AP Photos.

(Legislative Analyst's Office [LAO]), they also analyze proposed laws that would have a fiscal impact on the state.[7]

Chief of Security

If the governor *calls a state of emergency* during a pandemic, drought, or after a natural disaster or terrorist act, they are authorized to suspend certain laws and use private property in the impacted area, and the locality becomes eligible for state emergency funds. During the COVID-19 pandemic that he declared to be a state of emergency, Governor Newsom assumed **emergency powers**, which were affirmed by the state Supreme Court.[8] He wrote "an unprecedented number" of executive orders that suspended or overrode state laws and regulations temporarily, such as imposing vaccination and mask mandates, a "police power" that tested the limits of freedom and patience of many citizens along the way.[9] Democratic legislators in May 2022 rejected a Republican attempt to terminate Newsom's emergency declaration, although only certain provisions of the executive orders he had issued—namely, those relating to hospitals, vaccination, and testing—remained in place by then.[10] The governor is required to end a declared state of emergency as soon as possible, and the legislature can also vote to end one.[11]"

The governor also promotes security as *commander in chief* of the state's 19,000-member National Guard, which may be called on at short notice for humanitarian, peacekeeping, or even combat missions. As an operational force rather than simply a strategic reserve force, the Guard is called on average once every three days to assist in emergencies.[12] For example, they drop water on fires, set up family assistance centers for wildfire victims, support COVID-19 testing sites, and restore order in the wake of civil disturbances—but generally they are not authorized to engage in domestic armed conflict. The State Military Reserve is the defense force placed under exclusive control of the governor; the land-based California Army National Guard and the Air National Guard, dedicated to cyberspace, space, drone, and air capabilities, provide support. The governor also can authorize troops to assist with international disaster response and recovery efforts, as they have done in Australia by fighting raging firestorms, in Mexico by locating earthquake victims, and for Ukraine, through 30 years of training events and then tactical support following the Russian invasion in 2022.

With few restraints, a governor also can modify sentences or reduce penalties associated with a crime by offering *clemency*: to pardon offenders or to "commute" (shorten) their sentences, even for death row inmates. For instance, prisoners may be granted the possibility of parole even if they were sentenced without it, and Newsom established a clemency initiative to pardon those who were "prosecuted for being gay," meaning convicted of vagrancy, littering, or sodomy, that is, crimes used to punish adults for consensual sexual activities. A *medical reprieve* is another type of clemency: entirely incapacitated convicts may be released to live their final days outside of prison. *Pardoning* means that the offense stays on the individual's record, but no further penalties or restrictions will be imposed, and certain rights (gun ownership, professional licenses) may be restored. Compared to Governor Jerry Brown's eight-year record of 1,350 pardons and commutations and Governor Schwarzenegger's total of 16, Governor Newsom has done the same for 263 people in his first four years (plus medical reprieves).[13] Newsom has also *suspended the death penalty*, an action that most Republicans oppose and Democrats support.[14] Finally, the governor has the authority *to extradite fugitives* from other states.

Sources of Power

A state governor's powers resemble those of U.S. presidents and are spelled out formally in each state's constitution, but the structure of California's plural executive introduces a different set of constraints. For instance, the governor sets policy priorities through the budget, but shares responsibility for day-to-day administration with other elected executive officers and career state employees who may have different agendas. To overcome this structural disadvantage, the governor must draw on other sources of power to be an effective leader.

One source of power is *institutional*, such as whether the governor's political party holds a *majority* in both the Assembly and the Senate, as well as the *numerical advantage of the majority*. Newsom's own Democratic party has held not just a majority, but a *supermajority* during all of his years as governor, meaning that they have possessed the votes to override his vetoes—although they have never attempted to do so. Another institutional factor is the *cohesiveness of parties* in the legislature, because the presence of many moderates may make a Democratic governor's job of reaching compromises harder, or rigid and extreme partisans who are unwilling to budge from their positions could potentially thwart a more moderate governor's plans by obstructing specific bill language or foiling supermajority votes. *Shared partisanship* among the executive officers can also provide more governing consistency.

Power can also stem from a governor's *popularity, personal qualities*, and *style*. The governor's reputation as a loyal partisan friend or possibly as an untrustworthy party traitor affects their ability to attract legislators' support for preferred bills. For example, Governor Schwarzenegger alienated fellow Republicans by working with Democrats and championing policies that defied his state party's official platform. Jerry Brown (2011–18) struck "no nonsense" notes of practicality and toughness, disappointing fellow Democrats in dire budget cycles but satisfying them with few vetoes throughout the years. Newsom initially distanced himself from the Democratic legislative majority by seizing the reins of government during the COVID-19 pandemic and during social unrest, yet they have embraced his "progressive" words and actions. Personal *charisma*, the *power to persuade*, the *perception of having a mandate* (a popular demand for change), and *strategic use of the media* can also go a long way in enhancing a governor's base of power. Varied, lifelong *political experience* can also be a source of strength, as it was for Jerry Brown.

THE CONSTITUTIONAL EXECUTIVE OFFICERS

Eleven other constitutional executive officers help run state government. Should the governor leave the state at any time, the *lieutenant governor* (LG) takes temporary control; should the governor resign, retire early, die, become disabled, or be impeached, the LG takes the gubernatorial oath of office. Eleni Kounalakis became the first woman in state history to sign a bill into law, made possible by Governor Newsom's out-of-state vacation. Topping the LG's lackluster list of titles is "president" of the Senate, which entails showing up to cast a rare tie-breaking vote and nothing more. The "governor-in-waiting" is also a voting member of the California State University (CSU) Board of Trustees and the University of California Board of Regents and sits on several other regulatory and advisory state boards ex officio, or automatically by virtue of their position. The LG's staff includes about fifteen people.

Second in power to the governor is actually the *attorney general* (AG), known as the state's "top cop" or chief law enforcement officer. Through the state's Department of Justice (DOJ), the AG employs deputy attorneys general to help represent the people of California in court cases, provides legal counsel to state officials, coordinates statewide narcotics enforcement efforts, enforces state firearms and gambling laws, fights fraud, assists with criminal investigations, provides forensic science services, and supervises all sheriffs, police chiefs, and state agencies to enforce the law adequately and uniformly. All told, approximately 5,800 people work for the DOJ. The office is inherently political not only because the state's lead lawyer is elected and may use the position as a stepping-stone

Eleni Kounalakis ✓
@EleniForCA

...

I am humbled to step in as Acting Governor today & be part of history as the first woman in California to sign a bill into law.

I remain more determined than ever to ensure that while I may be the first to do so, I will certainly not be the last.

👤 Buffy Wicks and 3 others

2:41 PM · Mar 31, 2022 · Twitter Web App

174 Retweets   **76** Quote Tweets   **1,224** Likes

When the governor leaves the state for any reason, the lieutenant governor temporarily assumes power.

Source: Office of Lt. Governor of California, Eleni Kounalakis via Twitter.

to bigger and better offices (AG is also said to be shorthand for "aspiring governor") but also because he or she privileges some causes above others. Former AG Xavier Becerra filed more than 110 lawsuits against the Trump administration 'with a high degree of success, cases that helped clarify the limits of federal power. Among the first persons of color to hold the office, Rob Bonta has prioritized racial justice by combating hate crimes; he has hired more attorneys to prosecute polluters and organized retail theft criminals and will expand victim services.

More than 550 employees assist the *secretary of state*, who acts as the chief elections officer and oversees all aspects of federal and state elections held within California. This includes registering voters, distributing voter information guides in ten languages, certifying the integrity of voting machines, compiling statewide election results, and certifying and publishing election results. With a statewide voter database called VoteCal, the secretary of state's office offers expanded voter registration services to make voting more "customer-friendly," including online registration (http://registertovote.ca.gov), pre-registration for 16- and 17-year olds, all mail-in ballot elections, individual ballot tracking, early voting (up to 29 days ahead of election day), secure ballot drop boxes, and same-day voter registration (i.e., on election day)—efforts that reflect the secretary's goal to make it easier, not harder, for people to vote legitimately. Counties are transitioning away from neighborhood polling places to all-purpose "vote centers" that open 10 days prior to an election where universal absentee ballots or walk-ins are accepted, and 2020 marked a rapid shift to all-mail elections, which is now permanent. The Political Reform Division of the secretary of state's office implements rules relating to proper disclosure of lobbying and campaign finance activity and makes that information available electronically (http://cal-access.ss.ca.gov, plus a user-friendly version at powersearch.sos.ca.gov). As keeper of official historical records, the secretary of state also charters corporations and nonprofits, maintains business filings, stores complete records of official executive and legislative acts, and safeguards the state archives. Public notaries, persons authorized to formally certify signatures, are commissioned through this state office. The office also maintains several registries, including domestic partnerships, advanced health-care directives, and "Safe at Home," a confidential address and name change program for victims of domestic violence and sexual assault, as well as reproductive health-care workers and patients.

Fragmentation of authority is most evident in the three separate offices that regulate the flow of money through the state government. The prominent *controller* ("comptroller" in some states) is the chief fiscal officer who pays the state's bills and continually monitors the state's financial situation by keeping track of money coming into and moving out of the state's accounts. State employees and vendors who sell services or goods to the state will see the controller's signature on their payment checks. Ultimately responsible for ensuring that certain moneys due to the state are collected fairly, the controller is the at-large, "fifth" member of the BOE and sits on more than 70 advisory boards and commissions relating to state payouts for employee pensions, construction projects, other large categories of expenses, and is a member of the Franchise Tax Board (the body responsible for collecting personal income and corporate taxes). The controller oversees a staff of nearly 1,600.

The second money officer is the *treasurer*, the state's banker who manages the state's investments, assets, and bond debt. Every year the state borrows billions of dollars to finance huge infrastructure projects, such as the rebuilding of bridges or schools, and this borrowing takes the form of bonds sold to investors. The treasurer manages the state's mountainous debt by selling and repaying bonds on an ongoing basis, trying to secure improved credit ratings that lead to lower loan interest rates and payments, and maintaining the state's financial assets. About 250 employees round out the treasurer's office. The treasurer also chairs or sits on 60 boards, most of which are authorized to raise and spend money on huge infrastructure projects relating to roads, water supplies, housing, and more.

The five-member *Board of Equalization* (BOE) completes the triad of money offices, but it is a mere shadow of its former self. Established by the state constitution in 1879 to ensure that property taxes were collected uniformly throughout the state, over time it became responsible for collecting over $60 billion in taxes and fees every year—about 30 percent of the state's annual revenues. After a 2017 government audit exposed questionable accounting and hiring practices and shady campaign donations, the legislature and governor used the budget process to demolish the BOE by moving 90 percent of its 4,700 employees into a brand-new agency: the Department of Tax and Fee Administration. A smaller slice of its workforce was reconstituted into the Office of Tax Appeals, a quasi-judicial entity designed to settle disputes between taxpayers and tax collectors. The BOE itself, consisting of the state controller and four other elected regional officials (three Democrats and one Republican after the 2022 elections), reverted to its original constitutional mandate, which is to equalize property taxes. About 200 employees assist the board today. Surely it is a matter of time before the BOE is eliminated through constitutional amendment, a recurring recommendation from constitutional revision commissions and the LAO.

In the same antitax spirit that led to the passage of Proposition 13, voters rebelled against spiraling auto insurance rates and elevated the Office of *Insurance Commissioner* from a governor-appointed subagency to a full-scale executive office in 1988. To protect consumers who participate in the world's fourth largest insurance market and pay over $340 billion a year in premiums, the elected commissioner is supported by 1,400 employees who oversee the insurance industry by reviewing and preapproving rates for car and homeowners' (property and casualty) insurance, investigating fraud, and resolving consumer complaints.[15] The commissioner also makes sure that insurance companies are solvent, licenses 450,000 agents and companies operating in California, and enforces rulings against violators. The department has asserted its role in reviewing health insurance rate increases, though the commissioner lacks authority to reject exorbitant rate increases and cannot force companies to reduce rates. In 2014, insurers spent fourteen times as much as opponents to crush a proposition that would have given the commissioner the power to authorize or "veto" health insurance rate increases.[16]

Charter schools, prolonged school closures with distance learning, and digital divides: these represent issues of "intensity and polarization" that concern the *superintendent of public instruction*.[17] As the state's only nonpartisan executive officer and the overseer of all public schools, including public charter schools, the superintendent heads the Department of Education (2,600 employees) and chairs the State Board of Education, developing education standards, curricula, instructional materials, and assessments.[18] The superintendent implements standardized student testing and reporting (through the California Assessment of Student Performance and Progress, or CAASPP) as well as high school exit exams; data collection on a range of education-related issues such as dropout rates; yearly funding initiatives for K–12 and community college education; and federal court opinions and U.S. education policy initiatives. Like other state constitutional officers tasked with coordinating policy among a snarl of governing bodies, the superintendent sits as on more than 100 education-related boards and commissions.

In May 2022, Tony Thurmond, Superintendent of Public Instruction, praised the effort to create a safe learning environment for students as he welcomed the donation of thousands of LGBTQ+ friendly books intended for 234 Bay Area school libraries.

Source: Justin Sullivan via Getty Images.

Although these executive officers are free to consult each other and frequently find themselves in each other's company, at no point do they meet as a governing board, and no institutional mechanism exists to coordinate their work. At times this arrangement makes for strange bedfellows, as Governor Schwarzenegger found during the 2009 recession when he wrote an executive order closing all state offices two Fridays per month. He soon discovered that his mandate legally could not apply to his elected executive branch colleagues, who promptly ignored it and kept their offices open. One lesson to be gleaned from this example is that an organizational structure that allows Democrats and Republicans to share executive power virtually guarantees that a crisis will cause differences in governing philosophies to surface and probably clash. In any case, California has assumed the character of a "one party state" whereby its Democratic leaders cooperate because they share the same basic set of values with respect to government's purposes and functions.

ADMINISTRATORS AND REGULATORS

A great checkerboard of agencies, departments, administrative offices, and boards form the state's "bureaucracy," or bulk of the executive branch. Almost all are linked to the governor through secretaries whom they appoint to head each major agency or directors who run departments. Governor Newsom employs a team of senior advisors who coordinate policy with appointees across different policy areas.

Every organization within the executive branch is designed to help the governor execute state law faithfully, but bureaucratic reorganization is periodically needed to streamline operations and abolish haphazard structures that have been added over the years. Citizens may not have noticed, but former Governor Jerry Brown reduced the size of state government by consolidating several entities. He aimed to make government "easier to manage, and more coordinated and efficient" so that it could provide "more cost-effective service"—the object of all reorganization plans, to be sure.[19]

The "**superagency**" scheme of Governor Pat Brown—the late father of Governor Jerry Brown—has stuck since the 1970s, with a few alterations. Seven superagencies act as umbrella organizations for the related departments, boards, and commissions nested within them: (1) Business, Consumer Services, and Housing; (2) Environmental Protection (EPA); (3) Government Operations; (4) Health and Human Services; (5) Labor and Workforce Development; (6) Natural Resources; and (7) Transportation. For example, the Transportation Agency houses six associated entities, including Caltrans, the DMV, and the state highway patrol. The state EPA oversees the California Air Resources Board, tasked with mitigating air pollution (including greenhouse gas emissions regulations related to AB 32) and implementing the state's carbon cap-and-trade program, plus five other offices that regulate or assess pesticides, toxic substances, and other health hazards. The remaining large departments also house critical divisions and employ many specialists: Corrections and Rehabilitation (CDCR, which runs prisons), Finance (governor's budget), Food and Agriculture, and Veterans Affairs (see Figure 5.2). In all, about 215,000 full- and part-time public employees constitute the state administration or "state bureaucracy," a number that grows and shrinks with the economy.[20]

About a dozen salaried state commissions and boards possess *independent* advisory, regulatory, or administrative authority and are led either by gubernatorial appointees who must be confirmed by the Senate or are chosen by legislative leaders. Among these are the Public Utilities Commission (PUC), regulating all private companies in California to ensure they safely, affordably, and reliably provide essentials such as electricity, gas, transit, communications, and water. About 320 boards, councils, and commissions also help run state programs, manage public works, such as fairgrounds or the L.A. Coliseum, or handle professional licensing for teachers, dentists, accountants, and so forth. Most consist of four or five members, and some meet only twice a year. Full turnover of a board's membership rarely occurs during a governor's term; thus, competing ideological viewpoints can be represented on boards depending on who appointed whom. In addition, many organizations operate autonomously, meaning that they don't need to consult the governor or other elected executives before acting on an issue, although it's the elected officials who are ultimately responsible for actions taken. Together, unelected authorities across 200 state agencies make rules or establish regulations affecting Californians in virtually every imaginable way, from making beaches accessible to determining where waste can be dumped.

FIGURE 5.2 ■ Organization Chart of California's Executive Branch

CALIFORNIA STATE GOVERNMENT – THE EXECUTIVE BRANCH

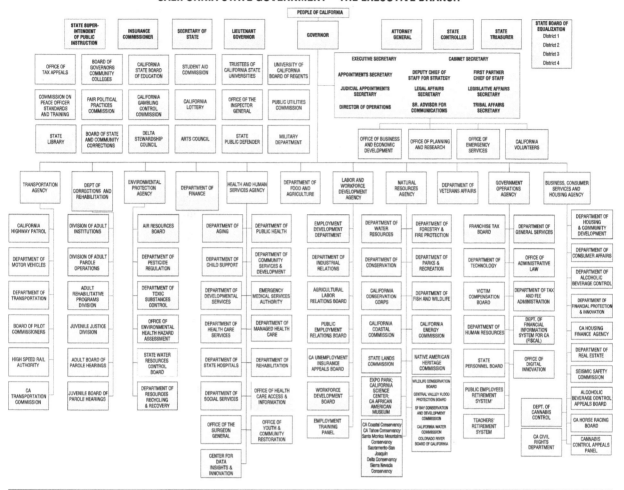

Source: Adapted from "California State Government—the Executive Branch," California Department of Technology, updated September 20, 2022, https://www.gov.ca.gov/wp-content/uploads/2021/12/Exec-Branch-Org-Chart-1.14.22_fully-remediated.pdf.

CONCLUSION: LEADING STATE GOVERNMENT

California's plural executive, which divides leadership for the state among nine elected constitutional offices, blocks one person from amassing "all the power" and enables separately elected individuals to accumulate and use "more accurate knowledge" to carry out their specific mission (as one framer of the 1879 revised state constitution put it[21]). On the plus side, the division of labor provides checks against the concentration of authority, but on the negative side, this arrangement perversely obscures individual accountability. Most Californians believe governors are all-powerful and blame them when things go awry, even if under normal circumstances they have no more authority to tell a treasurer what to do than the secretary of state does, although the governor shoulders the most responsibility for state spending.

In a state of emergency, however, the governor's normally larger share of power is vastly inflated, and accountability for decisions is clear. As Governor Newsom faced down a global pandemic and mass social uprisings, he tested the boundaries of that power as never before. To slow the spread of an unpredictable virus that threatened to overwhelm the state's health-care system, unilaterally he ordered all Californians to stay at home, shut down businesses, halted evictions, and suspended other regulations, overriding civil liberties in the name of safety and the greater public good. As social unrest overtook cities mid-year, he also worked with mayors to install the National Guard in cities around the state. Republicans who resented his actions launched a recall against him, but a big win only enhanced his 2022 reelection bid.[22]

Today the dominance of one party—Democratic—among constitutional offices helps bridge the accountability gap in that voters are able to affix responsibility for governing decisions to the party in power. On the flip side, Republicans are shut out of state leadership entirely and are unable to effectively challenge the ruling party, except in media, sometimes in court, and during elections—and lately, most political contests have been far from close.

Overall, the governor sets the tone for state administration through legislation signed or vetoed, appointments, annual budgeting, and sometimes executive branch reorganization, all in the service of managing "the big picture." Through more specialized roles, the constitutional officers formulate their own initiatives and maximize their own staff and budgets to reflect their priorities; shared partisanship and core governing values certainly helps them coordinate their efforts and mutually agree on policies. Latent tensions tend to surface during crises and economic hard times, especially if officials represent different parties, and occasionally their ambitions may put them at odds. But all in all, California's executive officers coexist in pursuit of the same basic goal: to allow the state and its people to prosper.

California's quasi-national status also provides a ready-made audience nationally and internationally for policy-oriented executive officers, many of whom seek national office. Their responses to national decisions by the Supreme Court, president, and Congress are closely watched by legislators in other states and are often viewed as monstrous by conservatives and as exemplary by liberals. Although the basic structure of the Golden State's executive branch resembles that of other states, the ways in which California's leading players maximize their roles—as global economic and environmental policy drivers and in past years as chief antagonists to the Trump administration—help set California politics apart from the rest.

KEY TERMS

Department of Finance (DOF): organization in the governor's office that compiles information about state agency finances and population demographics and constructs the governor's version of the state's annual budget.

Emergency powers: under the state's 1970 Emergency Services Act, the governor assumes "police power" and is authorized to exercise broad lawmaking and executive powers (such as through issuing executive orders) to remedy the situation.

Executive: an official who possesses the power to carry out or implement laws and policies.

Executive orders: a governor's formal instructions to state employees about how to implement a state law or policy.

Gubernatorial: of or relating to the governor.

Line-item veto: a governor's ability to cross out or veto items within a spending bill, also known as "blue pencil authority."

Superagency: large state agency that oversees smaller departments, boards, and commissions relating to a general area of state policy, headed by a secretary.

6 THE COURT SYSTEM

When a person living on the streets can't afford to pay an $80 ticket for trespassing on railroad tracks, should they also have to pay court processing fees, surcharges to subsidize court operations, and a $300 civil fine for not showing up in court, penalties exceeding $800?[1] State justices in a landmark 2019 California case decided "no": it is unconstitutional to use the criminal process to collect fines that impoverished people cannot pay, a violation of due process and equal protection rights.[2] In 2022, maximum civil fines were reduced from $300 to $100, and fines assessed before July 1, 2022 were forgiven.[3]

Excess fees also fuel racial and ethnic economic gaps. Persons of color are many times more likely to be searched and cited for offenses, and also jailed for not paying fees.[4] Legislators acknowledged these systemic disparities when they abolished twenty-three different court fees from state law (AB 1869). Most local governments, however, still rely on many types of late fees and other surcharges to keep their traffic programs running.

Fundamentally, the state courts' place in a separated system of powers is to provide "fair and equal access to justice for all Californians." Former Chief Justice Tani Cantil-Sakauye, who retired in January 2023 after serving a twelve-year term, points out that in their roles, judges must defend the constitution against enemies that could take the form of unconstitutional laws, bias, oppression of people, discrimination, or the elimination of rights.[5] Judges also verify that the rules, laws, and policies that the executive and legislative branches produce and the initiatives that the voters approve are constitutional or lawful. In one of the largest court systems in the world (and certainly the largest in the United States), over 2,000 judicial officers and

17,500 court employees handle at least 4.4 million cases annually, about 40 percent lower than expected because of pandemic-related impacts from 2020 to 2021.[6] Chances are good that all Californians at some point in their lives will engage the justice system directly to resolve family matters resulting from divorce or child custody disputes, through jury duty, or because of a traffic violation—the top reasons people connect to California's courts.

THE THREE-TIERED COURT SYSTEM

As in the federal judicial system, California courts are organized into three tiers, and the legislature controls the number of judgeships. At the lowest level are trial courts, also known as *superior courts*, located in each of California's fifty-eight counties. In a trial court, a judge or jury decides a case by applying the law to evidence and testimony presented. Working at this level are 1,750 judges and about 250 subordinate judicial officers, such as commissioners, and they deal with virtually all 4.4 million civil and criminal cases that begin here. Compared to ten years ago when over 8.5 million cases were in the system, judges' caseloads have become more manageable, but numbers are expected to increase as pandemic restrictions recede.[7]

Most citizens who use the courts are involved in resolving minor **infractions** for which a fine rather than jail time is imposed, including traffic violations such as texting while driving. Infractions, which are heard by a judge only, make up about 80 percent of the superior courts' docket. A recent rule change allows traffic violators who challenge their tickets to avoid paying their fines until a trial is held, and court administrators are considering moving all minor traffic violations out of criminal courts and into the civil courts. The next-higher level is a category of crime called **misdemeanors**, for which the maximum punishment is a $1,000 fine and up to one year in a county jail. Examples include drunk driving, vandalism, and petty theft. Finally, an accused criminal may be charged with a **felony**, which is a serious and possibly violent offense, punishable by a state prison sentence or potentially death—although Governor Gavin Newsom has halted all executions while he is in office. Examples of felonies include murder, robbery, rape, and burglary of a residence. County district attorneys (DAs) bring cases against the accused, and those who cannot afford to pay for their own legal defense are entitled to help from a public defender. Historically California's DAs have had a high conviction success rate (around 80 percent).[8] Sentencing outcomes depend on the severity of the crime, the offender's criminal history, and the court's discretion.

Civil suits, on the other hand, usually involve disputes between individuals or organizations seeking monetary compensation for damages, usually incurred through injuries, breaches of contract, or defective products. A *small claims* case is filed by a person seeking $10,000 or less, and attorneys are not allowed to be present at the court hearing. *Limited* civil cases involve damages valued at less than $25,000, and *unlimited* civil matters exceed that threshold. The large number of civil lawsuits in the state, over 635,000 even during COVID-19,[9] reflects a general acceptance of litigation as a "normal" way to resolve problems. The state attorney general can also bring civil cases against companies that break environmental, employment, or other types of state laws, or individuals who commit professional violations. Civil suits typically result in monetary judgments, not jail time, and the state does not supply legal representation for citizens who are involved in civil cases. The state does, however, support some legal defense assistance through "legal aid" services, portions of which go for eviction defense and to help families navigate the citizenship process and avoid deportation.

Juvenile, family, and probate cases are specific types of civil cases that are also heard in superior court. Family matters typically involve divorces, marital separations, and child custody cases. Parties might also ask a judge to rule on a family member's mental competence, settle an inheritance dispute, or legally change a name. A single judge or a trial jury may decide a case at this level.

For any large government system, pivoting quickly in the midst of a crisis is enormously difficult, but former Chief Justice Cantil-Sakauye supervised significant changes to help overcome challenges created by COVID-19—especially those that vulnerable populations have faced. In 2020, the chief justice extended criminal trial deadlines, suspended jury trials (no jury service required), and suspended evictions and foreclosures. Hearings were held remotely, and in a continuing effort to increase access to justice, defendants and witnesses have the ability to appear remotely in criminal proceedings (trials excepted) at least through January 1, 2024.[10] Traffic ticket payment services were made available online. By 2021, indigent and low-income individuals could apply to have fees and fines from infractions reduced in accordance with their *ability to pay*, a significant shift. Online "self-help" resources continue to be available on the http://www.courts.ca.gov website to help citizens obtain legal aid in civil cases, prep for court appearances, request repayment plans, avoid going to court altogether, and learn about immigration rights, services boosted by budget surplus dollars.

In a collaborative court, a team—usually social workers, lawyers, drug treatment program representatives, and the judge—work with a defendant to secure treatment for harmful behaviors (such as drug abuse) that have led to criminal activity. Judges oversee the process through regular court hearings.

Source: California Courts via YouTube/Public Domain.

During COVID-19 court closures, the chief justice also encouraged settling cases out of court thorough **alternative dispute resolution** (ADR), also known as mediation or legally binding arbitration, which offers a quicker way to decide cases and avoid the cost of hiring a private attorney. **Collaborative courts** have also become an important tool in dealing with repeat offenders. These "problem-solving courts" operate through superior courts, combining judicial case processing, drug and alcohol treatment services, social services, and monitoring—providing "wraparound services"—to help individuals rebuild their lives and avoid recidivism. Among over 400 collaborative courts in California are combat veterans' courts, drug courts, and sex trafficking prevention courts to treat and support victims of exploitation. When a former soldier pleads guilty to driving under the influence (DUI), for instance, in Veterans Court, they may be placed on parole and ordered to enroll in a program to treat alcoholism or possibly be treated for posttraumatic stress disorder (PTSD) while being monitored closely, in lieu of paying a fine or serving jail time. Those who have committed violent crimes must first serve their sentences and then can be accepted into the collaborative court system. A new county-based system will be enacted in 2023 for those suffering from severe mental illness or substance abuse: severely impaired Californians will be diverted to *CARE courts* where they can experience treatment-based wraparound services (medication stabilization, behavioral health care, and housing, for instance).[11]

If the losing party in a case believes the law was not applied properly, they may ask the next-higher district *court of appeal* to hear the case. There are no trials in district appellate courts, although three-judge panels commonly hear lawyers argue cases. Spread across six different geographical areas in nine court locations are 106 appellate justices who review contested cases for errors, improprieties, or technicalities that could lead to reversals of the lower courts' rulings, yet they affirm rather than reverse judgments in about 80 percent of cases. About 18,000 cases are filed each year and they "dispose" of about 20,000 (many take longer than a year to resolve). In 2020–21, the appellate courts published 9 percent of their written decisions, opinions that clarify and actually establish government policy because the state supreme court rarely overrules them.

The highest judicial authority is vested in a seven-member *supreme court*, whose decisions are binding on all California courts. Headquartered in San Francisco, supreme court justices also hear oral arguments in Los Angeles and Sacramento for cases appealed from the intermediate-level district courts throughout the year, but they automatically review death row cases and exercise original jurisdiction over a few other types. Of 6,500 cases appealed to it in the 2020–21 term, the court issued a mere 59 written opinions, accessible through the court's website. The justices are not required to review every case and therefore have wide discretion over case selection, concentrating on those that either address important questions of law or promote uniform judgments across the system. By law they must, however, analyze complex death penalty case records to generate internal memoranda and written opinions that often exceed one hundred pages apiece. Noting that it can take more than twenty years to exhaust the appeals process in death sentence cases, in 2016, a slight majority of voters declined to repeal the death penalty—reflecting declining public support for it over time.[12] In any case, two months into his term, Governor Newsom placed a moratorium on the death penalty, granting all current 674 death row inmates an indefinite reprieve, and signed a new law ensuring that those with intellectual disabilities will not be sentenced to death.[13]

Automatic appeals aside, justices spend considerable time choosing cases, and justices employ staff attorneys to assist them. Their interpretations of the law define the boundaries of acceptable behavior for businesses, government, and citizens. As the principal supervisor of the lower courts, the chief justice shoulders more responsibility than the other justices. As spokesperson for the judicial branch, they deliver the yearly *state of the judiciary address* to the legislature and act as its "chief lobbyist" during the budget process. Before retiring, Cantil-Sakauye praised the "unprecedented investments" in the courts made through the 2022–23 budget cycle, a turning point from previous decades of acute underfunding; for the first time in decades, for example, all judgeships authorized by law were fully funded. The court's reputation at any given time therefore reflects state spending but also its collective policy decisions, both in the legal questions the justices choose to address or ignore and in their interpretation of the wording and intent of specific laws. The former chief justice characterized California courts as "more than a place that resolves disputes. We have become centers for social justice."[14]

Webcasts of state Supreme Court oral arguments became a regular practice in 2022. Here, then-Chief Justice Tani Cantil-Sakauye (top center) listens to arguments with associate justices Martin Jenkins, Patricia Guerrero (elevated to Chief Justice in late 2022), Carol Corrigan, Joshua Groban, Goodwin Liu, and Leondra Kruger.

Source: CA Supreme Court/Public Domain.

ON AND OFF THE COURT

An attorney who has practiced law in California for at least ten years may become a judge, but individuals usually enter the position through gubernatorial appointment rather than by first running for office. Those who are interested in becoming judges may apply through the governor's office. A state supreme court ruling coupled with a law (AB 1024) allows undocumented immigrants to be admitted to the state bar and to practice law in California.

A governor has ample opportunity to shape the long-term ideological bent of the judiciary by selecting individuals whose partisanship and political principles are reflected in their judicial philosophies. When then-Attorney General George Deukmejian (1982–91) was asked why he was running for governor, he replied, "Attorney generals don't appoint judges. Governors do."[15] Governors tend to choose judges whose outlooks or judicial philosophies reflect theirs, and they build their legacy by shaping the demographic composition of the bench, which today remains disproportionately male, middle-class, and White, in contrast to the state's heavily multiracial/ ethnic prison population (Table 6.1). Continuing Jerry Brown's legacy of significantly diversifying the bench, Newsom's appointees reflect a wide variety of backgrounds and experiences. He boosted gender equality by ensuring half of all appointees are female; additionally, 8 percent identify as LGBTQ, 4 percent are veterans, and an unprecedented 58 percent are persons of color.[16] Vacancies are unpredictable. Governor Schwarzenegger made 627 judicial appointments over seven years, and in his latter eight years, Governor Brown appointed 644, over a third of all state judges (Figure 6.1).

Supreme court replacements tend to follow life cycles as most justices remain for decades, subject to a retention election every 12 years. Schwarzenegger appointed two of the

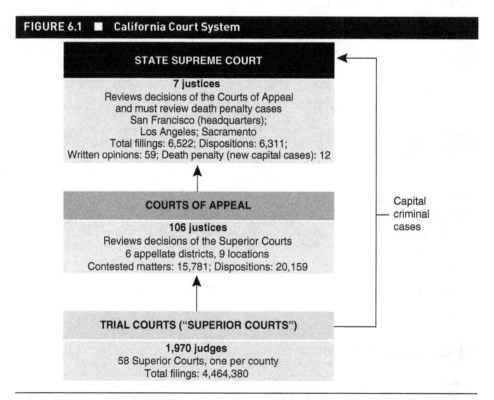

FIGURE 6.1 ■ California Court System

STATE SUPREME COURT

7 justices
Reviews decisions of the Courts of Appeal
and must review death penalty cases
San Francisco (headquarters);
Los Angeles; Sacramento
Total fillings: 6,522; Dispositions: 6,311;
Written opinions: 59; Death penalty (new capital cases): 12

COURTS OF APPEAL

106 justices
Reviews decisions of the Superior Courts
6 appellate districts, 9 locations
Contested matters: 15,781; Dispositions: 20,159

TRIAL COURTS ("SUPERIOR COURTS")

1,970 judges
58 Superior Courts, one per county
Total filings: 4,464,380

Capital criminal cases

Sources: "2022 Court Statistics Report: Statewide Caseload Trends, 2011–12 through 2020–2021," Judicial Council of California, 2022, https://www.courts.ca.gov/documents/2022-Court-Statistics-Report.pdf.

TABLE 6.1 ■ Diversity of California's Justices and Judges (in Percentages)

Court (Persons Reporting)	Female (N = 659)	Male (N = 1,048)	Black or African American (N = 144)	Hispanic or Latinx (N = 200)	Asian (N = 149) or Pacific Islander (N = 5)	White (N = 1,077)	Native American (N = 8) or Other/More than One (N = 91)	Information Not Provided (N = 33)
Supreme Court (7)	57.1%	42.9%	42.9%	14.3%	14.3%	28.6%	0%	0%
Court of Appeals (94)	40.4	59.6	11.7	7.4	5.3	70.2	5.3	0
Trial Court (1,606)	38.4	61.6	8.1	12.0	9.2	62.8	5.9	2.1
Total	**38.6**	**61.4**	**8.4**	**11.7**	**9.0**	**63.1**	**5.8**	**2.1**

Source: California Courts, "Demographic Data Provided by Justices and Judges Relative to Gender, Race/Ethnicity, and Gender Identity/Sexual Orientation," December 31, 2021, https://www.courts.ca.gov/documents/2022-JO-Demographic-Data.pdf.

Note: Supreme Court data current as of fall 2022. Patricia Guerrero and Kelli Evans are included, whereas Tani Cantil-Sakaouye is excluded.

seven supreme court justices including the Chief, Cantil-Sakauye, thereby fortifying the then-conservative court with his selections. Cantil-Sakauye's decision not to seek reelection to a second 12-year term in 2022 means that Democrats Jerry Brown and Newsom's appointees have refilled all but one of the seats and tilted the court in the opposite ideological direction. New elements of diversity have been added with the elevation of Patricia Guerrero, the first Latina and a first-generation citizen of Mexican parentage, to Chief Justice; and the appointments of Goodwin Liu, born to Taiwanese immigrant parents; Leondra Kruger, a Black woman in her 40s; Martin Jenkins, also Black and the first openly gay justice; and Kelli Evans, also Black and the first openly lesbian justice, who was raised in public housing by her grandmother—the court's newest member whose retention election would be in 2026.

Superior court judges serve six-year terms, and if they were first appointed to office and not elected, they must become nonpartisan candidates for their offices when their terms expire. They can run for as many six-year terms as desired. Longer terms are intended to increase the judiciary's independence and stability over time by reducing the frequency of distracting campaigns that can create potential conflicts of interest with campaign contributors. Contested elections are rare, and unopposed judges usually win.

Appointees to the six appellate courts and the supreme court also require the governor's nomination, but they must first be screened by the State Bar's Commission on Judicial Nominees (nicknamed the "Jenny Commission"), a state agency whose members represent the legal profession, and then be confirmed by the Commission on Judicial Appointments (*not* the state Senate). Together they evaluate appointees' fitness for office. Confirmation allows a justice to fulfill the remainder of their predecessor's twelve-year term, but that person must participate in a nonpartisan **retention election** at the next gubernatorial election, at which time voters are asked to vote "yes" or "no" on whether the judge should remain in office; no challengers are allowed. They may seek unlimited terms thereafter and must face the voters every twelve years.

Voters rarely reject judges. Defeat requires public outrage fueled by provocative, media-driven campaigns, as three supreme court justices discovered in 1986. Having earned reputations for being "soft on crime" at a time when rising crime rates were rattling the public, Chief Justice Rose Bird and two of her colleagues were targeted for their opposition to the death penalty. For the first time in California history, three justices lost their retention bids, and Governor Deukmejian replaced them with conservative justices.

Although judges almost never lose elections, they are not immune to campaign or interest group pressures. Progressives realized this when they established nonpartisan judicial elections in 1911, but many judges must run retention campaigns in which independent "super spenders" or rich ideologues try to influence election outcomes. In their primary role as defenders of law and order, judges are expected to be independent arbiters of justice, but elections can jeopardize their impartiality. In the thirty-eight states that rely on elections for choosing judges, the exorbitant amount of money now pouring into judicial campaigns—even retention elections— alarms court observers. Nationwide in 2019–20, almost $100 million was spent to influence the composition of state supreme courts, and special interest groups spent 36 percent of all spending, rates that continue to swell over time.[17]

Judges can also be dismissed for improper conduct or incompetence arising from a range of activities, among them bias, substance abuse, or sexual harassment. Hundreds of complaints are filed each year with the Commission on Judicial Performance, the independent state agency that investigates allegations of judicial misconduct. The commission does not review a justice's record but focuses instead on personal behavior that may warrant a warning letter, formal censure, forced retirement, or removal. Only a tiny fraction of judges face disciplinary action; the great majority have internalized the norms of judicial propriety that are imparted through law school and the legal community.

COURT ADMINISTRATION

Like the U.S. federal court system, the state judicial branch is headed by a chief justice. However, a formal voluntary organization, the *Judicial Council of California*, which the chief justice chairs, sets policy for the state's court system. The 21 voting members (plus nonvoting advisors) of this public agency are tasked with establishing rules and procedures in accordance with ever-changing state law, setting fiscal priorities, accommodating citizens with diverse needs, modernizing practices, and recommending improvements to the system. The council controls the court's approximately $5.2 billion annual budget. A subagency of the Judicial Council, the Administrative Office of the Court (AOC), is made up of staff members who actively implement the council's policy decisions. Administrators throughout the state manage the court system by supervising a supporting cast of thousands who help run the court system day to day. Among many other activities, they keep official records, hire interpreters, schedule trials, and develop programs to address issues affecting court caseloads and court operations, such as foster care or domestic violence.

JURIES

Barring a traffic violation, jury duty tends to be the average citizen's most direct link to the court system, and in a normal year, roughly 6,500 juries will sit in judgment at trial.[18] The COVID-19 pandemic closed the courtrooms to normal business and many proceedings were shifted online, the number of trials plunging to under 2,000 in FY2021, but operations are recovering. Normally, names of prospective jurors are randomly drawn from lists of registered voters and also provided by the Department of Motor Vehicles. Under the "one day or one trial" program, prospective jurors are excused from service at the end of a single day if they have not been assigned to a trial, and they only need to respond to a summons to serve once a year. If assigned to a trial, jurors consider questions of fact and weigh evidence to determine whether an accused person is guilty or not guilty. Convincing citizens to fulfill their duty to serve as jurors isn't easy, and juries tend to overrepresent those who have relatively more time on their hands, such as the elderly, the unemployed, and the wealthy. About 9 million people are summoned to serve on juries each year in California, although only half of them are eligible and able to sit on a trial; in all, almost 100,000 people are sworn in as jurors annually.[19] All jurors are compensated $15 per day starting with the *second* day of service plus thirty-four cents for mileage one way. There are no plans to raise this rate, although it is well below the national average of approximately $23 for the first day of service.[20]

Grand juries are impaneled annually in every county to investigate the conduct of county and city officials (examined by *criminal grand juries*) and also local governments (investigated by *civil grand juries*). Each "watchdog" jury contains 19 members, except for Los Angeles's two 23-member bodies. During their one-year terms, grand jurors research claims of corruption (illegal, improper, or wasteful practices), perform audits, issue reports, recommend improvements to local programs, and sometimes indict government officials for misconduct, meaning they uncover sufficient evidence to warrant a trial.

CRIMINAL JUSTICE AND ITS COSTS

About 90 percent of cases never make it to trial. High costs and delays associated with discovery, investigations, filings, and courtroom defense encourage out-of-court settlements and mediation, and the chance to receive a lesser sentence for pleading guilty results in plea bargains that suppress prison crowding. In spite of this and declining crime rates over three decades, the state's prisons were bursting at the seams for years.

Policing practices combined with mandatory and enhanced sentencing laws were largely to blame for the blistering growth of the prison population—a trend that finally has been reversed. In 1994, voters were scandalized by the abduction and murder of 12-year-old Polly Klaas, a crime perpetrated by a man with a long and violent record. Klaas's family and others lobbied vigorously for tougher sentencing of repeat offenders, and their efforts culminated in the "**three strikes and you're out**" (or "three strikes") law: anyone convicted of a third felony was sentenced to a mandatory prison term of twenty-five years to life without the possibility of parole, with enhanced penalties for second-strikers. Twenty years later, approximately 42,500 inmates were serving time for second and third strikes, most of which were nonviolent offenses.

Under federal court orders, the population was forcibly reduced through an assortment of measures, including the reclassification of crimes, resentencing under new laws, early release of prisoners, and the transfer of prisoners to county jails and **probation**. Voters have passed three initiatives to address "mass incarceration," or the imprisonment of large numbers of people who are disproportionately men of color. One, the three-strikes law was revised to impose a life sentence only when a new third felony conviction is serious or violent, and it also authorized resentencing for current inmates if they were locked up for nonviolent offenses. Two, some drug-related crimes were reclassified as misdemeanors (from felonies), enabling inmates to be resentenced, and all nonviolent offenders to become eligible for **parole** consideration; and it awards sentencing credits for good behavior and rehabilitative or educational achievements. Three, voters also decriminalized marijuana cultivation, use, and distribution. Notably, a law to replace the cash bail system with a risk-based release and detention system was repealed through a referendum driven by the bail bonds industry in 2020.[21]

Governor Brown and the legislature also crafted the "Public Safety Realignment" law in 2011 to meet a federal court mandate to reduce the prison population to 137.5 percent of capacity. **Realignment** policy has shifted the responsibility for jailing low-level nonserious, nonviolent, nonsexual (so-called 3N or *triple-non*) offender adult felons to county governments, and thousands of state parolees were transferred to county probation departments. These shifts continue, and so does the shortening of probation terms.

While COVID-19 reduced opportunities for criminal activity along with the prison population, reforms have also contributed to fewer arrests. These days the average daily inmate population statewide hovers around 100,000 and about 43,000 are on parole.[22] One consequence of realignment is that state prisons are now packed with the most violent, most serious offenders, and neither the costs of incarceration nor relatively high recidivism rates have come down.[23] Several major studies have shown that at least in the short term, prison downsizing has not affected overall violent crime rates in California, which remain at historic lows, but property, organized retail, and car thefts have risen and gun-related homicides spiked in communities of color during the pandemic.[24] Hate crimes are also mounting.[25]

To help prevent crime and also address high **recidivism** rates (reoffenses), Bachelor's degree programs are being permanently funded at seven institutions in conjunction with California State University system, a restaurant management training program is opening in Solano State Prison, and one-time funds are being pumped into rehabilitation and reentry programs.[26] Court fees have been cut back. A new law also enables nonviolent inmates who participated in a conservation camp fire crew to have their criminal records expunged so that they can be hired as firefighters (AB 2147). At the same time, budget surpluses are also being used to fund officers' emotional health and well-being and more money is being put toward community policing programs (Box 6.1).

BOX 6.1
FAST FACTS ON CALIFORNIA'S CRIMINAL JUSTICE SYSTEM

Budget 2022–23: $14.75 billion (general fund), $18.8 billion (total)*

Average cost per inmate, 2021–22: $106,131*

Staff, 2020–21: 56,000* (65,300 in 2022–23)

Average daily number of inmates: 97,000

Average daily parolee population: 43,825

Prisoners on death row: 674 (including 21 women)

Number of prisons: 34 minimum to maximum security, and including 1 medical prison, plus 35 adult firefighting camps, 1 community prisoner mother facility, and 1 female rehabilitative correctional center

Mean age: 41.9

Gender of inmates: 96.2 percent male, 3.8 percent female

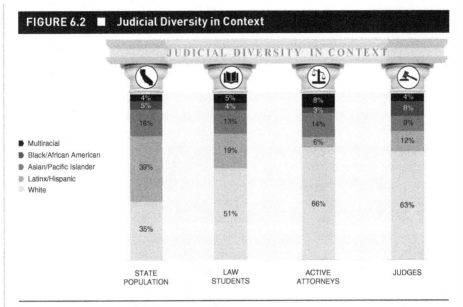

FIGURE 6.2 ■ Judicial Diversity in Context

Source: California Courts, "Demographic Data Provided by Justices and Judges Relative to Gender, Race/Ethnicity, and Gender Identity/Sexual Orientation," December 31, 2019, https://www.courts.ca.gov/documents/2020-JO-Demographic-Data.pdf.

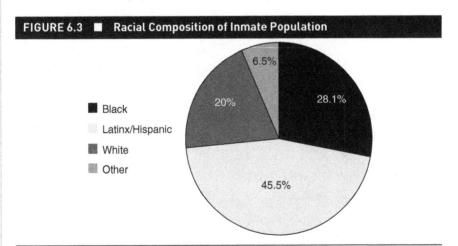

FIGURE 6.3 ■ Racial Composition of Inmate Population

Source: California Courts, "Demographic Data Provided by Justices and Judges Relative to Gender, Race/Ethnicity, and Gender Identity/Sexual Orientation," December 31, 2019, https://www.courts.ca.gov/documents/2020-JO-Demographic-Data.pdf.

Sources: Larger figures have been rounded. Division of Correctional Policy Research and Internal Oversight, "Offender Data Points: Offender Demographics for the 24-month period ending December 2018," CDCR (January 2020), and CDCR, "Average Daily Population, Month of January 2020"; California Dept. of Justice, "Crimes and Clearances, 2018" (interactive), Accessed June 27, 2020, https://openjustice.doj.ca.gov/exploration/crime-statistics/crimes-clearances.

*"How Much Does it Cost to Incarcerate an Inmate?" LAO, updated January 2022, https://lao.ca.gov/PolicyAreas/CJ/6_cj_inmatecost. Most recent and reliable report available.

Note: Figures have been rounded. All figures are for month-end June 2022 unless noted.

Longer sentences bring about an aging prison population with expensive health issues, and under the Eighth Amendment's prohibition against cruel and unusual punishment, inmates are the only population in the United States guaranteed the constitutional right to receive adequate health care—although the quality of that care is often in doubt. Prompted by a class-action lawsuit in 2001 alleging dire conditions, a federal receiver was placed in charge of the medical system, and the state was forced to make $8 billion in upgrades, which included building an inmate medical complex in Stockton.

Corrections budgets have climbed and stabilized, but underfunding of the correctional system is the default option for state lawmakers because prisoners are prioritized by no one: spending cuts to prisons represent a rare convergence point for those on the left, who would prefer more spending on rehabilitation and crime prevention programs, and those on the right, who tend to equate spending with unfair comforts for criminals who deserve to pay for their crimes. Moreover, the lack of lobbying on behalf of inmates—the kind perfected by most special interest groups—and virtual absence of public sympathy are problematic in a political system that is responsive to such pressures. In fact, cuts to prisons and corrections are the only ones that a substantial majority of citizens consistently say they would make in order to balance the annual budget.[27] This attitude may also stem from a popular misconception that prisons and corrections are *the* top spending category in the state budget, but at 6 percent of general fund spending, this area is the fifth largest in the state budget (health and human services is about six times larger).[28] One consequence of fiscal neglect has been the deterioration of prison infrastructure. Half of all state prisons were built before 1980 and need repairs totaling an estimated $11 billion.[29] A shrinking inmate population has eased the decision to close several prisons in need of repairs; one has shut down and four more closures are planned.

At over $106,000 *per inmate*, California pays far more than other states on average per offender, although fixed costs for security personnel, infrastructure, and medical care, along with a declining population, push up this annual average.[30] The "marginal" cost of incarcerating a person is closer to $13,000 per year, inclusive of living costs only. For each inmate, approximately $33,000 goes to health expenses, including pharmaceuticals and medical, mental, and dental care. About $45,000 per prisoner goes to "security" or staff salaries and benefits, and the remainder covers facilities, food, record keeping, rehabilitation, administration, and educational and drug treatment therapies—associated costs that have not shrunk along with the prison population, mostly because of compliance with federal court orders to deliver adequate health care and also compensation for prison guards and staff that only increases with time, not to mention COVID-19 health and sanitation protocols. Expenditures also cover supervising and treating adult parolees. As for approximately 650 young offenders, the state has shifted responsibilities for serving all youth "across the juvenile justice continuum" to *counties* and $100 million is being dedicated to detention and rehabilitative services at the county level.[31]

California continues to reckon both with the unequal treatment of individuals throughout policing, courts, and correctional systems, and the lack of trust in them—conditions that bear inestimable costs. For example, in recognition of the fact that officers kill about 200 people in California annually, only half of whom have guns, a recent law (AB 392) significantly changed the rules for use of force by prohibiting California law enforcement officers from using deadly force when they consider it "reasonable" as opposed to using only when it is "necessary."[32] A new law requires all officer-involved shootings resulting in the death of an unarmed civilian to be investigated by the state's Department of Justice, no longer by local officials. Laws also mandate diversity training for peace officers and forbid certain chokeholds, and prohibit the use of race, ethnicity, or national origin in sentencing (AB 2542), making it possible for sentences to be challenged for racial bias. These and other changes are meant to address systemic inequities that have been widely documented and also encompass crime victims, for whom voters passed "The Victims' Bill of Rights Act of 2008: Marsy's Law," adding entitlements to constitutional protections such as restitution (repayment), support services, and being notified of defendants' whereabouts, among other rights.[33] Budget surplus dollars have recently been allocated for permanent and mobile victim trauma centers (Figures 6.2 and 6.3).

CONCLUSION: ACCESS TO JUSTICE

Like a high-pressure system that changes the weather, the effects of civil disturbance following the murder of George Floyd and the COVID-19 pandemic provided momentum for alterations in policing, the California courts, and the corrections system. Signs of change are visible across the board.

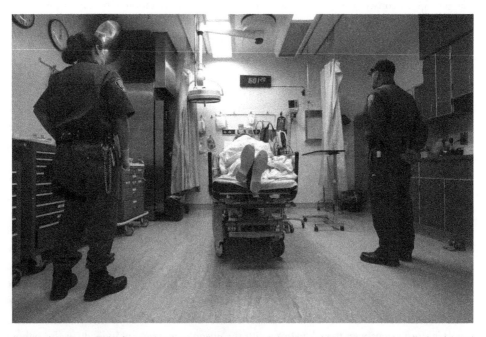

An aging inmate population has made prison medical care a costly business; the average annual medical and dental cost per person is $33,000, with much higher price tags for specialized care—for example, it costs about $1 million a year to care for and guard a prisoner lying in a vegetative state not only because of necessary medical equipment and round-the-clock care but also because of the high-security environment.

Source: AP Photo/Rich Pedroncelli.

Along with sentencing guidelines approved by the people, former Governor Brown's efforts to shrink the prison overpopulation to federally mandated levels began to address some of the racial and ethnic biases that have shaped California's criminal justice system historically. These efforts have been pursued with greater urgency, as Democratic legislators and Governor Newsom have committed to addressing systemic biases that prevent fair and equal law enforcement as well as impartial judgment by the courts. More bills are in the works. And with a surprise tax revenue windfall for at least two consecutive years, the state has pumped cash into officer health and training programs, victims' services, and education, therapy, and reentry programs for inmates. For the first time in many years, California courts are operating at full capacity, while arrests, trials, and the inmate population have declined significantly.

Whether all these measures achieve their intended effects has yet to be demonstrated.[34] Lower recidivism or higher rates of reintegration into a community after prison could signal that programs are working, for instance. For now, actual outcomes such as high recidivism rates and the fact that the incarcerated population is about three-quarters ethnic minority signal the complexity of public problem-solving, a task that also requires addressing poverty, under-education, unemployment, access to mental health care, and homelessness. Such social problems are manifest in all kinds of crimes and are inherent indicators of all Californians' quality of life, and closing gaps that are both real and perceived will require grappling with inequities at their political, economic, social, and cultural roots.

California policymakers face criminal justice issues that exist in all states but on a much larger scale; they have wrestled with them using the muscle of the ballot box, laws, and the budget. However, only a governing approach that comprehensively addresses the relationships among these issues can bring about fair, equitable, and accessible justice for all Californians.

KEY TERMS

Alternative dispute resolution (ADR): an alternative to a court trial; mediation or legally binding arbitration to which two parties freely agree to submit, usually led by a retired judge or trained arbiter.

Civil suits: lawsuits involving disputes between individuals or organizations that seek monetary compensation for damages, usually incurred through injuries, breaches of contract, or defective products. Types involve *small claims* and *limited* and *unlimited* civil matters.

Collaborative court: specialized "problem-solving courts" that operate through superior courts, combining judicial case processing, drug and alcohol treatment services, and monitoring to help individuals rebuild their lives and avoid recidivism. Examples include combat veterans' courts, mental health courts, homeless courts, drug courts, and domestic violence courts.

Felony: a serious or violent offense, punishable by a state prison sentence or possibly death. Examples include murder, robbery, rape, and burglary of a residence.

Infraction: a minor crime in which a fine rather than jail time is imposed, including traffic violations such as texting while driving.

Misdemeanor: an intermediate level of crime, for which the maximum punishment is a $1,000 fine and up to one year in a county jail.

Parole: after part or most of a sentence has been served and after a review by a parole board, an incarcerated person may be deemed no longer a threat to society and conditionally released to serve the remainder of a sentence outside of an institution, under supervision, as an alternative to or in lieu of prison time; a form of early release.

Probation: as part of a person"s initial sentence, an inmate may be released from prison or avoid incarceration and be supervised by an officer, with certain conditions to be met (e.g., not reoffend, find a job).

Realignment: a California state policy established by legislation and ballot measures in which low-level offenders in state prison are transferred to county jails and probation departments.

Recidivism: the act of recommitting crimes or reverting to criminal behavior after a period of incarceration or rehabilitation.

Retention election: a nonpartisan election in which a judge must face the voters (when an appointee reaches the end of a term they were appointed to fill; normally every six years for a superior court judge and every twelve years for an appellate court judge), at which time voters are asked to vote "yes" or "no" on whether the judge should remain in office; no challengers are allowed.

Three strikes law, or "three strikes and you're out": under laws passed as Proposition 36 and revised under Proposition 47, anyone convicted of a violent or serious third felony is sentenced to a mandatory prison term of twenty-five years to life without the possibility of parole, with enhanced penalties for second-strikers.

7 OTHER GOVERNMENTS

Thousands of governments operate within California's borders. Unnoticed by most residents, the state's counties, cities, special districts, and regional governments share responsibility for delivering essential services that both protect and enhance residents' quality of life—from maintaining police forces to making sure clean water flows beneath paved streets and from every tap. These governing bodies stretch scarce taxpayer dollars across a huge range of services that residents mostly take for granted: regular trash pickup, cemeteries, bus routes, sewage treatment, and street lighting are among the multitude of services either provided, managed, or contracted out to private companies by a gigantic patchwork of small governments in California. Their abundance reflects historically high demands for services, citizens' willingness to pay specific taxes but not higher general taxes, and strong desires to maintain control over local matters. Bottom-up, local solutions are thus joined to state and federal mandates in a functionally segmented system—one that works with surprising efficiency considering the enormous number and scope of issues encompassed and lean budgets. Illinois, Ohio, Pennsylvania, and Texas contain greater numbers of local agencies[1]—but the complexity and depth of regulation arising from them in California is virtually unmatched.

COUNTY GOVERNMENTS

Almost half of California's fifty-eight counties were created in the constitution of 1850, and in 1907, a portion of San Diego County was cleaved off to form Imperial County, the last county added to the list. County boundaries have remained static for about a hundred years while their populations have changed dramatically. All are considered subdivisions of the state, as they operate health and welfare-related programs authorized by the state government and provide critical services to the people within their boundaries. The relationship between the state and counties is

MAP 7.1 ■ California, 2020 Population by County*

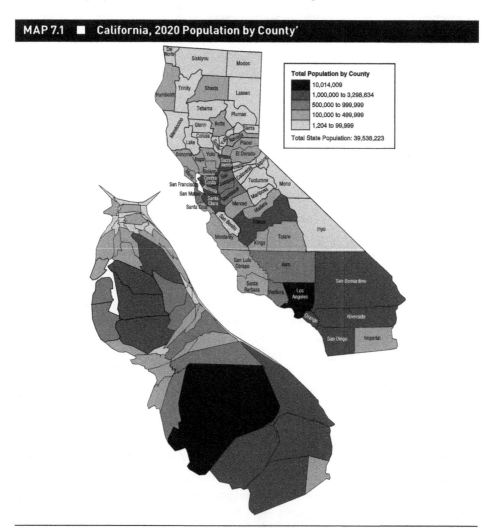

Total Population by County
- 10,014,009
- 1,000,000 to 3,298,634
- 500,000 to 999,999
- 100,000 to 499,999
- 1,204 to 99,999

Total State Population: 39,538,223

Source: "C-1 Summary Population and Housing Data: 2020," 2020 Census State Redistricting Data (P.L. 94-171) Summary File, U.S. Census Bureau, August 12, 2021, Extracted by the Department of Finance, State of California.

Notes: Geographic area and population are two variables used to measure the size of California's fifty-eight counties. Geographic boundaries are shown in the top map with shadings for population density, and the lower "cartogram" illustrates the relative distribution of population by county.

like that of a restaurant owner (the state) who creates a master menu, gives its fifty-eight "top chefs" (boards of county supervisors) a wad of cash, tells them to buy the ingredients and prepare all the meals according to the plan, and then makes them serve the finished dishes to their customers (California residents).

BOX 7.1
FAST FACTS ON CALIFORNIA'S OTHER GOVERNMENTS

Number of counties: 58

Number of cities: 482

Number of federally recognized tribes: 109

Number of public school districts: 1,029, containing 10,545 schools

Number of independent (elected) special districts: 1,922*

Number of dependent special districts: 1,700 plus 1,400 joint powers authorities (JPAs)*

Largest county by area: San Bernardino, 20,052 square miles

Smallest county by area: San Francisco, 47 square miles

Five largest cities by population:

Los Angeles, 3,898,747

San Diego, 1,386,932

San Jose, 1,013,240

San Francisco, 873,965

Fresno, 542,107

Largest county by population:

Los Angeles, 10,014,009

Smallest county by population: Alpine, 1,204

Number of chartered cities: 121 (25%)

Number of general law cities: 361 (75%)

Number of cities with directly elected mayors: 149 (30%)

Sources: "C-1 Summary Population and Housing Data: 2020," 2020 Census State Redistricting Data (P.L. 94-171) Summary File, U.S. Census Bureau, August 12, 2021, Extracted by the Department of Finance, State of California; "Learn about Cities," California League of Cities, 2020, https://www.cacities.org/Resources/Learn-About-Cities; "Fingertip Facts on Education in California, 2020–21," Department of Education, State of California. "California Tribal Communities," California Courts, State of California, https://www.courts.ca.gov/3066.htm.

*Numbers vary depending on what kinds of districts are counted. Dependent, independent, and JPAs actively report to the State Controller's Office yearly, totaling 5,185 in their online database as of June 2022 (100 governmental nonprofits are excluded from this count). Data collected by the State Controller, "Special Districts Raw Data for FY 2019–20," updated October 31, 2021, https://bythenumbers.sco.ca.gov/Raw-Data/Special-Districts-Raw-Data-for-Fiscal-Years-2019-2/c2qj-ad4e.

Each county can be pictured as a partially finished jigsaw puzzle, with a defined outer frame surrounding empty patches and oddly shaped clusters that take up most of the space. The completed sections represent cities, and they fill some counties almost completely and others only partially. Three counties contain no cities at all (Alpine, Mariposa, and Trinity counties). San Francisco is the only combination city/county, having consolidated the functions of both into one government. The blank spaces are considered **unincorporated** because they fall outside city boundaries, and all counties contain swaths of unincorporated areas, where more than 20 percent of Californians live (see Map 7.2 for a visualization of Los Angeles County). County governments directly provide essential services and local political representation to those residents.

Original county lines bear no relation to population density or economic activity today, and all counties are expected to provide the same kinds of services to their constituents regardless of population size or geographic area. This means that the largest county by population, Los Angeles, with 10 million people, maintains the same baseline agencies, elected officials, and responsibilities as tiny Alpine, with a population of 1,200. The state legislature endows each county with the responsibility to provide for residents' safety, health, and welfare and can either delegate functions to the counties or revoke them. No county or city could "secede" or break away to form an independent state without the permission of the California legislature and the U.S. Congress, but local ballot measures directing officials "to explore" that option have been used to publicize local grievances with state politics and policies.[2]

The constitution permits general law and charter counties, with the main difference lying in how officers are selected and organized. Each county is governed by a five-member *board of supervisors* (San Francisco's board has eleven members and a mayor). Supervisors face nonpartisan elections every four years, and most are reelected overwhelmingly unless they cannot run due to term limits, and that depends on whether voters in a specific county have enacted such limits via local initiative. Many termed-out state lawmakers prolong their political careers as county supervisors, putting their knowledge and "institutional memory" about state issues and systems to good use by helping run the state's largest subgovernments. The supervisors can make and implement local laws, but the **county administrator** (akin to a city manager) is responsible for the day-to-day administration of a county's operations. Forty-four counties are the *general law* variety, organized according to state statute. Each county must elect a sheriff, district attorney, and assessor and may appoint or elect a variety of other officers, such as a medical examiner and public defender. Including San Francisco, fourteen counties are organized under *charters* that allow flexibility in governing structure: apart from elected supervisors and the officials named previously, they can determine the other types of offices, whether they will be combined (will they have a recorder/clerk or assessor/recorder/clerk?), whether they will be appointed or elected, and whether they will be elected at-large or by district.

County officials such as the sheriff and assessor help the board of supervisors supply basic but vital social and political services in many areas:

- *Public safety:* courts, jails, probation, public defense, juvenile detention, sheriff, fire, emergency services, animal control services

- *Public assistance:* housing, state welfare programs, nutrition assistance (CalFresh), Medi-Cal, in-home supportive services

MAP 7.2 ■ Los Angeles County, Unincorporated and Incorporated Areas

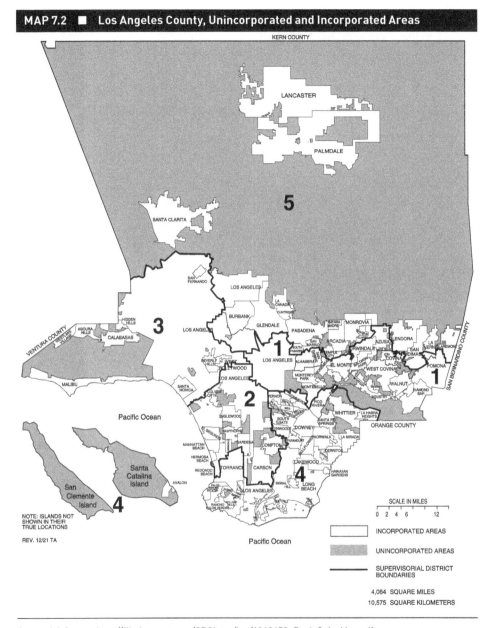

Source: LA County, http://file.lacounty.gov/SDSInter/lac/1043452_BasicColorMap.pdf.

- *Elections and voting:* voting processes, voter registration, signature verification

- *Tax collection:* county, city, special districts, school districts

- *Environment and recreation:* parks, sports, and entertainment facilities; open space; waste removal and recycling; air quality; land-use policy; water

- **Public health:** hospitals, mental health clinics, drug rehabilitation programs, vaccinations, COVID-19 testing

- **Education:** libraries, schools

- **Social services:** adoptions, children's foster care, homelessness assistance

- **Transit:** airports, bus and rail systems, bridges, road maintenance

- **Vital records:** birth, death, marriage certificates

Counties finance these operations by levying sales taxes and user fees and through state government funding, property taxes, and federal grants. They spend the most on public safety and public assistance (Figure 7.1). When state budget crises stem the flow of revenue, counties must lay off employees, cut services, and raise fees to make ends meet, and it takes years before the state restores funding to previous levels. Counties continually struggle to fulfill their state-mandated obligations—from preventing disease to ensuring foster children's safety—with relatively meager funding, and they relied heavily on federal funds during the COVID-19 pandemic to make up for revenue losses. Some of their financial woes today stem from their payment obligations to employees and future retirees for salaries and health and/or retirement benefits, which are consuming larger chunks of their budgets over time.

MUNICIPAL GOVERNMENTS

Communities in unincorporated areas of a county may want more control over land use in their neighborhoods, better services, or a formal identity. They can petition their state-chartered local agency formation commission, or LAFCO, to incorporate as a city or **municipality** if the residents generate enough tax revenue to support a local government. The median population

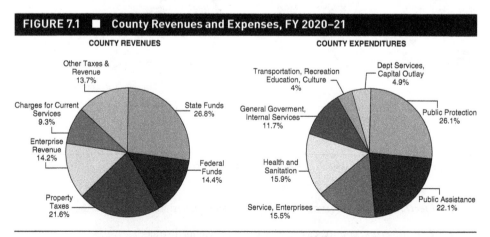

FIGURE 7.1 ■ County Revenues and Expenses, FY 2020–21

COUNTY REVENUES

- Other Taxes & Revenue 13.7%
- Charges for Current Services 9.3%
- Enterprise Revenue 14.2%
- Property Taxes 21.6%
- State Funds 26.8%
- Federal Funds 14.4%

COUNTY EXPENDITURES

- Transportation, Recreation Education, Culture 4%
- Dept Services, Capital Outlay 4.9%
- General Goverment, Internal Services 11.7%
- Public Protection 26.1%
- Health and Sanitation 15.9%
- Service, Enterprises 15.5%
- Public Assistance 22.1%

Source: Counties Financial Data 2020, Office of the State Controller, State of California, https://counties.bythe-numbers.sco.ca.gov#!/year/default.

Notes: May not add to 100 percent due to rounding.

*Reflects a range of minor revenue sources, including other taxes, fines, licenses, permits, fees, forfeitures, and use of money and property.

of a California city is 31,000, with a huge span between the smallest (Amador, population 200) and the largest (Los Angeles, population 4 million).

Much like counties, cities provide essential public services in the areas of public safety and emergency services; sewage and sanitation; public health; public works, including street maintenance; parks and recreation; libraries and schools; and land-use planning. Sometimes these overlap or supplement county programs: for example, a city might maintain its own library and also contain county library branches. If lacking their own facilities or in the interest of achieving greater efficiencies, cities can contract with counties for services, pool their resources in a *joint powers agreement* in which cities share services, or contract with private firms. A prevalent trend among cities has been to cut personnel, benefits, and public works costs through outsourcing. One such "**contract city**" is Camarillo, population 67,000, which purchases services for police protection, building and safety engineering, recycling and trash pickup, street sweeping and paving, and traffic signal maintenance, mostly from private contractors. Similarly, as municipalities in Orange County (OC) have grown, the OC Fire Authority has continued to provide critical fire services to them under contract, and county sheriffs have contracted to patrol thirteen OC municipalities that cannot afford their own police forces.

More than 75 percent of California's 482 cities are incorporated under general law, meaning that these "cookie cutter"[3] cities follow state law in form and function. The remaining *charter cities* are formed through city constitutions that grant local government supreme authority over municipal affairs and reflect local norms. This *home rule* principle permits municipal law to overtake state rules about a local government's organization. The City of Bell in the Los Angeles area serves as an uncomfortable reminder of this fact: using home rule to evade salary limitations that are set by state law, Bell's city leaders voted themselves exorbitant pay raises that technically were legal. When finally exposed, the city manager was raking in $1.5 million a year in total compensation—about nine times the governor's salary. In all, they stole more than $10 million from one of the state's poorest cities.[4]

Virtually every city is governed by a five-member *city council* that concentrates on passing and implementing local laws, called *ordinances*. Thus, unlike how state and federal governments separate powers among different branches to ensure checks and balances, city councils blend legislative, executive, and quasi-judicial functions (they hear certain appeals stemming from land use, for example), just as county boards of supervisors do. City councils rely heavily on small *boards, commissions*, and *task forces* filled by local volunteers or appointees to help recommend and set policy relating to the special needs of citizens and businesses. For example, Oakland has almost forty, including a Community Policing Advisory Board and a Youth Commission (to create appealing community programs for kids and youth). To facilitate public participation in public processes, all board members and commissioners must follow the *Bagley-Keene Open Meeting Act*, just as all city, county, and state governing institutions must abide by the *Ralph M. Brown Act*. These two laws mandate advance notice of all meetings, "open" meetings that do not take place in secret, and full public disclosure of the proceedings.

City council members are reelected every four years in nonpartisan elections, either by the entire city's electorate in an *at-large election* or by voters separated into *districts* or *wards*. A wide range of local governments, including cities, are moving to district-based elections because plaintiffs in lawsuits have successfully shown that racial and ethnic minority candidates are disadvantaged by at-large elections. In addition, many city councils are now subject to local voter-imposed term limits, and the list of term-limited cities grows each year. If the *mayor* is not elected at-large (meaning that the whole city votes for mayor), council members designate one among them to act as a ceremonial mayor, typically on a rotating basis for one or two years at a time. Each city makes its own rules regarding how long and how often city council members can act as mayor and whether the appointment will be automatic or by a vote. Automatic rotation creates opportunities for many young council members to assume that role. Ceremonial mayors lack veto power, and their vote on the council is equal to the votes of their colleagues. In place of an elected mayor, the council hires a manager to run city operations.

If the mayor proposes the city budget, has the power to veto city council actions, and can hire and fire high-profile appointees to help run city operations, then a *strong mayor* form of government is in place. Some 30 percent of California cities maintain this form of municipal government, partly because a sole individual can offer a clear agenda and be held accountable as the city's chief executive officer (CEO) for its success or failure. The far more popular *council-manager system* exists in nearly 70 percent of cities, an institutional legacy of Progressives who believed that efficient city management required technical expertise because "there is no partisan way to pave a street." In most cities, then, a council retains a ceremonial mayor but hires a professional **city manager** to budget for, manage, and oversee the day-to-day operations of a city. As a city's CEO, the city manager is authorized to make decisions independent of the council and thus wields great power behind the scenes. The office handles hiring and firing decisions and supervises all city departments. Most city managers possess a master's degree in public administration and have experience managing local government departments. Typically, the highest-paid city employee is the city manager, who earns more than $218,000 per year on average—although the numbers vary widely, with a handful making little (less than $20,000) and others making a lot (more than $300,000). The average annual wage for all types of California city employees is $80,880, but the pay scales vary immensely and so do the numbers of city employees, resident-to-employee ratios, and the types of professionals in any given municipality.[5] Others earning over $300,000 a year tend to be police chiefs, fire chiefs, or city attorneys working for large cities.

Cities depend heavily on taxes and fees to finance operations. Prior to Proposition 13, property taxes constituted 57 percent of combined city and county revenues annually; forty years later, property taxes represent roughly 17 percent of the average aggregate city budget. The bulk of revenues now comes from service charges for public utilities and transit; sales taxes; a variety of taxes and fees on hotels, developers, other businesses, and property use; and the state and U.S. governments. Bond money also enlarges budgets.

State representatives perform economic gymnastics to balance the state budget during hard times, and their routine used to include yanking property taxes and other fees previously committed to cities to backfill state budget holes. In an effort to stop such state "raiding" of local funds, cities and counties sponsored a constitutional amendment (Proposition 1A in 2004) to prevent state legislators from transferring locally generated property taxes, vehicle license fees, and sales taxes into the state's general fund. The state, however, can override some of those restrictions during fiscal crises to take what they deem necessary.

Ever since Prop 13 eliminated the ability of local school boards to raise taxes at their discretion, local governments have hunted for revenues continually. It's common to charge developers heavy fees for new construction projects or saddle them with the costs of constructing new streets, schools, lighting, sewers, or any infrastructure improvements related to population growth. These fees are then passed to homebuyers. **Mello-Roos fees** are assessed as a special lien against each property that will be in effect for 25 years on average, and the annual charges can vary dramatically from area to area and even house to house. In counties such as San Diego, the average homeowner in a Mello-Roos Community Facilities District pays about $2,000 more per year on top of property taxes.[6] Another strategy is to base land-use decisions on a project's net fiscal impact, a phenomenon known as the **fiscalization of land use**. In practical terms, this means that cities have incentives to entice and keep retail businesses that can generate substantial sales taxes, as local governments receive 1 percent of state sales taxes collected in their jurisdictions. Auto dealerships, shopping malls, and big-box retailers like Home Depot are, therefore, favored over low-income housing for people who will further stress city resources, or over service-based industries that will not generate tax revenue—in other words, decisions are made without regard to either the intrinsic value of, or need for, a project. Research by the Legislative Analyst's Office (LAO) has shown that this phenomenon does not seem to have affected recent land-use patterns significantly, but cities routinely use tax breaks, public financing, and low-priced land to entice business and spur the local economy.[7]

Borrowing large sums to build new stadiums or to rebuild schools, for example, has also become a favored tool for local governments of all types, especially school districts. Community debt typically takes the form of voter-approved *bonds* and requires two-thirds supermajority approval, or 55 percent approval for school bonds. Bonds are "sold" to lenders, and taxpayers are obligated to repay them with interest, usually after 20 or 30 years. Bond-related tax obligations are listed on residents' property tax bills and are based on a tiny percentage of the property's value. The state treasurer estimates that California city and county bond debt combined exceeds $531 billion, and K–12 school and community college district debt hovers around $324 billion.[8] In addition, voter-approved *parcel taxes* can be used to pay for large local programs. Residents pay a flat fee, or the tax is based on a property's square footage or other characteristic. These taxes are also attached to a property tax bill.

Debt can also take shape in long-term commitments to pay for hefty projects that may or may not generate income, such as a water treatment plant that local citizens pay for through higher sewage bills. The most common types of **unfunded liabilities**, a catchphrase that refers to whatever a city or county legally owes in future payments but does not yet have the financial reserves to cover, include the negotiated retirement and health care benefits owed to public employees, such as firefighters and police. In the past, generous employee labor contracts have often been based on optimistic projections of investment returns, but actual returns follow the economy as it zig-zags up and down. Today municipalities and counties owe billions of dollars in pension payments *plus* health care benefits, a looming problem for many. Residents in some cities, as in San Diego, have passed local initiatives trying to eliminate pensions and now offer 401(k) plans for new city employees. A few cities have declared bankruptcy.

San Bernardino and Stockton tried to wiggle out of their pension obligations through bankruptcy in 2012, but public employees' earned retirement benefits have been shielded by court decisions that amount to a "California Rule": promised pensions must be honored as ironclad throughout an employee's career and cannot be reduced without equal compensation.[9] For many California municipalities and counties, big questions about their long-term pension and benefits payouts remain (Figure 7.2).

City councils and county supervisors make local laws (their legislative function includes passing *ordinances*) and also execute laws by implementing plans or programs. The San Bernardino County Board of Supervisors meets twice a month, compared to Los Angeles's city council, which meets three times a week. At a typical meeting, local representatives listen to citizens' concerns, discuss pending regulations, decide land-use matters, pay tribute to community heroes, and approve expenses and payments for services.

Source: Renée B. Van Vechten.

SPECIAL DISTRICTS

A *special district* is a unit of local government serving a geographic area governed by a board for a specified purpose, such as running an airport or providing a community with street lighting or water. Abundant but obscure to the average citizen, special districts proliferate because they are created to meet critical needs that cities and counties lack the will or capacity to address. Like other local governments, they have unique jurisdictional boundaries, can sue and be sued, charge users for their services, and exercise the right to *eminent domain* (the taking of property for public use). Unlike most governments, however, they may cover only a portion of a city or stretch across several cities or counties. Created by law, about 2,000 special districts operate independently with their own boards of directors who are usually chosen by voters in low-profile, local elections, rendering them directly accountable to the people they serve.

A separate category of special districts includes 1,700 that are "dependent" on counties or cities for both their funding and leadership, meaning that local elected officials have the right to hire and fire members of those boards (and some even serve on them). Apart from these special districts, a related type of government body includes 1,400 **joint powers authorities** (JPAs): two or more local governments cooperating to offer a critical service across an area they define.

FIGURE 7.2 ■ City Revenues and Expenses, FY 2020–21

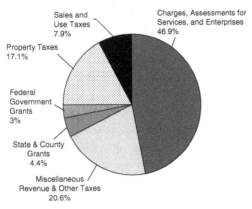

City Revenues

- Sales and Use Taxes 7.9%
- Property Taxes 17.1%
- Federal Government Grants 3%
- State & County Grants 4.4%
- Miscellaneous Revenue & Other Taxes 20.6%
- Charges, Assessments for Services, and Enterprises 46.9%

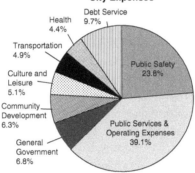

City Expenses

- Debt Service 9.7%
- Health 4.4%
- Transportation 4.9%
- Culture and Leisure 5.1%
- Community Development 6.3%
- General Government 6.8%
- Public Safety 23.8%
- Public Services & Operating Expenses 39.1%

Source: Cities Financial Data 2020, Office of the State Controller, State of California, https://cities.bythenumbers.sco.ca.gov/#!/year/default.

Notes: Includes the City/County of San Francisco. Figures may not add to 100 percent due to rounding. FY 2020–21 revenues reported by mid-2022 for all 482 cities totaled $91.95 billion, and expenses totaled $91.22 billion.

The majority of special district services are paid for through service charges, or property taxes and parcel taxes that initially require a two-thirds majority vote. Hospital, mosquito control, trash disposal, cemetery, fire protection, irrigation and water delivery, bus and rail transit, and utility districts are a few types. The Southern California Metropolitan Water District (MWD) epitomizes this type of fee-based service organization: created by the legislature in 1928, its mission is to provide adequate, reliable supplies of high-quality water to current and future residents in Southern California. A water wholesaler, it owns and operates major infrastructure, including the Colorado River aqueduct, hydroelectric plants, pipes, and water treatment facilities. Twenty-six cities and water districts buy more than 1.5 billion gallons of drinking water from MWD every day, supplying 19 million people in six counties. In addition to paying their local water district for the water they use, Southern California residents pay annual charges listed on their annual property tax bills for continuing MWD operations, even when water use is cut drastically because of drought conditions.

SCHOOL DISTRICTS

School districts constitute a separate but most familiar type of local government agency: more than 1,000 provide K–12 education for 6 million students attending over 10,500 different schools; an additional 73 districts encompass 116 community colleges serving over 2.1 million students.[10] Created by state law, nonpartisan five-member boards of education (Los Angeles's board has seven) govern their school districts by following the detailed operating instructions of the state's education code and heeding the State Board of Education's mandates. A superintendent manages the local system, which may be responsible for 600,000 students—as is the case in the gargantuan Los Angeles Unified School District—or fewer than twenty students. School boards handle issues relating to nearly every aspect of student life, from regulating students' cell phone use to defining nutritional standards to designing appropriate curricula, and they must weigh the concerns of vocal parents and special interests trying to influence their decisions along with the concerns of those who do not speak up so forcefully.

State-funded, K–12 public *charter schools* operate outside the jurisdiction of the local school board but remain open to all; almost 1,300 of them are organized by parents, teachers, and/or community groups to provide specialized education programs that may have an emphasis in the performing arts, sciences, languages, or college preparation, for example.[11] The school's mission is spelled out in its charter, or contract. The 1992 state law that permitted charter schools to form dictates that charter schools must be free and open to all students, and if a school receives more requests to attend than it has spots available, it must hold a blind lottery to determine which students can attend. Many in regular school districts view charter schools as competitors, and their contentious relationship continues to inflame disputes over applicable regulations and standards for accountability.

Proposition 98 dedicates approximately 40 percent of the state's general fund budget to K–12 and community college education, yet elementary and secondary schools rely on multiple source of funding. Using FY 2022–23 as a point of reference, over 73 percent of K–12 public school money is sourced through Prop 98 with state general funds and local property tax revenue. The rest is pulled from various places: approximately 7 percent from the federal government and about 20 percent from miscellaneous sources (including bond payments), the state lottery (a mere 1.2 percent), special local parcel taxes, and donations funneled through private foundations that have been formed to supplement operations by buying equipment or hiring specialized teachers (such as music or arts instructors) that districts cannot afford otherwise.[12] Due to gargantuan state budgets, per pupil spending has grown remarkably over five years: from $17,186 in 2018–19 to an estimated $22,893 in 2022–23.[13]

REGIONAL GOVERNMENTS

If a fast-food chef lives two cities away from their workplace because excessive rents near their job are unaffordable, how many buses should they have to ride to get home? Where should affordable housing be built? City and county borders can't fence in the universal issues affecting everyone's quality of life; issues such as housing, transportation, and the environment—or homelessness, traffic, and pollution—know no boundaries. To avoid trying to solve each of these thorny problems on their own, or risk having state policymakers dictate a "one-size" solution that might not fit, neighboring local governments can collaborate to attack common

Nearly 1,000 separate water districts in California are responsible for making sure that all residents and businesses within their boundaries have clean water for drinking and irrigation. These special districts draw or import water from reservoirs, lakes, or rivers, or operate pumps to extract local groundwater. They treat and test water flowing through their pipes to ensure it meets strict federal and state standards. Here, a water distribution operator manages the flow of irrigation water in Turlock Irrigation District's gravity-fed system.

Source: Photo courtesy of the Turlock Irrigation District.

problems more efficiently. **Regional governments** provide the spaces and places for local officials to cooperate in solving shared problems that transcend boundaries.

Regional governments provide permanent *forums* in which currently elected leaders in the same geographic areas can exchange ideas and information, plan, and coordinate public policy across county and city lines, especially those relating to sustaining the population and environment. Their governing boards are composed of mayors, city council members, and county supervisors, making them *intergovernmental* entities. They work by consensus and base their decisions on input from research specialists and advice from staff, federal departments, special districts, state agencies, tribes, and sometimes foreign governments.

Regional agencies can form voluntarily to deal with one or more issues, or state law can establish them for specific purposes, such as the coordination of public transportation across a geographic area. Whether the organization develops from the bottom up or is established by state law, participants collaborate to solve their collective problems in these so-called *councils of government* (COGs). They are known by their acronyms, such as "SJCOG" (the San Joaquin COG) or "MCAG" (Merced County Association of Governments).

Some of the main functions a COG performs could be assumed by specific types of regional organizations, such as *transportation commissions* or *congestion management agencies*. One example is the Contra Costa County Transportation Authority, which uses local sales taxes for freeway expansions and improvements, emergency roadside call boxes, and the funding of buses and bicycle paths. Federally designated *metropolitan planning organizations* (MPOs) are another type of regional government: they are legally responsible for researching, designing, and finding funding for transportation plans covering large urban areas (over 50,000 people), and also addressing state climate goals. *Planning councils* exist for general purpose cooperation. For instance, fifteen member cities of Los Angeles's South Bay Cities COG (SBCCOG) were averaging $3,600 monthly payments for mediocre broadband to synchronize their traffic signals and transit systems and help provide reliable remote services like telemedicine and classes; by pooling their resources for high-speed internet, they now access nearly unlimited bandwidth for about $1,000 a month.[14]

Regional government may also take the form of regulatory entities that set rules for environmentally sensitive activities. State law authorizes these bodies to set rules and enforce them. For instance, California's thirty-five "air districts" ensure Californians breathe clean air by helping to control pollution from stationary sources (*air pollution control districts*, or APCDs) and promoting air quality (*air quality management districts*, or AQMDs) through comprehensive planning, air quality monitoring, grant programs, public education, and special permitting.

The Association of Bay Area Governments (ABAG), a COG uniting local elected officials from nine counties and 101 cities, practically does it all: by agreement they deal with energy efficiency, environmental protection, disaster resilience, equity challenges, provide some local services, and partner with the Bay Area AQMD; by state law, they enact housing allocations, establish trails, work against climate change through land use decisions, and coordinate regional transportation plans with the Metropolitan Transportation Commission.[15]

FEDERALISM

To what extent is California at liberty to act in spite of the federal government? Whereas all local governments are subordinate to the state, the states have a different relationship to the national government. The U.S. Constitution creates a system in which states possess independent governing power and share some responsibilities with the federal government. Although Congress can override the states on all matters named in the Constitution, which remains the supreme law of the land, the Tenth Amendment reserves "all other" powers to the states, meaning that they possess primary governing authority over areas such as education, family relations, elections, and commerce inside their own borders. Yet even in areas where they do exercise primary control, states' influence has diminished over time as courts have interpreted Congressional powers permissively, and as federal grant programs have grown. The U.S. Congress discovered long ago that *funding* is a convenient instrument for enticing states to adopt federal goals by granting or withholding money in exchange for their compliance. In this way, federal highway funds have been exchanged for lower speed limits and a minimum drinking age of 21—issues that only the states can legislate. A solid majority of conservative U.S. Supreme Court jurists are now turning the tide toward more state power with their decisions in cases regarding issues such as abortion rights (allowing states to regulate) and elections, among others. For Congress, laws and money are their keys for getting the states to follow their lead.

As California declared itself a sanctuary for undocumented immigrants (through SB 54), essentially shielding noncriminals from deportation by disallowing state law enforcement to cooperate with Immigration and Customs Enforcement (ICE), the Trump administration threatened to "cut off the flow of federal money" to California. However, the federal courts determined that the executive branch cannot weaponize funding by singling out states for punishment, and it also ruled that states have no obligation to be "conscripted" to enforce federal policies. In other words, states can only be *encouraged* to enforce federal laws.

For all its defiance, California remains dependent on the federal government to balance its ledgers—*especially* during emergencies. In a normal year, federal dollars represent almost *one-third* of total state government spending (about 32 percent) covering services that communities need and use: housing subsidies, medical care, school lunch, the cost of educating low-income students and those with disabilities, transportation projects, unemployment insurance, and much more.[16] In far from normal times, the federal government provided over $251 billion extra to the state to confront the pandemic and its effects.[17] Local governments normally reap *direct* federal funding, mostly in the form of grants, and they collected billions more for coronavirus relief.[18] For example, the Bay Area Rapid Transit (BART) system depends on ridership to pay employees and what it owes for all parts of the system; without $1.5 billion in relief funds that came after ridership fell 70 percent, BART service and expansions would have been decimated, with harsh impacts on the environment and riders (half of whom do not own a car and 75 percent who identify as non-White) for years.[19] Separately, individuals draw payments from the U.S. government as student financial aid and income support (tax credits, housing and food assistance, Medicare, Social Security benefits), as well as civilian and military wages, salaries, and retirement; and businesses and universities benefit from research contracts and grants.[20] During the pandemic, people received direct payments and benefits covering health care, unemployment, food, and more. All told, federal awards to California exceeded an estimated *$603 billion*, money that helped propel the state's economic recovery.[21]

States must play by federal rules if they accept money from the national government or if a project requires a federal permit or approval, generally speaking. Congress can impose obligations through laws ("Acts"), federal administrators can create regulations derived from those laws, courts can issue orders, and presidents can write executive orders that apply to states. For instance, Caltrans, the state agency that fixes freeways and builds transportation infrastructure, usually must comply with hundreds of federal requirements, starting with the National Environmental Policy Act (NEPA), transportation laws and those relating to the physical environment and land use (clean water and air, noise, coastal zone management), regulations of animals and their habitats such as the Endangered Species Act, and cultural directives including executive orders about Native American sacred sites. California is also subject to **unfunded mandates**: federal laws ordering that a service be provided or a new standard be followed, but no funding is supplied for implementation. Mandates add substantial "hidden" costs to social services, transportation, education, health care, and environmental cleanup.

Mandates also can take the form of *preemptive rules (regulations)* or laws preventing a state like California from taking certain actions, such as aggressively regulating the environment. For 50 years, the U.S. Environmental Protection Agency (EPA) has allowed California to impose stricter mileage and greenhouse gas emission limits on vehicles sold in the state—even tougher than the federal government's standards, enabling California to cut pollution and colonize the roads with zero-emissions cars and light trucks.[22]

Cooperation between state elected officials and federal representatives and their leaders in the U.S. Senate and House of Representatives can facilitate more favorable federal policies and funding levels, but which parties are in the majority and the White House largely determines who is influential. One of eight House members is from the Golden State (52 total), but they must negotiate with Senators (each state has two, equally) and the president. Given California's major share of the population, position as a gateway to the Pacific, significance to the military, and importance to the nation as an agricultural hub and economic powerhouse, federal funds will continue to backfill permanent and growing needs, and the tug of war between the state and the federal government over authority to determine certain issues will continue, as it has since the creation of the federal government.

BOX 7.2
CALIFORNIA'S LANDMARK CLIMATE CHANGE LAW: AB 32

California set itself apart yet again when the state's majority Democratic legislature joined Republican Governor Arnold Schwarzenegger in crafting the Global Warming Solutions Act of 2006, otherwise known as Assembly Bill 32 (AB 32), the world's first law establishing a program of regulatory and market mechanisms to curb emissions of greenhouse gases (GHG). Voters beat back an initiative to rescind it in 2010 (Proposition 23), but businesses and antiregulatory interests continue to strongly oppose its related costs. AB 32 promotes a low-carbon, sustainable economy by prioritizing efficient, renewable energy sources that improve air quality, and authorizes the state's Air Resources Board (ARB) to comprehensively devise and manage programs to lower GHG emissions.

Most notably, ARB has enacted the nation's first cap-and-trade program for GHG emissions. Modeled on other successful market-based pollution reduction programs, California's version is designed to reduce the overall amount of GHGs by setting an upper limit, or cap, on the aggregate amount of statewide emissions from 85 percent of GHG sources. About 360 "polluters" (businesses creating carbon and other gases linked to climate change, representing 600 facilities) were initially given trading credits, or allowances, for the normal amount of GHGs they produce. Chevron's Richmond refinery is the biggest source; the University of California is another large emitter. Every year the total cap on statewide emissions declines by 2–3 percent, and the total number of allowances also declines, providing incentives for polluters to invest in more efficient technologies or fuels that will reduce their own emissions, thereby creating for them a surplus of carbon trading credits that they can sell at a quarterly online auction. Companies in capped industries must register and report their emissions annually, subject to independent verification, and ARB has designed the process to protect against collusion, cheating, and price manipulation. A few Republicans joined Democrats in voting to extend the system through 2030, and since 2012, the carbon credit auctions have generated billions of dollars for environmental programs. The global pandemic severely weakened the cap-and-trade market, but it has recovered. Advocates of the system extol the facts that no new taxes are directly assessed, businesses have flexibility to alter their practices to be compliant, and revenues support "green" initiatives. Opponents bemoan the new layer of regulations and paperwork and costs of compliance, dubbing them "carbon taxes" that are passed along to consumers. California and Quebec, Canada, linked their cap-and-trade auctions in 2014.

Initially, a tight coalition of automobile, shipping, manufacturing, and energy industries fiercely accused the new law of going too far by setting stricter standards than the federal government—because the federal EPA had never set a GHG emission standard. After initially denying California a waiver from the Clean Air Act that would allow it to set its own tougher standards, on June 30, 2009, the EPA under the Barack Obama administration reversed the ruling, giving California and thirteen other states the green light to proceed with implementation and enforcement of laws like AB 32. Governor Schwarzenegger crowed, "A greener, cleaner future has finally arrived."* Since then, the Trump administration tried denying the waiver and the Biden administration reversed course again. Having far surpassed the original reductions goal of 15 percent lower emissions by 2020, state lawmakers continued their crusade against climate change by passing SB 32 (in 2016), resetting ambitious carbon emissions targets to 40 percent below the 1990 level by 2030 (ultimately 80 percent below by 2050), by creating a new framework for building more sustainable communities (SB 375), and setting reduction targets for livestock-related methane (SB 1383). They also set a "zero carbon" threshold for 2045, whereby 100 percent of California power is supposed to come from renewables (SB 100), complemented by an ARB rule requiring that all diesel cars and trucks sold in the state be zero emission by then. ARB's Clean Miles Standard now compels all ridesharing companies to start electrifying their fleets starting in 2023, aligning with Governor Newsom's executive order ending sales of all internal combustion passenger vehicles by 2035. Higher living expenses are associated with the stricter standards (e.g., increased gas prices), but data show the state is inching toward its goals with emissions now around 3 percent below 1990 levels, making the 40 percent reduction target seem a long way off (Figure 7.3).

FIGURE 7.3 ■ 2000–19 Emissions by Sector

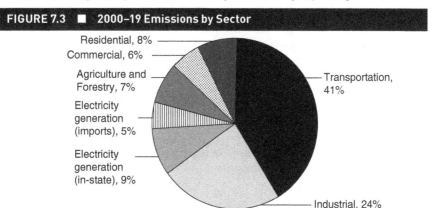

Source: "Current California GHG Emission Inventory Data (2021 Edition)," Air Resources Board, State of California, accessed July 14, 2022, https://ww2.arb.ca.gov/ghg-inventory-data.

Note: Total California emissions for 2019: 418.2 million metric tons of carbon dioxide equivalent, and were projected to decrease further in 2020.

Sources: "AB 32 Global Warming Solutions Act of 2006," Air Resources Board, State of California, September 28, 2018, https://ww3.arb.ca.gov/cc/ab32/ab32.htm; "California Cap and Trade," Center for Climate and Energy Solutions, accessed July 14, 2022, https://www.c2es.org/content/california-cap-and-trade./; "Governor Brown Establishes Most Ambitious Greenhouse Gas Reduction Target in North America," Office of Governor Edmund Brown, Jr., Press Release, April 29, 2015.

*"Governor Applauds EPA Decision Granting California Authority to Reduce Greenhouse Gas Emissions," Office of the Governor, State of California, Press release, June 30, 2009.

TRIBAL GOVERNMENTS

An often overlooked class of government functions alongside state and local entities and also under the thumb of the federal government: that of sovereign tribal nations. Tribal governments operated in relative obscurity until fairly recently. Isolated on 100,000 acres of mostly remote and frequently inhospitable reservations throughout California, the state's 109 federally recognized tribes had minimal impact on neighboring cities or state government. Native groups were defined politically by their interaction with the U.S. Congress and federal agencies such as the Bureau of Indian Affairs, as well as by prior case law that treated them as wards of the federal government rather than as sovereign nations. In the main, California governments could (and did) ignore them.

Gaming changed all that. Although states cannot tax tribal nations, as bingo halls flourished in the 1970s and blossomed into full-scale gambling enterprises by the late 1980s, states began looking for ways to limit, eliminate, charge, influence, or otherwise control this new growth industry, one whose environmental and social effects on surrounding communities were proving significant.

After the U.S. Supreme Court ruled in 1987 that tribes do indeed have the right to run gambling enterprises on their lands, Congress exercised its supreme lawmaking authority (to which tribes are subject) and wrote the *Indian Gaming Regulatory Act (IGRA)*, a law that restricts the scope of gaming and defers regulatory authority to the states. The IGRA also stipulates that tribes within a state and the state itself must enter into compacts to permit certain forms of gaming irrespective of tribal sovereignty. In California, casinos with 350 or more slot machines are considered Class III gaming operations and are subject to compacts. Class II gaming includes card rooms and bingo played for monetary prizes (Figure 7.4).

California voters overwhelmingly approved Proposition 1A in 2000, a state constitutional amendment that formalizes the right of federally recognized tribes to operate gaming operations

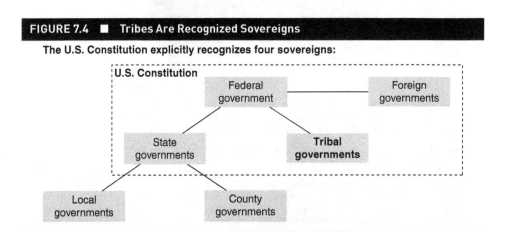

FIGURE 7.4 ■ Tribes Are Recognized Sovereigns

The U.S. Constitution explicitly recognizes four sovereigns:

Source: K. A. Spilde, J. B. Taylor, and K. W. Grant, II, *Social and Economic Analysis of Tribal Government Gaming in Oklahoma* (Cambridge, MA: Harvard Project on American Indian Economic Development, 2002). Reprinted with permission of the authors.

on tribal lands, which includes lands acquired (or taken into trust) with the federal government's consent.[23] The governor negotiates or renegotiates gaming compacts, the legislature must ratify them, and they may be challenged through referenda, subject to the voters' will.[24] As of mid-2022, California had ratified gaming compacts with 75 out of 109 tribes (four were in legal dispute); 66 casinos were operated by 63 of those tribes, plus card rooms and a smattering of satellite slot arcades that do not require compacts.[25] Voters rejected a 2022 ballot measure to enable online and mobile sports betting, a direct competitor of tribal gaming; a record $407 million was spent to influence the outcome. The state's casino industry is exceeded in size only by that of Nevada, and more than half of the state's slot machines are located in three Southern California counties: Riverside, San Bernardino, and San Diego.

A federal court has ruled that a state cannot force tribes to share their revenues; California can only negotiate payments for items that benefit tribes or directly offset local and state costs, such as promoting antigambling programs. Seventy-two tribes without casino operations receive an annual payout from the Indian Gaming Revenue Sharing Trust Fund (to which large gaming tribes contribute) amounting to $1.1 million per tribe annually.

Gaming enterprises have transformed tribal governments into major political players at both the state and national levels, enabling them to lobby and to donate heavily to candidates, political parties, and state initiative campaigns, especially those that affect tribal gaming.[26] Direct political representation has come much more slowly, however; James Ramos, former chair of the San Manuel Band and San Bernardino County supervisor, became the first California Native American legislator when he was elected to the Assembly in 2018. He has championed efforts to promote Native American voter participation and widen education about tribal history and affairs, and created a new Feather Alert system to help with locating missing indigenous persons.

Clearly, "tribal sovereignty" has limits with regard to both federal and state law. Today the conservative-led U.S. Supreme Court is revisiting the relationship between tribes and states. For example, the Court held in 2022 that "Indian country within a state's territory is part of a state, not separate from a state," thereby elevating states' inherent jurisdiction over tribal lands and potentially disrupting tribal criminal justice systems.[27] Thus, the states' authority appears to extend to prosecuting crimes on reservations. By executive order, both Governors Brown and Newsom advanced government-to-government consultations with tribes to create opportunities for "meaningful input in the development of policies, processes, programs, and projects," and participating state officials must complete training so that they have some knowledge about tribal sovereignty.[28] Under (federal) Public Law 280, California cannot regulate affairs on tribal lands, which are governed by tribal councils.

Led by a chairperson, councils are vested with executive, legislative, and judicial powers and maintain full control over tribal membership, which range from 5 to 5,000 registered members in California, totaling more than 50,000 in all (and more than 70,000 self-identify as Native American). Relative prosperity for gaming tribes has transformed those tribal governments into fully staffed operations that implement federal assistance and grants covering health care and education, and lands improvement projects, such as widening roads and building bridges. They have increasing institutional capacity to provide services that the state can't or won't provide; however, California local governments are obligated to provide services such as law

Joined by Assemblyman James Ramos (fifth from left) of the San Manuel Band of Mission Indians and other tribal leaders on the site of the California Indian Heritage Center in West Sacramento, on June 18, 2019, Governor Newsom formally apologized for the violence, mistreatment, and neglect inflicted on Native Americans throughout the state's history.

Source: AP Photo/Rich Pedroncelli.

enforcement, road access and repairs, and emergency services. Tribes are important participants in regional planning, and their enterprises generate jobs, tax revenues, and charitable donations to local communities.

Tribes have proven to be more vulnerable to the ravages of pandemics than the general population, and still suffer from a long history of colonization, genocide, and staggering dispossession of their lands, as reflected in persistently high poverty rates overall. In 2019, Governor Newsom formally apologized to Native Americans for the state's "historical mistreatment, violence, and neglect" of them, including an early state-sponsored "war of extermination" prosecuted through murderous bounty hunts, forced assimilation programs, systematic denial of civil rights, and state-sanctioned kidnapping and legal enslavement that outlasted the Emancipation Proclamation. It is a symbolic step that is part of the largely untold story of Native Americans in California.[29]

CONCLUSION: THE STATE'S INTERLOCKING SYSTEMS

California's state government is much more than a mega-institution with a few major components. Thousands of local and regional entities are responsible for countless directives that have immediate impacts on everyday life—laws and rules that are crafted by thousands of people working in elected and unelected capacities across county, city, special districts, school districts, and regional governments, as well as in tribal nations. Operating mostly out of sight, their day-to-day work attracts little attention from either the public or the media, but in ways both small and large, their decisions directly condition the health and livelihoods of communities throughout the state. These entities safely dispose of millions of cubic feet of trash daily, kill mosquitoes that spread disease, and assume responsibility for solving innumerable collective action problems that transcend boundaries but require local input and cooperation to solve. When they're doing their jobs right, virtually no one hears about them.

The state's government should therefore be viewed as a complex organism, with thousands of identifiable working parts that have specialized and localized functions. Each part contributes to the welfare of the whole, either singly or in conjunction with others, but never in total isolation. When dissected, the system appears as a bewildering mess of overlapping boundary lines, yet with remarkable success, these interrelated systems provide essential services that citizens need and will continue to demand.

As the Coronavirus pandemic ripped through counties, cities, special districts, schools, and tribes, their dependence on state on federal dollars took on new, humongous dimensions. Normally the U.S. government supplements critical projects and emergency services in communities across the state, but the explosion of needs during the Coronavirus public health crisis blew away past records. State government funding for basic services also continues to be a critical lifeline. *Interdependence* is a hallmark of the modern state.

KEY TERMS

City manager: a professional public administrator who oversees the day-to-day operations of a city, usually in charge of supervising all city departments and both preparing and implementing the city's budget.

County administrator: a professional public administrator who oversees the day-to-day operations of a county, usually in charge of supervising all county departments and both preparing and implementing the county's budget.

Contract city: a municipality that outsources (or contracts with) one or more neighboring local governments to provide city services.

Fiscalization of land use: a city practice whereby land-use decisions are driven by the need to collect sales tax revenues, which leads to favoring large retailers

and decision making without regard to the intrinsic value of, or need for, a project.

Joint powers authority (JPA): a regional governing entity formed by two or more governments that enacts a binding agreement to provide services (also known as a joint powers agreement).

Mello-Roos fees: fees on new construction to support infrastructure development, usually paid monthly by homeowners for a period of time (such as twenty-five or 40 years).

Municipality: another word for a city or township that has its own (local) government.

Regional governments: planning organizations that bring together local elected officials to facilitate the exchange of ideas and information, enabling them to plan and coordinate their policies across county and city boundaries. Councils of government (COGs) are a type of regional government.

Unfunded liabilities: financial obligations for payouts in the future but insufficient funds have been set aside to cover them.

Unfunded mandates: laws that require a lower-level government or agency to provide services, but no funds are supplied by the higher-level government to implement them.

Unincorporated areas: geographic areas of a county that lie outside city boundaries and are governed by a county board of supervisors.

THE CALIFORNIA BUDGET PROCESS

Annual budgeting at the state level is a grueling, multistage process of translating social and political values into dollars, a set of interrelated decisions that creates winners and losers. A budget is a statement of *priorities*, the result of intense *bargaining*, and the product of an *educated guessing game* about future income and economic trends that provides risk-averse politicians with incentives to respond to the most vocal and powerful interests. All the while, larger economic conditions provide an evershifting context for decision-making that can set the stage for massive heart attacks (due to an economic disaster that creates deficits and requires sudden and terrifying cuts, for instance), or just mild heartburn (from conflicts over how best to use unexpected surpluses). National politics can also leave marks on the state budget.

COVID-19 threw lives into chaos and businesses and jobs into limbo, and ultimately, the inflow of federal relief dollars salvaged the state's $202 billion 2020–21 budget. Then in 2021, another surprise: an unanticipated budget **surplus** materialized (the state revenues collected during that budget year exceeded the amounts spent). Billions flowed into the state's treasury while the wealthiest companies and individuals profited during a surging economic recovery. A shockingly bigger surplus of nearly $98.5 billion arrived in 2022, triggering an obscure rule that voters had imposed in the 1970s: the "**State Appropriations Limit** (SAL)" or **Gann Limit**.[1] With the SAL, normally the state can spend up to a certain amount per year based on a complicated formula that is tied to the state's population size in 1978, and if (for two years running) there is more money to spend over that threshold, then the excess must be refunded to taxpayers, or be spent on specified items (schools, emergencies, and infrastructure spending qualify), or taxes must be cut.

In FY 2022–23, riding this rogue wave of prosperity and mindful that the economy could backslide into recession, instead of reducing taxes that would be almost impossible to restore in harder economic times, Democratic lawmakers and Governor Gavin Newsom seized the moment to address problems that had festered for years. After setting aside rebates for taxpayers, state debt payments, and budget reserves to satisfy the SAL, they spread the wealth through spending on people, business, the environment, and infrastructure. Mostly through one-time spending made possible by the state's historic $308 billion budget and with a greater focus on equity, they expanded housing and Cal Grants for college students, increased supplemental social security and welfare payments, widened health care access for low-income residents, beefed up rental assistance and homelessness programs, boosted the TK–12 education budget to newfound levels, addressed wildfire and drought risks, created grants for struggling businesses and farms, and devised a five-year infrastructure plan to reboot schools and build a low-carbon future.

No matter the circumstances, however, many Californians wonder, "Why are my taxes so high? Why does the state spend so much money but it never seems to have enough?" This chapter examines the budgeting process and the role of taxes in it, and explores the reasons for California's budgetary dilemmas that, more often than not, force representatives to make hard choices among alternatives to preserve what they value.

CALIFORNIA BUDGETING 101

California's fiscal year (FY) begins July 1 and ends June 30. By law, a new budget must be passed by June 15, or lawmakers are supposed to forfeit their pay. The governor must then sign the budget by July 1, or the state cannot write checks for services or goods in the new cycle. In past years, the budget was routinely completed late, triggering more uncertainty and panic for Californians dependent on state services, but the on-time budget eleven years in a row (2011–22) attests to the power of one-party government (that is, with Democrats dominating both the legislative and executive branches), as well as rules (the budget now passes with a simple majority—rather than a two-thirds—vote).

Advance work begins in the governor's *Department of Finance (DOF)*, an office staffed by hundreds of professional analysts who continuously collect data about state operations. Each branch of government and executive department itemizes its own programmatic budget needs, from personnel to project costs, including items such as habitat restoration (Department of Fish and Game), in-home care for people with disabilities (Department of Public Health), and trial court funding (judicial branch)—merely a sampling from among thousands of state government activities. The DOF's projections about how much money will be available through taxes and fees provide baselines for estimating how much *must* be spent on major existing programs and how much *can* be spent on new desired programs or services. *Mandatory spending* already committed through existing laws, such as Medi-Cal health coverage, absorbs most of the annual budget, leaving limited room for legislators to fight for the leftover *discretionary funds* used to cover all other state services, from monitoring the safety of amusement park rides to sheltering victims of domestic violence.

Guided by the governor's initiatives, political values, and stated objectives, the DOF prepares a budget by assigning dollar amounts to state programs and services. The governor submits a proposed budget to the legislature by January 10, which will take the form of a **budget bill** and be routed to the legislature's own Legislative Analyst's Office (LAO) for scrutiny. Heeding recommendations from policy specialists in the LAO and anticipating the governor's updated version that accounts for actual tax receipts (the **May Revision** or "May Revise"), Assembly and Senate budget committees and subcommittees develop their own version of the budget throughout the spring. State administrators and budget analysts testify before the committees, as do officials, lobbyists, and citizens representing every sector of society and local government as they seek protection for existing benefits or beg for more.

Once the budget committees finish their work and a conference committee has resolved their differences, legislative leaders and their staff members negotiate with the governor and staff to reach compromises over the final numbers in the comprehensive budget bill. How much will be committed to building housing at state colleges and universities? Expanding or cutting mental health programs or after-school care? Funding additional CAL Fire staff? Hundreds of decisions like these play into negotiations both in committees and in high-level negotiations that routinely include the party leaders from both houses. When the same party controls the governorship and both legislative chambers, minority-party leaders will ultimately be excluded from the top-level negotiations if their votes are not ultimately necessary for passing the budget. Thus, the **Big Three**, or the governor, the speaker, and the Senate president pro tem (all Democrats), have been the key negotiators since 2011.[2]

State Senators Susan Rubio and Anthony Portantino debated as their chamber worked on passing the historic $308 billion state budget in June 2022.

Source: AP Photos/Rich Pedroncelli.

After the Assembly and Senate vote on the final budget bill, it is subject to the governor's *line-item veto power* (see Chapter 5). Agreement among Democratic legislative leaders and Governor Newsom on spending has made line-item vetoes almost wholly unnecessary, although they occur with regularity when the two branches are led by members of different parties. Soon after the ink is dry, the governor then signs a series of "**trailer bills**"—several bills amounting to hundreds of pages that package together a multitude of necessary policy changes to the state laws and codes outlined in the budget plan.

MECHANICS OF BUDGETING: REVENUE

A budget reflects the governor's and legislature's educated guesses about how much money the state will collect in taxes, fees, and federal grants during the coming year, as well as the state's commitments to spending or saving what it collects. All budgets are built on economic data, assumptions, and formulas designed to produce accurate forecasts about incoming dollar amounts and the demands for the services and goods covered by those amounts. Relatively small numerical shifts in these formulas can equal hundreds of millions of dollars, or those estimates can be off by double digits; for example, the state controller reported that revenues in July 2022, the first month of the 2022–23 fiscal year, had fallen short of projections by 10.9 percent, equating to $1.4 billion.[3] Discrepancies like these simply cannot be estimated precisely in advance. Nevertheless, sophisticated assumptions about how much will be coming into the state's coffers serve as a foundation for balancing the budget—or at least making it temporarily *appear* balanced at the moment it's signed into law.

Revenue is another word for income. The largest revenue streams are provided by *taxes* and *fees*, and in FY 2022–23, these amounted to a projected $222.7 billion in general fund revenues.[4] Taxes are deposited into the state's main account, the **general fund**, or redistributed to county and local governments. Special fees and taxes are also collected but go into separate funds, such as gas taxes that are funneled into the transportation fund; these were expected to total another $66 billion in 2022–23. It should be noted that property taxes are raised at the local level and are mainly used to fund schools and local governments; they do not augment the general fund. The amount of taxes collected will rise and fall with the economy, creating unpredictable revenue swings (Table 8.1).

The state relies on three major sources of taxes, all of which are highly sensitive to larger economic trends. The "big three" include *personal income taxes*, also known as the PIT; *sales taxes*; and the *corporate tax*.

PIT represent the greatest portion of state revenues in California (as they do for all but a few states), totaling a projected $141.5 billion in FY 2022–23, about half of all taxes and fees collected (49 percent). California's personal income taxes are *progressive*, meaning that tax rates increase along with income so that people at the higher end of the income scale are charged a greater percentage in taxes than those at the lower end.

On top of base taxes, marginal tax rates (as of mid-2022) for single or married individuals range from 1 percent to 12.3 percent, and they are indexed to inflation.[5] To illustrate how this works, excluding credits and exemptions for self and dependents, a single person making

TABLE 8.1 ■ Five-Year Infrastructure Plan, Department of Motor Vehicles (DMV) Budget Detail, 2022–27. In 2022, the state committed to spend more than $52 billion over a five-year period to modernize, repair, or build public structures and facilities, much of which has needed to be fixed for years. This small "budget detail" shows nearly $250 million in planned projects for just one of the many state entities—the DMV—that will receive money for stated needs.

Description of Work	Location(s)	Total Amount
Field Office Replacement	El Centro ($63m), San Diego County ($57m), San Francisco ($33m), Bakersfield ($13m), Orange County ($28m), Inland Empire ($4m)	$200 million
Field Office Reconfiguration	Pleasanton ($12m), Santa Barbara ($18.3m), San Pedro ($1m), Hollywood ($1m)	$32.3 million
Planning and Site Identification	Statewide	$3 million
Elevator Modernization	Sacramento Headquarters	$13.7 million

Source: Gavin Newsom, "California Five-Year Infrastructure Plan," Office of the Governor, State of California, 2022–23, https://www.ebudget.ca.gov/2022-Infrastructure-Plan.pdf.

Note: Figures have been rounded.

$18,000 would pay a base tax of $93.25, plus a 2 percent "marginal rate" on the amount over $9,325. A person in the next bracket would pay a 4 percent marginal rate, up to the highest bracket of 12.3 percent for those making over $625,369. Millionaires also pay 1 percent extra to help fund mental health services. This policy of "soaking the rich" means that California relies disproportionately on higher-income taxpayers to fill its coffers, although taxpayers can receive various exemptions and credits to offset the total they owe. In fact, in 2019 (the most recent data available), more than 8,500 Californian taxpayers with incomes of over $200,000 paid rates of zero to less than 1 percent because of the deductions, credits, or tax breaks they were allowed to take.[6] Even so, the top 1.7 percent of personal income tax filers—those with incomes of over $500,000 that year—paid over *half* of all income taxes in California.[7]

Retail sales and use taxes are the second-largest source of California's income, accounting for 17.3 percent of all revenues in 2022–23 (including special funds). Consumer spending on everything from phones to cars directly affects how much money is available to cover state expenses. Optimistically, sales and use taxes were projected to total almost $50 billion, an amount based on the base state sales tax rate of 7.25 percent. Of the 7.25 cents levied on every dollar spent on goods, 6 cents go to the state (some of which fund local activities), and 1.25 cents are reallocated to local governments. Sales tax rates average almost one percent higher in many locales because voters have approved extra county and city taxes (8.17 percent is the mean; 7.75 percent is the median).[8]

Revenues from *corporation taxes* were expected to decline from the previous year to $38.5 billion (13.3 percent of all state income). The remaining revenues from a smattering of lesser sources include regular and special taxes collected on cars and trucks, insurance, fuel, tobacco, alcohol, and cannabis; these were estimated to come in at $26.2 billion (9 percent of all revenues), and the remainder comes from regulatory fees, licenses, surcharges, and fines imposed on a wide range of activities (professional licensing and credentialing, energy, other commerce); these total approximately $32.6 billion (11.3 percent of all revenues).

The pool of money available to spend in a given year is also potentially filled by other streams, including cash borrowed through *bond* sales, *surpluses* from the prior year, *transfers* from reserve accounts, and the federal government. *Federal grant money* is funneled through the federal fund, representing billions of dollars from the U.S. government that subsidize specific programs, such as food assistance or job retraining, or recently for the COVID-19 public health response, or to local entities to prop up essential services such as low-income housing or transit projects. Prepandemic, California benefited from a staggering $125.7 billion from the federal government (2019–20). After COVID-19 hit, billions more poured in from Washington, D.C. to help counter the miseries of coronavirus, with more going straight to cities and counties. Today, when the anticipated $143 billion of federal dollars are combined with all sources, the entire state budget in FY 2022–23 is actually a jaw-dropping *$451,529,600,000* (Figure 8.1).[9]

MECHANICS OF BUDGETING: EXPENDITURES

The state expected to spend a record $308 billion in the 2022–23 year. What does it cover? *Education*, predominantly, and initiatives and statutes have more or less locked in annual funding levels. Except in times of recession or fiscal emergency, Proposition 98 mandates a minimum spending threshold that usually results in close to 40 percent of the budget being dedicated to K–12 schools and community colleges, systems that include nearly 5.9 million schoolchildren and 2.1 million full- and part-time community college students. In 2022–23, Prop 98 funding for K–14 exceeded $110 billion, leaping up from the levels of just three years prior. Heading into the school year, that translated into K–12 per-pupil funding of $17,011, almost 43 percent higher than in 2019. Taking federal, state, and local funds into account, a total of $128.6 billion was committed to elementary and high school education, or $22,893 per student (all-inclusive).[10] Prop 98 funding for California Community Colleges exceeded $12.6 billion (or $18.2 billion from all sources). The two major public university systems, California State University (operations and positions funded with almost $12 billion) and the University of California ($46.4 billion), are the largest components of the "higher education spending" category, for which resident tuition has been frozen or incrementally raised since 2011. About $105 billion from general, special, and bond funds covered all education in FY 2022–23, representing a third of all state expenditures.[11]

Health and human services eat up the next largest slice of the budget pie. With $101 billion allocated, a third (32.9) percent of all state expenses in 2022–23, this enormous budget category encompasses a range of essential services for the state's most vulnerable and at-risk populations: Medi-Cal, food assistance, residential elder care, COVID-19 response, children's health care, and benefits for foster youth and the disabled. Federal government fund transfers for welfare and other payments to the state are supplemented and redistributed through state agencies like the Department of Social Services, which manages the CalWORKS public assistance program. Medi-Cal coverage (the state's version of Medicaid) was expanded under the national Affordable Care Act (ACA),

FIGURE 8.1 ■ State Revenue, FY 2022–23

General Fund and Special Revenues, 2022–23 = $288.7 billion

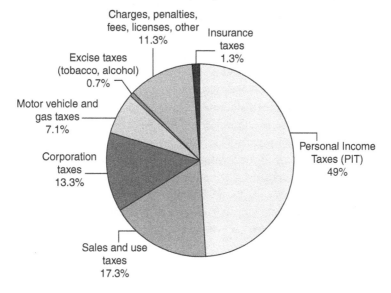

Charges, penalties, fees, licenses, other 11.3%

Insurance taxes 1.3%

Excise taxes (tobacco, alcohol) 0.7%

Motor vehicle and gas taxes 7.1%

Corporation taxes 13.3%

Personal Income Taxes (PIT) 49%

Sales and use taxes 17.3%

Type of funds to be spent in 2022–23 from all sources (projected July 2022) = $451.529 billion*

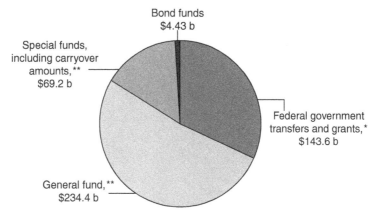

Bond funds $4.43 b

Special funds, including carryover amounts,** $69.2 b

Federal government transfers and grants,* $143.6 b

General fund,** $234.4 b

Sources: "California Budget 2022–23 Summary Charts, Revenue Sources," Department of Finance, State of California, http://www.ebudget.ca.gov; "Schedule 8" and "Chart B, Historical Data, Budget Expenditures," DOF, State of California, July 2022.

Notes: Percentages in the top chart are based on general fund and special fund revenues of $288.7 billion (bond funds excluded). Figures may not add to 100 percent due to rounding.

*Federal funds are included as expenditures in Chart B. $3.5 billion transferred to budget reserve accounts not included.

**This figure includes a portion of prior year carryovers (surplus).

and included 14.6 million people at the beginning of 2022. A new state law extended coverage to all low-income adults over age 50 as of mid-2022, and the state budget deal struck a month later opened Medi-Cal to all low-income residents, regardless of immigration status, changes that are projected to give 700,000 more people access to vital health care. The program continues to cover Californians with disabilities and the state is eliminating "asset tests" (wealth qualifications) for them by 2024. Medi-Cal is expected to insure almost 40 percent of the state's population by then. Covered California, the state's own (self-sufficient) insurance marketplace that was set up as part of the ACA, helps connect residents to affordable health care coverage (Figure 8.2).

The $18.7 billion Transportation Agency (2022–23) manages the state's *transportation* infrastructure, encompassing Caltrans, the California Highway Patrol, and the Department of Motor Vehicles. Much of its budget is derived from federal funds and also special funds in the form of fuel taxes, which finance the construction of state highways, mass transit projects, bridges, and maintenance of 52,000 miles of road and highway lane miles plus related infrastructure (such as drainage). As hybrid, electric, alternative fuel, and zero emissions (ZEV) vehicles have swarmed the roads, less and less money has been generated through gas taxes for fixing deteriorating roadways—a common situation across the U.S. In 2017, lawmakers raised California's fuel excise taxes (SB 1; it later survived a referendum vote) as most other states have done. Though unpopular, this stable revenue stream is expected to generate more than $50 billion for basic road repairs that will require at least $90 billion over ten years (see Table 8.3).[12] Funding from the federal Infrastructure Investment and Jobs Act will help hammer away at the long inventory of needs through 2027.

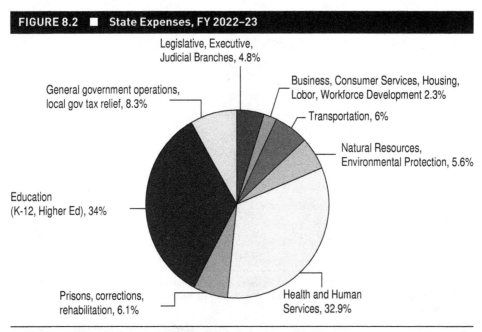

FIGURE 8.2 ■ State Expenses, FY 2022–23

Legislative, Executive, Judicial Branches, 4.8%

Business, Consumer Services, Housing, Lobor, Workforce Development 2.3%

General government operations, local gov tax relief, 8.3%

Transportation, 6%

Natural Resources, Environmental Protection, 5.6%

Education (K-12, Higher Ed), 34%

Prisons, corrections, rehabilitation, 6.1%

Health and Human Services, 32.9%

Source: "California Budget 2022–23 Summary Charts, Total State Expenditures by Agency," Department of Finance, State of California, http://www.ebudget.ca.gov.

Notes: Percentages are based on combined general, special, and bond fund expenditures of $307.916 billion. Figures have been rounded.

State government also incurs *general* and *operational* costs, most of which takes the form of salaries and health care for state employees, and the retirement systems that manage pension funds; these categories include tax collection and information technology functions, along with debt payments. About 3.8 percent of the general fund budget is dedicated to paying interest on both general obligation or lease-revenue bonds.[13] Just under 5 percent of the total annual budget is used to run the courts, executive branch offices, and legislature. Another 4 percent is committed to the operation of departments and commissions dedicated to regulating sectors such as utilities, cannabis, campaign finance, food, agriculture, and providing veterans services.

Including special funds, $18.8 billion goes to the *prison system*. Corrections cover inmate medical care and rehabilitation programs, as well as prison guard salaries and operating costs. As discussed in Chapter 6, on average it costs over $106,000 annually per adult inmate in California, a price tag that includes expensive medical care and correctional officer compensation, as well as a declining prison population which concentrates fixed costs. Through budgeting, more emphasis is being placed on probation services, restorative justice, and continuing COVID-19 safety protocols.

Confronting climate change and building a "more resilient, just, and equitable future" are among the priorities shaping the budgets for *natural resources* and *environmental protection*.[14] Combined, these areas represent more than 5.6 percent of all expenditures, or over $17.1 billion in 2022–23. Activities center on greenhouse gas (GHG) emission reductions and cap-and-trade, environmental restoration projects, recycling, permitting, air monitoring, promoting energy resilience, hazardous waste storage and disposal, fighting and protecting against wildfires, monitoring water quality, addressing drought, and so forth.

Finally, billions more dollars are directed to protecting workers (safety and labor law enforcement, training); distributing unemployment checks (the state failed dismally in this area during the COVID shutdown); regulating professions; supporting businesses and farms (tax credits, grant programs); providing emergency response to natural disasters and COVID-19; funding public defenders; creating affordable housing; and addressing homelessness, among hundreds of other purposes—and in combination with all other state actions, invite debate over the merits of government power (Figure 8.3).

MECHANICS OF BUDGETING: DEFICITS AND DEBT

The state commits to a spending plan before it knows how much will actually arrive in its coffers. Legislative and Department of Finance analysts do their best to predict how much unemployment compensation, welfare, housing assistance, health coverage, and a host of other services and benefits will be needed, but the costs of these services depend on how the economic winds blow. A struggling economy typically means that more residents lose jobs and pay less income taxes; financially distressed consumers also spend less, so the state's sales tax collections falter. Meanwhile, the state has already committed to a spending plan, but government expenses in the form of unemployment checks, health coverage, and other social services spike during economic hard times, and these imbalances translate into billions of dollars that policymakers cannot quickly replace.

When expenses exceed revenues in a fiscal year, *deficits* result. Legislators and the governor must hit the negotiating table to "close the budget gap," which they can accomplish through reducing

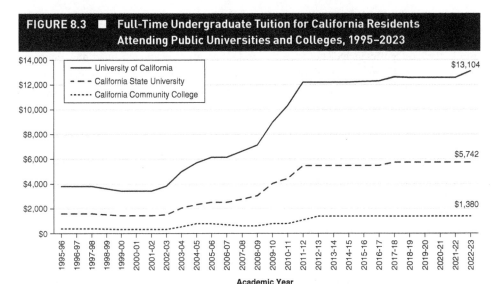

FIGURE 8.3 ■ Full-Time Undergraduate Tuition for California Residents Attending Public Universities and Colleges, 1995–2023

A Tuition Stability Plan for all University of California campuses, approved in 2021, keeps tuition and fees stable and predictable for current and incoming classes, remaining flat until the student graduates, for up to six years.

Most fees are waived for two years for all full-time community college students who are residents of California. The fee per unit was $46 in AY 2022–23.

Source: California Legislative Analyst's Office.

Notes: University of California (U.C.) figures include both system-wide tuition and Student Services Fee. The *Tuition Stability Plan* for all U.C. campuses, implemented in fall 2022, keeps tuition and fees stable and predictable for current and incoming classes, remaining flat until the student graduates, for up to six years. Most fees are waived for two years for all full-time community college students who are California residents. The fee per unit was $46 in AY 2022–23.

benefit checks, cutting state workers' salaries and/or benefits, eliminating or reducing services, changing tax policies, borrowing huge sums, deferring payments to schools or other government agencies into the future, or a combination of these. To ensure the numbers balance out, at times state officials have resorted to "gimmicks," such as unrealistically assuming a high employment rate or overestimating tax revenues. Governor Jerry Brown pushed back on those tactics in June 2011 by vetoing the budget for the first time in state history, citing "legally questionable maneuvers, costly borrowing and unrealistic savings," and demanded revisions.[15] To pass the budget on time, the legislature complied.

Structural budget deficits can also occur when imbalances are either anticipated or built into a budget and carry over to the following year, further deepening the hole and underscoring the fact that every budget builds on the prior one. Big, long-term commitments which lack a secure funding source can help break the state's budget during an economic recession. A structural deficit that existed from 2000 was finally plugged with state program reductions, higher revenues from an improving economy, and a temporary sales tax hike (Prop 30), all of which brought state spending in line with its income. To avoid going over a "fiscal cliff" (a sudden drop-off in revenues that results in deficits) when the economy sours eventually, lawmakers can opt for **one-time investments** (or "one-time spending" projects) using lump sums that are immediately available, rather than creating yearly spending obligations. The state's $52 billion five-year infrastructure plan takes this approach.[16]

California state government carries several types of **debt**, or large amounts that need to be paid back to lenders or creditors. **Bond** funds are borrowed dollars that supplement the budget and are designated for specific purposes; they provide revenues and also represent long-term debt. Two basic types, **general obligation bonds** (meaning the general public is obligated to repay them) and **lease-revenue bonds** (used to build public works that generate money) generally cover investments in infrastructure that shape the quality of life and commerce, such as better roads and water supplies. When times got tough in the late 2000s, to cover general fund expenses the state "raided" special accounts and also deferred payments that had been guaranteed to schools with promises to repay what it borrowed, resulting in a different kind of debt known as **budgetary borrowing**. That amounted to a $35 billion "wall of debt" that took a decade to pay off. Then there are **unfunded liabilities**: pension and health care promises made to state employees in labor contracts. Future benefit values are difficult to pinpoint because fund levels depend on fluctuating rates of return over time, human longevity, and unknown future costs. They are hardest to tame, but in good economic times, the state has continued to chip away at mounting obligations, as seen in the $2.9 billion contribution (2022–23) to the state's employee retirement fund (CalPERS).

Borrowing to finance megaprojects has become so commonplace that the average bond measure is in the $5 billion range, and the state now carries over $78 billion in **general obligation (GO) bond** debt principal plus $43 billion in interest payments, for a total of $121 billion in GO bond commitments. Many more billions have been authorized and have yet to be sold.[17] Most of the state's long-term **debt** comes from voter-approved GO bonds dedicated to school construction and remodeling, public transportation projects (including a record-setting $19.9 billion omnibus transportation bill approved in 2006), and environmental and natural resource projects, such as beach restoration or above-ground water storage. These measures veer sharply from the "pay-as-you-go" schemes typically used to finance large infrastructure projects in the past. Bonds will cost about twice their "face value" in the long run because of compounded interest, though the long-term cost is lower (about $1.40 paid for every $1 borrowed) if inflation is taken into account and if the state treasurer can rely on good state credit ratings to secure low interest rates.[18]

Notably, by 2022 the state's financial situation had recently improved to the point where it did not need to rely on outside lenders to meet financial obligations during the year, and its fat reserves provided padding for possible economic shocks. Mandatory annual deposits into the **Rainy Day Fund** resulted in a sizeable cushion; it had stored nearly $37.2 billion in the Budget Stabilization Account, school system stabilization account, and other budgetary reserves (Table 8.2).[19]

POLITICAL CONSTRAINTS ON BUDGETING

The budgeting process is far more than a series of steps. By nature it is political, involving numerous factors that condition and constrain policymakers' ability to make decisions collectively. These factors help explain how budgets can be out of balance by billions of dollars within weeks of their passage, and why millions of Californians are skeptical of elected officials' ability to solve problems and they remain dissatisfied with the budget in any form.

Above all, the budget reflects the *larger economic climate*. State governments suffer the same economic miseries when the U.S. economy falters, and rise with the tide when the economy recovers. High unemployment rates destroy PIT and sales tax proceeds, the two largest but highly variable sources of

TABLE 8.2 ■ Types of Debt		
Category	**Description**	**Main Types or Forms**
Bond debt	Long-term loans to cover infrastructure that shapes quality of life and commerce; bonds over $300,000 must be authorized by voters; are repaid in future (often five, twenty, or thirty years) with interest; state debt is managed by the state treasurer	General obligation bonds Lease-revenue bonds* Other; self-liquidating special funds
Budgetary borrowing	Long-term loans taken or payments deferred to cover shortfalls in an annual budget	Bonds for economic recovery Underfunding of mandated programs or unpaid costs to local governments and schools Deferred costs and payments Internal loans or borrowing from special funds
Unfunded liabilities*	Promised benefits for current and future state worker (teachers, etc.) retirees, negotiated and set in labor contracts but underfunded based on obligations; note that costs are subject to change over time	Underfunded (future) pension payouts for state employees (CalPERS, CalSTRS, UC and CSU, Judges) Future health care for retirees Pooled Money Investment Account (PMIA) loan

Sources: California State Treasurer's Office, "Bond Debt Summary as of July 1, 2020," https://www.buycaliforni-abonds.com/state-of-california-ca/documents/view-file/i27?mediaId=442538; LAO, "Structuring the Budget: Reserves, Debt and Liabilities," February 5, 2019, https://lao.ca.gov/Publications/Report/3925#State_Debts_and_Liabilities; DOF, ebudget 2020.

*"Lease-revenue" refers to debt incurred for facilities construction that will be repaid through revenue generated by the activities or projects being financed.

**CalPERS is the California Public Employees' Retirement System; CalSTRS is the California State Teachers' Retirement System, partially funded by the state. Health care costs will be affected by changes to the federal Affordable Care Act.

revenue on which state government stakes its fortunes. As the tax burden has shifted away from corporations and onto high-income individuals who largely rely on earnings from capital gains and business activity, the tax base has become even more volatile. As mentioned earlier, the 300,000 tax filers making $500,000 or more, *the top 1.7 percent of taxpayers, paid 51.6 percent of the state's income taxes.* Thus, the entire state budget critically depends on the financial fortunes of this elite class.[20]

The *political climate* also influences what kinds of programs receive funding and how much. Changing public opinion can cause certain issues to gain political traction; sometimes this happens in response to sudden events, elections, or environmental crises. Crime dominated the political agenda in the 1990s; the drought and wildfires now lead. Affordable housing, homelessness, immigration, and climate change command the special attention of Democratic lawmakers, and they use tax money to address big social problems through government programs. Furthermore, lawmakers know who their loyal supporters are, and they privilege some interests over others. Citizens who don't share the values of those in charge will view these choices as wasteful, offensive, or just plain ridiculous.

Anyone who has observed lawmaking up close will know that *special interests* and their *lobbyists* also unduly prevail throughout the process. Businesses, labor unions, and local governments all send swarms of policy experts and lobbyists to educate and inform state lawmakers and their staff about the anticipated effects of proposed budget changes on their clients. The information and relationships they leverage help determine what benefits they might receive or not, and sometimes they also threaten to use the initiative process to achieve what legislators might not deliver. Well-organized special interest groups are behind some of the initiatives deliberately designed to limit legislators' budgeting flexibility; for example, a coalition of educators successfully endorsed Proposition 98, which guarantees minimum funding levels for public education (roughly 40 percent of the general fund).

Term limits have also contributed to the tangle by continually restocking the legislature with many novice lawmakers who need time to develop a big-picture view of how systems in the state interrelate and how cuts in one area will affect others. It takes more than one budget cycle for a legislator to see how the process unfolds; it takes much longer to grasp how different constituencies are affected by changes. Prop 28 has enabled more legislators to develop more seasoned perspectives as they stay in the same office over time (up to twelve years).

Use of the ballot box, or *ballot-box budgeting*, has fundamentally reshaped budgeting practices throughout the state as well. Proposition 13 is a case in point. Prior to 1978, cities, counties, and schools relied heavily on property taxes to finance their budgets, which provided strong incentives to raise taxes continually. When Prop 13 capped property taxes at 1 percent of a home's or commercial building's purchase price and limited property assessment increases to no more than 2 percent per year, local governments were forced to look for other ways to cover the cost of services (now mainly sales taxes and fees), and state government assumed responsibility for refilling local government accounts and funding schools. However, when times got tough in the early 1990s, the state substantially changed the way it allocated education funds, resulting in the redirection of yet more revenues away from local governments. Local governments are always searching for stable sources of revenue, and because of their reliance on sales taxes and fees, their budgets can be devastated by emergencies—as they were by the coronavirus pandemic initially (the federal government supplied billions in recovery funding). Other ballot measures, such as mandatory minimum sentences (three strikes and automatic sentencing enhancements), unintentionally impose costly obligations on the state that drive up prison budgets and affect communities of color more harshly—reasons laws like these have been curtailed recently. Under Proposition 2, the state is also required to pay down debt each year and set aside amounts in a "rainy day" fund for emergencies.

In all of this, *rules matter*. Today the *two-thirds supermajority vote requirement to raise any tax or fee* can hamstring the majority Democrats, who—unless they hold supermajority status in both houses, as they have since 2016—must secure a few votes from the minority Republicans, who consider raising taxes a nonstarter. In the absence of a supermajority, unless 54 Assembly members and 27 Senators are willing to hike sales taxes or vehicle license fees, the majority party needs several minority-party members' votes to implement such increases.[21] Ironically, however, it takes only 50 percent plus one to *reduce* taxes and fees. Until 2010, one rule mattered above all others: a two-thirds vote requirement for passing the budget. With the power to kill the budget, minority-party members seized on this as their only opportunity to meaningfully influence public policy and force the majority to meet their demands. Overdue budgets became routine. In 2010, Californians lowered the *threshold for passing the budget* to a *simple majority*, meaning 50 percent plus one (41 Assembly members and 21 Senators), thus shifting the burden of constructing a balanced budget entirely to the (Democratic) majority. Budgets have been on time ever since, but Republicans have been sidelined.

Generally speaking, representatives would rather give their constituents what they want than risk losing the next election because they voted for a law that caused their constituents to lose an important state service, such as in-home elderly care for an aging mother; they don't want to be blamed for a lower unemployment check or loss of health care coverage. Thus, *risk-averse politicians* who may want to promote the general welfare but shy away from making painful cuts to in-demand services help drive up deficits.

TAX BURDEN: HIGHEST IN THE NATION?

It is a common complaint among Californians that they pay the highest taxes in the United States. By one estimate, California's ranking in the top five (in 2022, behind New York, Connecticut, Hawaii, and Vermont) in terms of overall tax burden tends to justify that view: on average, Californians spend at least 11.3 percent of their personal income on all types of state and local taxes, but the percentage of income that people pay in taxes isn't equally distributed.[22] For example, the lowest-income *and* the highest-income households pay the largest share of sales, excise, and property taxes as a percentage of their incomes, whereas those across the middle pay relatively less.[23] Escalated living costs for all mean increased tax bills, and most Californians consider themselves overtaxed: six out of ten say they pay more to state and local governments than they feel they should.[24] The bottom line is that one's perception of being overburdened is heavily influenced by both the kinds and rates of taxes one pays, and although some states do have a much lower effective tax burden, including a dozen with either no income or state sales taxes, burdens vary widely among individuals and also among states, none of which have the same blend of taxes (Figure 8.4).

The statewide base sales and use tax rate of 7.25 percent is the highest in the nation (the national median is 6 percent), but when local taxes are added (cities and counties can charge additional voter-approved increments), California drops out of the top ten, averaging 8.2 percent (compared to 7 percent nationally).[25] What's taxed or not differs greatly among the states: California doesn't levy surcharges on food or services, whereas other states do not tax clothes or do tax certain kinds of services. California charges the highest total gasoline taxes (see Table 8.3), with Illinois and Pennsylvania in second and third place, respectively.[26]

Corporate taxes are relatively high on paper, but many firms pay a fraction of the 8.84 percent main rate because of available tax credits in the tax code. Lawmakers also suspended a portion of the

FIGURE 8.4 ■ The Annual Budget Process

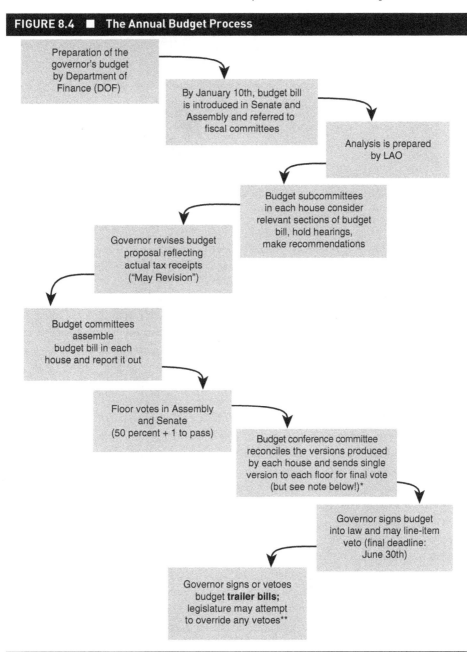

Preparation of the governor's budget by Department of Finance (DOF)

By January 10th, budget bill is introduced in Senate and Assembly and referred to fiscal committees

Analysis is prepared by LAO

Budget subcommittees in each house consider relevant sections of budget bill, hold hearings, make recommendations

Governor revises budget proposal reflecting actual tax receipts ("May Revision")

Budget committees assemble budget bill in each house and report it out

Floor votes in Assembly and Senate (50 percent + 1 to pass)

Budget conference committee reconciles the versions produced by each house and sends single version to each floor for final vote (but see note below!)*

Governor signs budget into law and may line-item veto (final deadline: June 30th)

Governor signs or vetoes budget **trailer bills;** legislature may attempt to override any vetoes**

*More typically, the Senate and Assembly **leaders debate and negotiate with the governor** over final figures, with their staff members working overtime. If a conference committee meets, usually three people from each house participate. From this point, permutations of the process occur with regularity.

**Leaders in each house help members construct many separate "*budget trailer bills*" that contain new policies or formalize legal changes reflected in the final budget figures. Trailer bills are processed through the houses, and the governor signs (or vetoes) each one. The legislature may attempt to override the governor's vetoes, but achieving the required two-thirds threshold is rare.

Source: Public Works, County of San Luis Obispo.

13 percent state diesel sales tax for a year to provide businesses some relief from high pump prices (October 1, 2022–23). California's notoriously high personal income tax rates are also misleading: the 13.3 percent marginal top rate is among the highest in the nation, but it is only paid by those making more than $1 million annually, and deductions and tax credits often reduce their tax burden significantly. At the other end of the scale, targeted, refundable earned income tax credits help low-income residents, and for half of all taxpayers who make less than $40,000, their income taxes rates compare favorably nationwide.[27] Due to Proposition 13, Californians pay among the lowest property tax rates in the nation; still, their yearly tax bills based on the excessive purchase price of a home can be higher than in other states overall, especially when they are stuck paying Mello-Roos fees or other local bond or parcel tax add-ons. "Sin" taxes on alcohol are comparatively low: as of 2022, California occupied the median for beer taxes ($0.20 per gallon) and the lowest for table wine (also $0.20 per gallon, tied with Texas), but it should be noted that this category represents less than 1 percent of the state's revenues.[28] To raise the cannabis industry's competitiveness against a fierce illegal market, cultivation taxes amounting to $161 per pound were eliminated in 2022, and tax credits were created to help legitimate businesses get ahead.

These figures show that the amount of taxes paid varies greatly from individual to individual and among socioeconomic classes, and California lawmakers have tried to even out tax burdens by tinkering with the rules. Unlike "regressive" taxation systems in which middle- and low-income households effectively pay higher tax rates than the wealthiest households due to a higher percentage of their incomes disappearing through sales and excise taxes (systems in which income taxes are not graduated), California's tax code is more equitable than most. Although the state's higher sales taxes are regressive in nature, the income gap between rich and poor is narrowed somewhat through graduated tax rates, limiting deductions for high-income filers, not taxing groceries, and providing credits instead of exemptions, for instance.[29] In spite of these measures, however, income inequality in California continues to grow, and Black and Latinx families accumulate much less wealth than White families overall.[30] In sum, whether individual Californians pay more or less than taxpayers in other states depends greatly on how much they earn, homeowner status, whether they have recently bought a house, regional location, the type of vehicle they own and how much they drive, and what goods and services they consume. These factors also influence individuals' perceptions of being overtaxed at least as much as their attitudes about public spending and the proper role of government do.

TABLE 8.3 ■ State and Local Governments Rely on a Variety of Taxes (Rates as of July 1, 2022)	
Type of Tax	**Current Basic Tax Rate**
Personal income	Marginal rates of 1% to 12.3%*; additional 1% surcharge for taxable income over $1 million
Sales and use	7.25% (state)*, but an average rate of 8.17%, varies by locality (add-ons by cities and states, ranging up to 10.75%)
Property	1% of assessed value, plus charges for voter-approved local debt (assessed value typically grows by 2% per year)
Corporation	8.84% of net income apportioned to California (10.84% for certain banks and financial companies)
Cannabis taxes	15% excise tax on sales (cultivation taxes ended June 30, 2022)
Vehicle license fee	0.65% of depreciated vehicle value (but note other registration fees depending on vehicle type and whether newly purchased: "Road Improvement Fee" for ZEV; "Transportation Improvement Fee" of $28 to $196 in 2022 [rates are tied to Consumer Price Index]); base registration fee; California Highway Patrol fee; county or district fees possible
Tobacco and vaping products	$2.87 per pack of twenty cigarettes; 61.74% of wholesale cost for vaping (vapor) products, e-cigarettes, any product containing tobacco or nicotine
Alcoholic beverage	Varies by beverage, from 20¢ per gallon of wine or beer to $3.30 per gallon of spirits under 100 proof; $6.60 per gallon of spirits 100+ proof
Vehicle fuel	53.9¢ per gallon (plus 2.25% state sales tax (about 12¢), plus local sales tax, plus 2¢ per gallon UST fee; federal tax of 18.4¢ also collected)**
Diesel fuel	41¢ per gallon (plus 13% state sales tax (about 23¢), plus local sales tax, plus 2¢ per gallon UST fee; federal tax of 24.4¢ also collected)**

Sources: "Tax Rates—Special Taxes and Fees" (as of July 1, 2022), Department of Tax and Fee Administration, State of California; "Tax Calculator, Tables, Rates, 2021 tax," Franchise Tax Board, State of California, July 1, 2022; "Estimated Gasoline Price Breakdown and Margins," California Energy Commission, State of California, August 8, 2022, https://www.energy.ca.gov/data-reports/energy-almanac/transportation-energy/estimated-gasoline-price-breakdown-and-margins.

*Includes temporary tax increases imposed by Proposition 30 (2012) and extended by Prop 55 (2016).

**"UST" refers to underground storage tank maintenance fees.

In addition, perceptions about whether the state overtaxes, overspends, or doesn't spend enough largely depend on beliefs about the proper roles of government and judgments about whether the state is achieving, can meet, or could fulfill those roles. When asked in a recent survey how they would prefer to use the budget surplus, the most popular choice among almost all California adults—Republicans and conservatives notably excepted—was to "increase state funding for education and health and human services" over refunding some of the money to the people.[31] The only category most citizens would slash is prisons and corrections—which federal courts have determined to be generally *under*funded historically.[32] However, it is worth noting that while Californians seem to have a penchant for keeping taxes low, time and again, it has been shown that while they oppose general tax increases, they are much more willing to support *specific* taxes if they are assured the funds are designated for purposes perceived as necessary and narrow in scope—as they did in 2018 for gas taxes and in 2012 and 2016 when they approved temporary sales and income tax hikes to pay for education.

CONCLUSION: BUDGETING UNDER VARIABLE CONDITIONS

As a U.S. state, California faces most of the same basic challenges as the other forty-nine, but as one of the world's largest "countries," its economy is intimately tied to global fortunes, and its fiscal dilemmas are comparable in scope and depth. Policymakers routinely deal with amounts in the billions, not just millions or thousands. The sheer volume of issues generated by nearly 40 million residents is staggering, and the majority of those issues are reflected, though not always resolved, in the state's annual budgets. Above all, annual budgets provide a blueprint for the state's priorities and the governor's values in particular. When one party controls both the legislature and the governor's office (Democrats 2011–present is a case in point), the budget clearly reflects that party's perspective, and it becomes easier for voters to hold that party to account for policy decisions and consequences.

Budgeting by nature is a rough-and-tumble business. Financial analysts in the executive branch's DOF and professional consultants in the legislative branch's LAO and in committees must perform the wizardry of forecasting without a magic crystal ball, relying on feedback, data, experience, statistical indicators, history, and tested formulas to predict the economic conditions for the coming year. Political representatives must then square their ideals with economic realities and reevaluate their preferences in the context of what is politically possible. Choices must be made, bargains must be struck, and solutions must be fashioned through compromise—these days, principally among Democrats. Legislators' behavior is guided by rules, such as vote thresholds that could ease the reaching of bargains or marginalize minority party members if their votes aren't needed (as Republican members know). Budget meltdowns, delays, and harsh spending cuts during the late 2000s illustrated that effective governing requires rules that will facilitate rather than obstruct compromise.

After negotiations have ended, the legislature has passed the budget bill, and the governor has signed it into law, the spending plan (surpassing $300 billion in 2022–23) is then assaulted by forces largely beyond the government's control. National and international crises may trigger severe and unanticipated drop-offs in tax revenues, leaving the state in the lurch. In times like those, representatives have almost no fiscally sensible ways to deal with such short-term crises because they cannot legally cut services immediately without undermining the state's contractual commitments to people and companies. On the other hand, an unanticipated surplus allows state officials the opportunity to fulfill more promises. Although the budget is normally assembled for the coming year only, unexpected windfalls have put the state on firmer footing to weather a downturn and to make 3- and 5-year plans. Its very design conditions future choices: commit to new programs with ongoing obligations or one-time spending only? Peel back taxes temporarily or permanently? California's brand of politics is clearly reflected in the choices and compromises that emerge from the annual budgeting process; quasi-national in scope and dwarfing those of every other state, the budget unveils the complexities of an immense and active state government.

KEY TERMS

Big Three: the governor, the Assembly speaker, and the Senate president pro tem.

Bond: a debt instrument enabling a state or local government to raise capital, usually for large projects, by borrowing large sums of money and committing to repay the principal and the interest by a specified future date (usually twenty or thirty years). A bond can be a piece of a large loan that is financed by multiple sources.

Budget bill: the proposed annual spending plan for the state's next fiscal year, formulated as a massive bill that must be passed by the legislature and signed into law by the governor.

Deficit: expenses exceed revenues in a given fiscal year, meaning not enough money is collected to cover spending commitments.

Debt: an amount that is owed; bond debt exists as borrowed amounts that accumulate interest.

Budgetary borrowing: long-term loans taken or payments deferred to cover shortfalls in the annual budget.

General fund: the state's main "bank" account, into which tax revenues are deposited.

General obligation bonds: a type of bond that is backed by the full faith and credit of a state or local government and will be repaid by taxpayers (see "bond"). Usually covers investments in infrastructure, such as library or road construction, school upgrades, or water projects.

Lease-revenue bonds: debt incurred for facilities construction that will be repaid through revenue generated by the projects being financed.

May Revision (also known informally as the "May Revise"): an updated version of the proposed annual budget that accounts for actual tax receipts; the governor's Department of Finance prepares and submits new budget estimates to the legislature by May 14.

One-time investments (or one-time spending): a lump sum that is dedicated to a project for a specific amount of time, as opposed to a permanent spending commitment that automatically renews by law annually (or needs to be renewed by lawmakers).

Rainy Day Fund: another name for the Budget Stabilization Account, mandated under Proposition 4; a budgetary reserve that is funded by annual state payments to be used in case of emergencies (such as during the "rainy days" of an economic downturn).

Revenue: another word for (government) income.

Structural budget deficit, or structural deficit: projected imbalances between income and expenses that are built into a current budget and carry over to the following year's budget.

Surplus: amounts of revenues collected that exceed the amounts spent, as with the annual state budgets in FY 2021 and 2022.

Trailer bills: bills that make the necessary policy changes to the state laws and codes outlined in the budget plan; these are passed after the budget bill is signed and are often lengthy and voluminous.

Unfunded liabilities: promised benefits for current and future state worker (teachers, etc.) retirees, negotiated and set in labor contracts but underfunded based on obligations.

9 POLITICAL PARTIES, ELECTIONS, AND CAMPAIGNS

Your election ballot arrived in the mail. Do you toss your completed ballot in a *mailbox* (no stamp needed) or hand it to a county election official at a ballot *drop-off location* that opens 28 days ahead of Election Day? Push it into a secure *dropbox*? Register and then vote *in person* on a machine at a *vote center* when they open 4 to 10 days before the election, or go to your *neighborhood polling place* on Election Day if you're in a county without vote centers? Since California moved to universal vote-by-mail elections, everyone has more choices about how to vote. That's by design. Public safety concerns around COVID-19 accelerated reforms already underway thanks to the 2016 Voter's Choice Act, a state law that localizes flexibility and convenience for California voters—at least for those who do not vote in person.

Elections help repackage millions of voices in the same way that political parties do: through them, diverse interests are voiced, aggregated, and translated into policy. Without them, the scale and scope of conflict produced by countless unorganized groups would be unmanageable. Equity would be unachievable. Without elections, citizens would lack a civil means to hold their representatives accountable.

Many Californians remain unconvinced that their voices matter or that these institutions are the best outlet for working out their intentions, goals, and grievances. Even when given the option of joining a political party that is "a good reflection of their political views," 58 percent of survey respondents said they would prefer to remain unaffiliated.[1] Moreover, the category of **"No Party Preference"** voters who register without a political party affiliation remains robust, surpassing 25 percent in 2018 but falling slightly short of that mark today. Overwhelmingly, Californians think they make better public policy decisions than elected officials do, placing their faith in an initiative process that allows them to bypass state government—although less than half trust their fellow voters to make good public policy decisions through the ballot box.[2]

Although Californians have been fairly united in their general distaste for politics and parties and at best are ambivalent about politicians, they are unevenly divided over the proper role of state government and tend to live near others with whom they agree socially and politically. An ideological **east–west divide** has formed along liberal–conservative lines, whereby the more urbanized and suburbanized coastal regions are heavily liberal to moderate (favoring strong roles for government) and trend Democratic, and sparsely populated, rural, inland and far northern counties are much more conservative (favoring small roles for government) and strongly Republican. This active fault has displaced the old north–south divide that is still visible in policy disputes over water distribution (and maybe sports rivalries) but little else. Urban Californians share more in common with other urbanites today, and inland residents have more in common with each other as well; their politics are reinforced by their sociopolitical environments (see Chapter 10 and Figure 9.1).

A DOMINANT-PARTY STATE

"Modern democracies are unthinkable save in terms of political parties," wrote political scientist E. E. Schattschneider in 1942.[3] Historically speaking, however, political parties in California have struggled for survival, not prospered, despite the outward appearance of being a Democratic stronghold. Much of the parties' troubles date to Progressive reforms in the early twentieth century deliberately designed to strip them of their power. Idealizing politics without partisanship, Progressives overhauled election law and established ways for voters to sidestep parties and representatives altogether with the initiative, referendum, and recall. As described in Chapters 2 and 3, other innovations included secret ballots, nonpartisan elections for local officials and judges, cross-filing at the state level for elected officials, and direct primaries that freed party members to choose their nominees without interference from party bosses.

The long-term consequences of the Progressives' attack on parties are still visible, and a good deal of the Progressives' antiparty program flourishes today: a version of the Progressives' cross-filing system has been revived with Top-Two primary elections, special interests in place of parties can affect some campaigns decisively through independent spending, all *local* elections remain nonpartisan, and candidates choose how to define themselves and when they run for office.

State parties have survived these challenges, and today California has solidified its reputation as a "dominant-party state" with Democrats regularly sweeping state and federal elections: they hold a supermajority in the legislature, the executive branch, and the Congressional delegation with both U.S. Senate and all but 12 of California's 52 U.S. House seats. As in other states where one of the two major parties has a virtual monopoly in elections—which some casually refer to as "one-party" states, a label usually reserved for autocracies—Democratic officials are motivated by a similar set of values that are generally shared by those who vote for them. The two major parties are well-formed opponents within state government but because of so few Republican representatives in Sacramento, most policy debates are among Democrats over

MAP 9.1   ■   California's East-West Partisan Divide

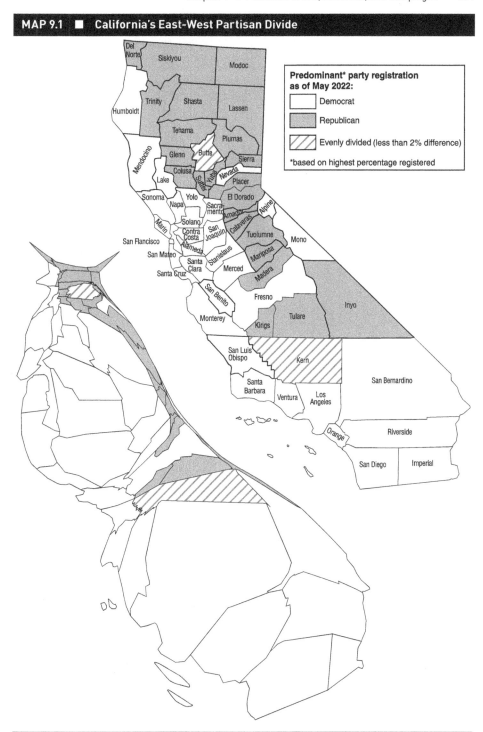

Predominant* party registration as of May 2022:

☐ Democrat

▨ Republican

▨ Evenly divided (less than 2% difference)

*based on highest percentage registered

Source: "Report of Registration: Registration by County," Office of the Secretary of State, State of California, as of May 23, 2022.

moderate or centrist policy approaches and "far-left" solutions. Average Californians lack deep attachments to political parties but generally favor "progressive" or liberal options over more conservative ones. These phenomena can be recognized through a more systematic examination

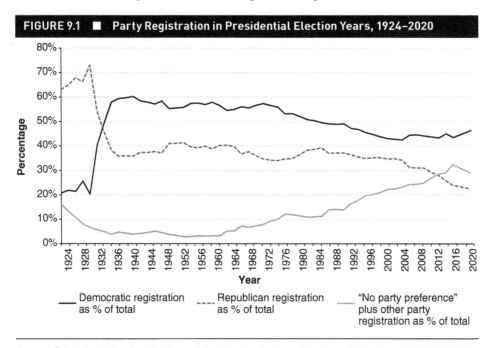

FIGURE 9.1 ■ Party Registration in Presidential Election Years, 1924–2020

____ Democratic registration as % of total

---- Republican registration as % of total

____ "No party preference" plus other party registration as % of total

Sources: "Historical Voter Registration and Participation in Statewide General Elections 1910–2020," Office of the Secretary of State, State of California, accessed October 29, 2022, https://elections.cdn.sos.ca.gov/sov/2020-general/sov/04-historical-voter-reg-participation.pdf.

Notes: Percentages are based on numbers from the closing date for registration in the general election. In previous years, No Party Preference voters registered as "Decline to State."

Source: Office of Secretary of State Alex Padilla.

of three interconnected parts of the party system: party *in the electorate* (PIE), party *in government* (PIG), and party *as an organization* (PO).

PARTY IN THE CALIFORNIA ELECTORATE

In one respect, a political party is made up of members who share similar beliefs about the role that government should play in their lives, but "party in the electorate" also refers to the generalized sentiment a party's members share about what it means to be a Republican, Democrat, or member of any other party. They also tend to know what policies and which politicians they *dislike* and form biases against "the other party." This is reflected in growing rates of *party polarization*, or strong differences between the major parties based on divergent political ideals and goals; dangerously, polarization can also be based on animosity for and distrust of other partisans.[4] Not everyone associated with a party shares these negative sentiments or desires the same policies, of course. Divisions or "factions" *within* the California Democratic Party have grown along with their political power at the state level; they are also visible in vigorous local debates over policing and addressing homelessness, and in the sensational 2022 recall of San Francisco District Attorney Chesa Boudin, whose criminal justice policies were too lax for the 55 percent of voters who blamed him for unpunished shoplifting, spikes in crime, and open drug use in the city.[5]

About 70 percent of registered California voters identify with the two major parties, Republican and Democratic, but that number is somewhat deceiving. According to statewide surveys, a majority of Californians think the state needs a robust third political party.[6] Because neither party has absolute majority status, the independent, No Party Preference voters provide the swing votes necessary for state candidates and ballot measures to win or lose, and generally speaking they side with Democrats.[7] Most district-based elections for Congress, Assembly, or state Senate are lopsided in favor of Democrats, and a few districts heavily favor Republicans. Some views are shared by solid majorities in all regions of the state, irrespective of party. Most people think taxes are too high, regard housing as unaffordable, and believe immigrants deserve a path to citizenship, for example.[8] While California is commonly labeled a "deep blue state" based on voter registration and election outcomes that have overwhelmingly favored Democrats, the reluctance of more people to join a party, a culture that favors individualism over blind party loyalty, and the defection of about one out of four people from the major parties add purple streaks to the state's blue political complexion.

In terms of party registration, California was an absolute majority-Democratic state between 1934 and 1989; since then, Democrats have made up the state's plurality party, topping Republicans by 22.8 percentage points in May 2022. Democrats today are first in registration with 47 percent of all registered voters, Republicans take second at 24 percent, and other parties collectively hold third place with a combined membership of 6.5 percent. Individuals who affiliate with no party constitute about 23 percent of the state's electorate.[9]

A thin slice of No Party Preference voters actually consider themselves purely politically independent (11 percent), with most of them leaning toward the Democrats (52 percent) rather than toward Republicans (37 percent), even as they profess to dislike the parties: 58 percent of independents rate the Democratic Party unfavorably, but they rate the Republican Party even more unfavorably at 69 percent. A plurality of them are moderate.[10] Exit polls show that 57 percent of independents voted for Joe Biden versus 35 percent for Donald Trump in 2020, and a majority of them rejected a recall of Democrat Gavin Newsom in 2021, evidence that corroborates political scientists' findings that self-identified independent "leaners" usually vote for the parties they say they tend to prefer.[11] More men have registered independent (59 percent); independents also tend to be young and college educated (48 percent college grads) and they are a diverse group (about half are persons of color).[12] Santa Clara, San Francisco, San Diego, San Mateo, and Imperial counties contain the highest percentages of No Party Preference registrants in the state (between 25 and 28 percent in 2022).[13]

Current members of the Democratic Party in California tend to be ethnically diverse, female, in the low-to-middle income bracket, and younger than in the past. As with independents, at least one out of two Democrats identifies as Latinx, African American, or Asian American, and the other half identify as White.[14] About one out of four likely Democratic voters has a household income of $40,000 or less per year; they are also more likely than Republicans to be college graduates (43 percent versus 30 percent), and a quarter of them are renters rather than homeowners. A disproportionate number of women are likely Democratic voters (just over 60 percent). The largest share of all likely young voters (age 18–34) are Democrats (28 percent).

Republicans, meanwhile, tend to be White and middle- to higher-income.[15] In contrast to Democrats and independents, 70 percent of likely Republican voters identify as White and are about evenly split between men and women.[16] Well over half (57 percent) are over the age of 55. Half of Republican likely voters make $80,000 or more annually (compared to 43 percent of Democrats).[17] Overall, these trends mirror those across the states.

Three out of four California Republicans describe themselves as **conservative**: they generally want strictly limited government, oppose taxes, respond more favorably to business than to labor, prefer strong restrictions on illegal immigration, and believe that "individual destiny should be in the individual's hands." Considered to be on the right-hand side of the ideological spectrum; they favor protecting an individual's right to own guns, and want lower taxes and fewer government services (79 percent of Republicans), and a majority believe that abortion should be illegal in most or all cases.[18] About half (49 percent) view immigrants as a benefit to California, but most oppose school districts designating themselves as "safe zones" for undocumented immigrants who are targeted by federal enforcement (83 percent).[19] Fully 80 percent of California Republicans believe it is not the federal government's responsibility to ensure all Americans have health insurance.[20]

California Democrats, on the other hand, tend to hold **liberal** views: 72 percent of them would pay higher taxes in exchange for more government services. They want the government to promote equal opportunity in education and the workplace, they want wider access to health care and overwhelmingly favor a government-offered health insurance plan that Americans can choose instead of private insurance (over 90 percent), and they support prochoice laws and oppose the overturning of *Roe v. Wade*. Overall they are more responsive to labor than to business. They feel laws covering the sale of guns should be more strict rather than less (83 percent).[21] Regarded as being on the left-hand side of the ideological spectrum, most Democrats say they are liberal (65 percent), and one in four consider themselves moderates (it should also be noted that the ambiguous labels of *progressive* and *liberal* are often used interchangeably, and the term does not refer to the Progressive Party of 100 years ago).

In contrast, independents are distributed across the ideological spectrum: 44 percent of likely independent voters describe themselves as moderate or *middle-of-the-road*, and equal proportions (about 28 percent) consider themselves liberal or conservative. More (59 percent) would prefer to pay lower taxes for a state government that provides fewer services than higher taxes for more services; but only one in three independents believe that it's not the federal government's responsibility to provide health insurance, and 76 percent would favor a government health plan option.[22] Three out of four were opposed to overturning *Roe v. Wade*. On climate change, a scientific issue that has become politicized, 80 percent of independents regard global warming as a serious or somewhat serious threat to the economy and quality of life for Californians, compared to almost all Democrats (96 percent) and only 53 percent of Republicans who hold that view.[23]

PARTY IN GOVERNMENT

Those most responsible for advancing a party's brand name through policymaking are current elected officials: the party in government. Approximately 20,000 officials in California hold elective office; of them, 132 occupy state government seats and 54 people represent Californians in the U.S. Congress in Washington, D.C. The most visible decision makers—the governor, Assembly members, state Senators, and Congress members—pursue agenda items that become associated with a party's name through fulfilling their chief purpose: *to organize government in order to achieve their policy aims*. Through their messages and decisions and also by what they choose not to do, those in positions of power communicate what it means to be a member of a particular party. Homegrown (former) U.S. House Speaker Nancy Pelosi and Governor Newsom have helped carve their Democratic Party's policy priorities into law, and current U.S. House Speaker Kevin McCarthy has tried to do the same for Republicans.

The Assembly and Senate have been majority Democratic almost continuously since 1971, interrupted only once by Republican rule in the Assembly in 1995–96, and Democrats have maintained a near-lock on supermajority status in recent years (see Chapter 4). A high degree of ideological polarization is evident in lawmakers' votes, especially with regard to taxation and spending: Democrats are more willing to raise certain taxes (income taxes paid by millionaires or gas taxes, for example), and Republicans are unwilling to raise them, period, instead insisting on shrinking government through cutting services. Republicans operate from a minority position as only 28 state lawmakers out of 120 (mid-2022), and they signal their policy positions through their opposition to major Democratic initiatives. Majority Democrats control policy debates over feature issues such as guarding reproductive rights and the climate, but factions within the majority party also have the power to curb its freedom to rule: moderates have helped temper the party's impulse for excessive business regulation in favor of protecting labor interests, for instance.

Termed-out representatives continue to exert influence in their parties and over policy at the local level as county supervisors, city council members, and other local elected officials, although those positions are technically nonpartisan. More Republicans are elected at the local level than the state level, and these offices provide training grounds for higher office.

BOX 9.1
HOW TO PARTY IN CALIFORNIA

To qualify as a new political party in California, a group must first hold a caucus or convention at which officers are elected, and a name is chosen. After filing a notice with the secretary of state, qualification may then proceed either by petition or by registration. Petitioners need to gather 1,114,661 valid signatures,* a number equal to 10 percent of the votes cast at the most recent gubernatorial (governor's) election, and they must file those petitions in several counties at least 135 days before the next election. The more complicated registration option requires that 0.33 percent of registered voters complete an affidavit of registration at least 154 days prior to the next election (or 123 days prior to a presidential election) where they indicate their preference for the new party, affidavits that must be verified by county elections officials. A party maintains its qualified status by retaining enough registered members according to the elections calendar (Figure 9.2).

Registered Parties in California, 2022

- **American Independent**: http://www.aipca.org
- **Democratic**: http://www.cadem.org
- **Green**: http://www.cagreens.org
- **Libertarian**: http://www.ca.lp.org
- **Peace and Freedom**: http://www.peaceandfreedom.org
- **Republican**: http://www.cagop.org

Parties That Have Failed to Qualify

- God, Truth, and Love
- California Pirate Party
- The Hogwash Party
- Reform Party
- Superhappy Party
- United Conscious Builders of the Dream

Source: California Secretary of State, "Qualified Political Parties," accessed July 1, 2022, https://www.sos.ca.gov/elections/political-parties/qualified-political-parties.

*This number changed after the 2022 elections.

PARTY ORGANIZATIONS

The concept of party also encompasses formal organizational bodies and their rules. It should be noted that when citizens register to vote, they actually become members of their *state* parties, organized according to election codes in the fifty different states and the District of Columbia. This is why citizens are given the option to register when they visit the Department of Motor Vehicles, a *state* agency. The national organizations known as the

FIGURE 9.2 ■ Registration by Political Party in California, 2022

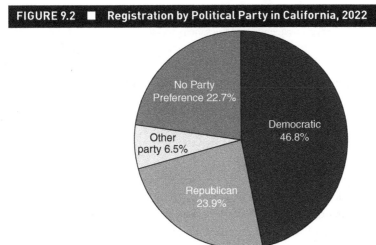

Source: "Primary Election Statement of the Vote, June 7, 2022," Secretary of State, State of California, n.d., https://www.sos.ca.gov/elections/prior-elections/statewide-election-results/primary-election-june-7-2022/statement-vote.

Democratic National Committee and Republican National Committee have little to no control over the state parties.

Party organizations are well suited to fulfill another key party role: that of *nominating candidates for election and getting them elected*. At the top is the party *state central committee*, responsible for coordinating the local bodies that exist below it, for strategizing to win seats, and for assisting candidates with funding and other resources. These committees run their respective state conventions every year.

A state party chair acts as CEO of the party, and members of the state central committees include current statewide elected officials, nominees for statewide office, county-level party officials, and appointed and elected members from across the state. Democratic members of their state central committee number about 3,000, evenly divided between men and women and roughly balanced among age groups and races/ethnicities. The Republican state central committee has approximately 1,400 members, and there are no gender, age, or race/ethnicity quotas. Beneath the major state party organs are 58 *county central committees* for each party, also organized by the state election codes. Further down are local and regional clubs that are home to dedicated party volunteers. The Democratic Party organizes these clubs by Assembly district. In the past few years, rifts have developed between the more leftist and centrist factions of the party: they wrestle over how to bring down housing costs and deal with homelessness, whether to establish universal health care, how to protect laborers without losing businesses to other states, how to regulate law enforcement, how to reform education, and how to promote equity and attack inequality. Republicans are unified in their defense of gun rights, opposition to gas taxes, and support of businesses as engines of the economy.

In California as elsewhere, *informal networks* formed by interest groups, media outlets, campaign donors, and other elites, such as termed-out officeholders, also influence how party organizations behave and how they are perceived.[24] Working through ideologically based networks and groups, powerbrokers guide agenda priorities, help decide who is recruited or endorsed for elective office, pressure competitors to drop out of a race to clear the field for a preferred front runner, or donate money directly to the party and candidates. Perhaps most importantly, these activists also shape elections behind the scenes through massive **independent expenditures**: money spent to influence election outcomes, such as through paid social media, ads, or mailers, *without* candidates' knowledge or input.

ELECTIONS: CONTINUITY AND CHANGE

Like political parties, elections are a keystone of democracy, and voters continue to find ways to improve them, usually in order to address what they perceive as unfair advantages held by groups or individuals. Elected officials also occasionally readjust the rules that regulate the conduct of parties or candidates, though they risk being seen as self-serving. Sometimes those reforms perform as intended, but unanticipated or unintended consequences often follow.

Propositions 11 and 14, already discussed elsewhere in this text, illustrate such outcomes. For example, after the U.S. Census was taken, newly redistricted maps in 2012 and 2022 forced many incumbents into the same districts, which caused an unprecedented number to decline to run for reelection (26 opted to call it quits midterm or not run again in 2022), a "great resignation" of sorts.[25]

Proposition 14, the Top-Two primary, triggered a different set of outcomes. For years, reformers tried to enlarge the electorate by unlocking primary elections so that independents could participate. In a normal **partisan primary election** for various offices (but not the U.S. presidency), independents play no role; only party members can nominate their own candidates who will later compete head to head with the other party's nominees in the general election. If six Republicans jump into a Senate primary race, only one will receive enough votes to become the Republican nominee for that district (an incumbent is invariably renominated). That person will face the Democratic nominee in a **general election**, usually held in November.

Until 1996, the state had a *closed primary* system, meaning that only voters who declared their party affiliation prior to the election could participate in their own party's elections. At the voting station or polling place, a person would receive a Republican or a Democratic ballot listing party candidates for each office. Independent voters could not vote for partisan nominees, although they could vote on statewide initiatives, local measures, and nonpartisan offices. Proposition 198 (1996) changed the rules but only temporarily. Californians approved the *blanket primary*, a type of open primary, in which all registered voters could vote for any candidate. In 1998, primary election voters were given a single ballot listing each office and every possible candidate for it, just as in a general election. Two years later, the U.S. Supreme Court ruled the scheme an unconstitutional violation of political parties' First Amendment right to free association. A *modified closed primary* took its place, and independents' votes counted if a party allowed it.

In June 2010, California voters decided again to switch to a system that resembles an *open primary*, similar to the one Washington state adopted in 2004. In exchange for his vote to pass the budget in 2009, Republican Senator Abel Maldonado demanded the legislature place a constitutional amendment on the ballot creating a nonpartisan "**Top-Two**" primary, also known as a *voter preference election*. The system is not a traditional political party primary, because the names of all candidates for an office appear with their party labels (they have the option to list it or not but virtually all do so), and any registered voter may consider all candidates and choose one who doesn't share the voter's party identification. In essence, it's a free-for-all that has been nicknamed the "jungle primary." Even if one candidate receives a majority of all votes cast for that office, the two highest vote-getters advance to the general election for a runoff, be they two Republicans, two Democrats, one from each party, or otherwise—and there were twenty-eight *intraparty* matchups in the November 2022 elections featuring top-two candidates from only one party.[26]

Although reformers hoped to disrupt the status quo by encouraging the election of more representative candidates whose policy positions would be closer to those of the average or "median" voter, thereby producing less polarized and more moderate delegations of legislators, the Top-Two primary has fallen short of expectations.[27] Most voters "stay in their lane" and do not cross party lines when voting.[28] But it has not been a failure. There is evidence that the quality of challengers is higher in intraparty contests,[29] and in certain matchups, the more centrist candidate prevails over the more ideologically extreme one, as seen in a growing number of Assembly and Senate Democrats who identify with the "Mod" or "Moderate Caucus"; these lawmakers tend to block certain business regulations and tax increases. Still, it is not clear whether their election can be attributed solely to the Top-Two system, and party leaders typically strive to keep their members in line on important votes and discourage behavior that undermines party unity.

Prop 14's underwhelming outcomes may also be attributed to the difficulty average voters have in discerning candidates' positions, and ideological polarization that is reflected in voters' general distaste for the opposing party's candidates.[30] An unrelated effect of Prop 14 is that *third party candidates* or those who identify with minor political parties, such as the Green Party, have virtually no chance of winning seats, although some of them make it to general elections where one of the major party candidates does not face another major party candidate. In 2019, deposed Assembly Republican leader Chad Mayes renounced his party affiliation, filed as a No Party Preference candidate, and won in 2020, but so far, he is the only statewide candidate in history to have done so.

Another momentous reform has been *term limits* for elected state officials, which have generated a slew of electoral consequences since their adoption in 1990 (Chapter 4). The game of political office musical chairs now extends to all levels of government: competition has increased for down-ticket elections, such as big-city mayorships and seats on county boards of supervisors, and pitched contests over congressional seats have also multiplied as the pool of experienced candidates looking for jobs continues to swell. About two-thirds of all statewide officials attempt to run for another office within two years of being termed out. In the crusade to stay in office, it is also fairly common now for incumbents to be challenged by members of their own party or even their own colleagues—rivalries that used to be adroitly managed by party leaders or preempted by the advantages of incumbency that scared off good challengers, meaning those with experience and money.

Special elections to fill vacant seats are commonplace due to term limits, as politicians leave one office for another that opens up. A "domino effect" occurs when a state senator runs for an open U.S. Congress seat and a member of the Assembly then runs for the vacated state Senate seat; this then creates a third election needed to fill the empty Assembly position, and so on down the line. These elections aren't free: a stand-alone special Assembly election can cost taxpayers around $2 million, and voter turnout for state elections is usually dismally low, averaging *just over 19 percent* turnout with all-mail elections.[31] (Note that candidates who win a special election with over 50 percent of the vote are considered elected, and no runoff election will be held.) The attempted recall of Governor Newsom cost over $200 million.[32]

Inventive reforms continue to reshape California elections. Los Angeles County's Registrar-Recorder/Clerk was the first in the nation to design a publicly owned voting system that launched in the March 2020 primary elections, enabling deployed military, overseas citizens, and disabled persons to vote remotely, but only if they were registered in the County of Los Angeles (and nowhere else).[33]

New models for elections also aim to expand the electorate through innovations such as *vote centers* that were first proposed under the Voter's Choice Act and were operational in many counties by the November 2022 general election. Vote centers either can be situated in neighborhoods for locals, or sited regionally and be open for all county residents. These centers replace traditional neighborhood polling booths with sites where, several days before Election Day (it varies by county, but ten or four days ahead typically), voters can drop off their ballot, get a replacement ballot, vote early in person, or register to vote conditionally (eligibility will be verified before the vote is counted). After testing the all-mail-ballot system in the 2021 gubernatorial recall election, the state made universal vote-by-mail permanent: all registered voters now receive a ballot at least 29 days prior to Election Day and they can either mail their completed ballot to their county registrar without a stamp, take it either to a staffed ballot drop-off location or a vote center, or put it in a secure ballot drop box in their county before the polls close at 8 p.m. on Election Day. Counties decide which options are available. A ballot must be submitted or postmarked on or before Election Day and received within seven days of Election Day for it to count. Research shows that mail-in ballot elections do not advantage either political party's turnout rates but have a modest, positive effect on turnout overall.[34] In addition, it appears that mail ballot elections help narrow the turnout gaps between traditional voters and underrepresented groups, but consolidating many polling places into one or a few local or regional vote centers, even if they are open several days before Election Day, effectively limits in-person voting options and tends to discourage turnout (especially among persons of color) by disrupting their habits.[35]

VoteCal, a centralized database connecting all fifty-eight county elections officials, as well as ballot tracking, have enabled the switch to universal vote-by-mail elections. Because voter information is now linked statewide, as of 2018, voters are able to register to vote on the day that they cast a ballot—also known as *same-day registration*—without running afoul of laws designed to prevent voter fraud. Because of VoteCal, a person can track their ballot, check to see if their mail-in or provisional ballot was counted, and see the reasons why it may not have been counted. VoteCal also enables *16- and 17-year-olds to preregister* to vote. An existing **motor voter law** reduces barriers to vote even further: Californians are *automatically registered to vote* when they renew their driver's licenses or register their cars with the Department of Motor Vehicles (DMV) unless they opt out. Californians can also register to vote via the internet; *online voter registration* is a service offered in forty-two states and D.C. To register in California, applicants can go to http://registertovote.ca.gov. If a person does not have a signature that can be accessed from a California driver's license record, then a hard copy of the form that the applicant fills out online will be mailed for a signature. The secretary of state reports that these reforms have helped bring about the highest levels of voter registration among eligible citizens since the 1950s.[36]

Eliminating obstacles to vote is a priority in California, and voters are NOT required to show a form of identification at the polls. Election fraud, such as impersonating someone or forging another person's name on a ballot, is a felony in California and remains extremely rare. Usually those cases will be referred to the FBI for investigation and possible prosecution. Virtually no credible allegations of widespread fraud have been substantiated in court or elsewhere because of natural and deliberate safeguards that include, among other things: specific inks used to print materials; special paper (made in Germany for the 2021 recall); step-by-step tracking of every ballot; electronic and manual signature checks; regular stress testing of machines; paper trails for machine voting; pollworker training; and security surrounding every stage.

The number and location of official ballot drop-off locations and voter dropboxes are determined by local county elections officials. Their placement depends on population concentration, voter convenience, proximity to public transportation, security, and availability of funds.

Source: AP Photos/Lea Suzuki.

Ash Kalra 🏹 ✓ @Ash_Kalra · Apr 23   ⋯

This morning, we had a great turnout for @alex_lee for State **Assembly**, @aishabbwahab for State Senate and @thesajidakhan for **District Attorney!**

Aisha Wahab and 5 others

Source: Photo by Ash Kalra via Twitter/Public Domain.

CALIFORNIA CAMPAIGNS

Given parties' relatively weak hold over Californians, the frequency of elections, a highly mobile population, and the immense size and density of districts, campaigns serve the important role of connecting citizens with candidates and incumbents. Across the state, virtually all campaigners face the same basic challenges: raising huge sums of cash to buy access to potential voters and convincing enough of those voters to reject their opponents.

Former Assembly Speaker Jesse Unruh once professed that "Money is the mother's milk of politics."[37] Indeed, incumbents cannot afford to stop raising money, waging what is known as the nonstop "permanent campaign." On average, a successful Assembly campaign costs close to $900,000, and an average winning Senate campaign about $1.3 million (with a wide range)—which means that candidates need to raise roughly $1,000 *every single day of the year* to be viable.[38] Actual costs depend critically on how strong the competition is and how threatened incumbents feel. The sums spent in open seat elections or by vulnerable incumbents can be steep, and incumbents often spend gross amounts even when they are unopposed or face "sacrificial lambs" who spend almost nothing in their own defense. For example, Democratic Assembly member Evan Low of Silicon Valley spent over $3 million to defeat a Republican challenger in 2020, while his opponent didn't even form a campaign committee (and thus didn't report any spending).[39]

Spectacular spending occurs around open-seat elections with no sure winner. Redistricting following the 2020 U.S. Census contributed to a proliferation of elections in which there technically was no incumbent, sparking hopes for newcomers and the retirements of incumbents who preferred not to face off against a colleague. Candidates for open seats collect and spend over $1 million on average; the most exorbitant races can cost each candidate several million. In one intense June 2022 Senate primary that came down to two Democrats, for example, former Insurance Commissioner and former Assemblyman Dave Jones raised and spent almost $1 million to secure a place in the Top-Two, and his competitor, Angelique Ashby, spent $800,000—previewing an expensive general election (which she ultimately won).[40] Costs are also higher when there is a good possibility that the seat could flip to the other party or be the race that denies the Democrats a supermajority, which can occur through a special or regular election (Table 9.1).

Candidates enjoy the constitutional right to spend as much as they want of their own money in pursuit of a political office; the two major state political parties may donate to candidates without limitations, and lobbyists are prohibited from contributing directly to individual candidates. If they raise more than they spend, then they can roll the leftover cash into another campaign committee and become competitive almost immediately. It is important to note that *there are no limits on how much can be donated to ballot campaigns*, and recall elections are exempt from contribution limits (meaning the campaigns urging "yes" or "no" to recall).

Most campaigns are financed through individuals, business- and union-related political action committees, and groups that must adhere to strict limits set by the Fair Political Practices Commission (FPPC), the nonpartisan body that regulates campaign finance and lobbying in the state. By industry, among the most reliable contributors to California campaigns are trade and public employee unions, banking and securities/investment firms, energy or oil and gas companies, general business (manufacturing, chemicals, food and beverage, tobacco), law, agriculture, real estate, health, and ideological or single-issue groups. Out-of-state entities are allowed to donate to individuals and initiative campaigns, and they, along with everyone else, must report how much they either donate or spend independently, plus the source of their contributions, a point the FPPC drove home in 2013 when they fined two out-of-state nonprofits $1 million for improperly reporting (hiding) their contributors' names.

To clarify these rules further, all campaign contributions and expenditures must be reported to the California Secretary of State's office, which makes all details about money flowing through the system publicly available (see http://cal-access.sos.ca.gov). The state's strong disclosure rules (dictating that information about donors must be made available to the public) survived a legal challenge after the U.S. Supreme Court ruling in *Citizens United v. Federal Election Commission* (2010) lifted a seventy-year-old ban on independent federal campaign expenditures by corporations and unions in the name of free speech. Large sums are now being spent in independently run *federal* (Congressional and presidential) campaigns without strict reporting and disclosure requirements, principally in the form of mass mailings, signage, and television and radio ads designed to defeat or endorse candidates. However, in California, large sums could already be spent independently on state elections, so these were minimally affected by *Citizens United*.

Why do candidates require colossal amounts of campaign cash? In California's populous districts, paid media are the only realistic way to reach large numbers of likely voters. Advertising is especially pricey in urban media markets already crowded with commercial ads. Most candidates invest heavily in this type of **wholesale campaigning**, or indirectly contacting voters through social media, the airwaves, and direct mail.

This is not to say that knocking on doors, attending community events, and "pressing the flesh"—types of **retail campaigning** that require a comfortable pair of shoes and a band of volunteers—are unimportant in modern campaigns. Personal, face-to-face contact is particularly

TABLE 9.1 ■ Cost of Campaigns for State Candidates, 2018 and 2020

Office & Year	Average Spent by General Election Winner	Average Spent by Open Seat Winners Only	Average Spent by Incumbents
Assembly 2018	$900,000 (n = 80)	$1,440,000 (n = 4)	$870,000 (n = 76)
Assembly 2020	$917,000 (n = 79)	$664,000 (n = 9)	$909,000 (n = 70)
Senate 2018	$1,065,000 (n = 20)	$1,370,000 (n = 6)	$935,000 (n = 14)
Senate 2020	$1,313,000 (n = 20)	$1,508,000 (n = 6)	$1,230,000 (n = 14)

Constitutional Offices in 2018	Winner (Total Amount Spent) (*incumbent)	Loser (Total Amount Spent)
Governor**	Gavin Newsom (D): $46,800,068	John Cox (R): $15,158,629
Attorney General	Xavier Becerra* (D): $6,575,787	Steven Bailey (R): $550,087
Superintendent of Public Instruction** (nonpartisan)	Tony Thurmond: $3,416,090	Marshall Tuck: $5,071,273
Lieutenant Governor**	Eleni Kounalakis (D): $10,463,994	Ed Hernandez (D): $3,378,765
Insurance Commissioner**	Ricardo Lara (D): $2,158,536	Steve Poizner (NPP): $3,261,287
Secretary of State	Alex Padilla* (D): $726,165	Mark Meuser (R): $313,771
Treasurer**	Fiona Ma (D): $2,176,687	Greg Conlon (R): $68,132
Controller	Betty Yee* (D): $898,818	Konstantinos Roditis (R): $26,200
Board of Equalization**	Ted Gaines (R): $377,855	Tom Hallinan (D): $45,345
	Malia Cohen (D): $127,145	Mark Burns (R): $26,685
	Tony Vazquez (D): $245,363	Marshall Rick (R): $12,824
	Michael Schaefer (D): $0	Joel Anderson (R): $339,860

Source: California Secretary of State, "Cal-Access: Candidates and Elected Officials, 2018 General," accessed July 1, 2020, http://cal-access.sos.ca.gov/Campaign/Candidates/list.aspx?electNav.=.63, and "Cal-Access: Candidates and Elected Officials, 2020 General," accessed July 15, 2022, https://cal-access.sos.ca.gov/Campaign/Candidates/list.aspx?electNav=71.

*Incumbent.

**Open seat.

Notes: Figures are reported for spending between January 1 and December 31 of the election year, covering both the primary and general elections. Candidates can voluntarily limit their spending in either or both the primary and general elections, but they sometimes exceed the limits. Dollars are unadjusted (real dollars) and figures have been rounded. Excludes Blanca Rubio (online record was unavailable).

beneficial in local contests in which friends and neighbors help turn out the vote. Social distancing crushed retail campaigning in 2020. The clear limitations of remote happy hours and Zoom fundraisers were flatly exposed, necessitating more wholesale campaigning.

Professional campaign managers and consultants help candidates build momentum and efficient money-raising machines by coordinating critical aspects of successful campaigns: access to donors, polling data, opposition research, media buys, targeted messaging, and volunteers. Still, neither high-priced campaign consultants nor "all the money in the world" guarantee a win: in her losing gubernatorial contest with Jerry Brown, Republican candidate Meg Whitman spent a total of $178.5 million, or $43.25 per vote, compared to Brown's $36.7 million, or $6.75 per vote. Whitman, former president and CEO of eBay, spent $144 million of her own fortune on the race.

Mailers that advertise a candidate's qualifications, positions, and messages are standard elements of a political campaign strategy to reach potential voters, including Spanish speakers in Devon Mathis's Central Valley district. In English, the mailer reads: "Inflation. Expensive Housing. Gasoline Tax. We need a leader who fights for the people like Assemblyman Devon, a veteran who puts people before politics. Answering the call to serve."

Source: Courtesy of Devon Mathis for Assembly 2022/Axiom Strategies.

CONCLUSION: A COMPLEX ELECTORATE

Parties, elections, and campaigns have been the instruments of change and the targets of reform. Historical disdain for parties lingers in California's state election codes and permeates the conduct of elections, surfacing in initiatives that seek to empower individuals over organizations, such as Proposition 14, the "Top-Two primary," which reformed primary elections by opening them to all voters, regardless of political party affiliation. It is also manifested in out-of-sight party organizations, active informal party organizations and independent influencers, and a solid chunk of No Party Preference voters. Drawing more young voters and persons of color into elections has been a shared goal of California officials, many of whom have helped revitalize registration and ballot access rules, an ongoing effort.

Political parties are far from dormant, however, and in legislatures they function as a practical means to coordinate the actions of like-minded people. Parties run elections and organize government action, and they still provide the most important voting cues for the average citizen—even those who reject political party labels. The ideological divisions they represent are real, and the fact that Democrats hold a distinct party registration advantage and have been sweeping state elections for more than a decade signals their solid advantage over Republicans, as well as Republicans' need to regroup in order to regain lost ground.

Democratic consolidation of power in California state government enables greater accountability in that at election time, voters can blame or reward the members of that party for the governance provided. On the other hand, one-party control leaves fewer "checks" against the excesses of power, and the party in charge runs the risk that their policies will tilt further and further away from the ideological middle, the space most Californians occupy. Furthermore, Democratic ascendancy should not be interpreted as the citizenry's wholesale endorsement of the ruling party's liberal policies; even if there is general congruence between a district's voters who consistently reelect incumbents, those patterns tend to mask the ideological diversity of Californians, many of whom don't vote, and fewer than half of whom positively identify as Democrats, and many of whom do not agree on how to solve fundamental issues in their own backyards, such as homelessness. Many citizens remain detached from and uninterested in state politics, a topic covered in the next chapter. Reforms designed to ease pathways to voting are unlikely to strengthen those partisan connections, but they do intend to increase political participation, however incrementally.

The COVID pandemic provided an opportunity for some of the bold changes California made in election systems, from easier registration, to early voting, to vote counting. Having followed in the footsteps of other states that forged innovative party and election reforms, California continues to engineer its own set of rules that is clearly unique and at times innovative, but not necessarily exceptional. It remains to be seen whether same-day voter registration, expanded motor voter registration, or switching to all-mail-ballot elections results in campaigns, candidates, and winners that embody the spirit of moderation and citizenship that Californians—indeed, most Americans—yearn for, or whether these will bring about the effective representation that citizens so strongly desire. The abiding hope is that they will—or that the *next* reform will.

KEY TERMS

Conservative: an ideological disposition to strictly limit government, taxes, and illegal immigration; general favoring of business interests over those of labor; and a belief that the individual—not government—should be financially responsible for his or her own well-being and destiny.

East-west divide: a political division manifest in geography (where people live), whereby the more urbanized and suburbanized coastal regions are heavily liberal to moderate and trend Democratic, and rural, inland counties are much more conservative and strongly Republican.

General election: a regular election, usually held in November; a major (run-off) election that features two candidates who have been chosen through a primary election, and after which the winner takes office.

Independent expenditures: money spent to influence election outcomes, such as on mailers or ads, without candidates' direct knowledge or input.

Liberal: an ideological disposition to more government services in exchange for higher taxes (such as wider access to health care); favoring government action to promote equal opportunity in education and the workplace; general favoring of labor interests over those of business.

Motor voter law: citizens are automatically registered to vote when they renew their driver's licenses or register their vehicle with the Department of Motor Vehicles, unless they opt out.

No Party Preference: a term designating that a citizen has chosen to register to vote without a political party affiliation.

Partisan primary election: a preliminary election in which candidates vie to become their party's nominee for elective office; the winners later compete head-to-head with the other party's nominees in the general election.

Retail campaigning: campaign activity involving direct, face-to-face contact with voters.

Top-Two primary: California's "open" voter preference election, in which any registered voter may select a top choice (one person) from among all candidates for office, and the two highest vote-getters advance to the general election for a runoff, regardless of party affiliation.

Vote by mail: a system of voting wherein voters receive their official ballots through the mail, and completed ballots may be dropped off at a voter's polling place, official dropbox, drop-off location, or vote center.

Wholesale campaigning: campaign activity involving indirect contact with voters through the airwaves and direct mail.

10 POLITICAL ENGAGEMENT

CITIZENS AND POLITICS

"ROEvolution!" "BLACK LIVES MATTER." "The Climate is Changing: WHY AREN'T WE?" Since 2017, in unprecedented numbers, Californians have thrust millions of signs in the air to protest anti-immigration policies and climate inaction, support LGBTQ+ rights, demand racial justice and police accountability, stand up for reproductive rights, and they have counterdemonstrated. More people have rallied, marched, and protested than ever before, helping California earn its reputation as a "state of resistance," one in which political power is tangible and exercised publicly.[1]

The Greek words *demos* and *kratos*, or *democracy*, translate literally as "the people rule." In a democracy, political power resides with the people, but they either delegate power to their representatives to make decisions, or exert power by themselves by approving or rejecting ballot initiatives. Democracy and voting go hand in hand, but self-governance takes shape in many other ways, including ordinary actions such as talking to others about who uses or abuses power and becoming informed about issues. Citizens try to influence the political system and each other by using social media and regular media channels, or by joining political parties (the subject of Chapter 9), nonprofits, or organized interest groups. Journalists and mass media play a critical role in connecting Californians to state and local governments by framing and distributing information that influences public opinion and political behavior. If the people's will, demands, and needs have any chance of being translated into public policies, then speaking out or taking some kind of action is imperative, as political decisions reflect the biases of those who show up and demonstrate that their interests matter. As this chapter discusses, certain groups possess unequal weight in the political system, and individual participation is associated with certain characteristics that are unevenly distributed across the population.[2]

PREDICTORS OF POLITICAL PARTICIPATION AND DISENGAGEMENT

Like other Americans, few Californians follow state politics closely. In fact many across the state "hate" politics, whereas the impulse to march, talk politics, vote, or "get involved" comes almost automatically to others. What accounts for the divergence?

Feeling that you personally have the power to make a difference, your sense of ***political efficacy***, is key to engaging a political system at almost any level.[3] Those who think they will never be taken seriously or believe that their efforts will be wasted don't usually vote, demonstrate, or email their representatives. On the other hand, those who experience the impact of unfair laws,

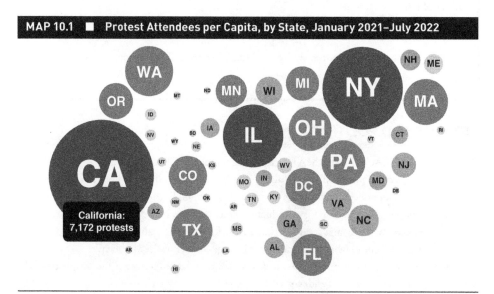

MAP 10.1 ■ Protest Attendees per Capita, by State, January 2021–July 2022

California: 7,172 protests

Source: Crowd Counting Consortium, data accessed July 2022. https://sites.google.com/view/crowdcountingconsortium/home?authuser=0.

recognize the immediate relevance of policy changes, and feel as if they can make a difference tend to become involved in politics. *Interest in politics* also helps activate people; interest levels are generally higher among likely voters across all racial/ethnic groups, and Californians who have "only a little" interest in politics tend to have measurably lower levels of participation. For example, *56 percent* of Latinxs have only a little interest in politics or "none" at all, compared to 36 percent of Blacks and Asian Americans, and only 27 percent of Whites—a nearly 30-point gap, one that has closed by about 7 points in the past 5 years but is reproduced in their political habits.[4] Similarly, politics matters "a great deal or a fair amount" to 55 percent of younger Californians (age 18–34), compared to 70 percent of older Californians (over age 55). Overall, however, political interest climbed after Donald Trump was elected U.S. president, which shows that one doesn't need to possess a natural liking for politics to care about it.

Socioeconomic variables strongly predict levels of political activity. *Education, age,* and *income* levels are positively related to participation, meaning that the more educated, older, and wealthier one is, the more likely one will pay attention to government affairs and try to affect political outcomes. *Home ownership* and *length of residence* are positively associated with civic behavior and activism; retirees and older residents who have lived in their own homes for more than two decades are among the most reliable political participants.

Race/ethnicity and *nativity* (whether one was born in the U.S.) are among the strongest predictors of political engagement and disengagement. California contains disproportionately large Latinx and Asian populations with high percentages born elsewhere, and foreign-born persons are less inclined to discuss politics, register to vote, carry a protest sign, or cast a ballot than are others.[5] Having friends and family who talk about politics and who value voting— aspects of *living in a* "pro-voting" *culture*—matters greatly for political activity; for example, Spanish speakers who hardly ever talk about politics with their friends are far less likely than other groups either to register to vote or actually vote.[6]

While disengaging from politics can certainly be a conscious choice, *not participating* is associated with many factors that often lie beyond an individual's control. Political science research shows that lower education and income levels are associated with fewer chances to be contacted or mobilized, language deficits, and having less disposable or "free" time, issues that disproportionately affect low-income workers who might hold down multiple jobs. Lower socioeconomic status is also correlated with a lower sense of confidence in one's power to change things (lower political efficacy), and continued disengagement can lead to even higher levels of frustration and political apathy—a cycle that can be hard to break.

In sum, these variables predict that certain kinds of people will be over- or underrepresented in California politics. On the whole, more Millennials and persons of color tend to be more disconnected from politics than White, well-educated, older homeowners, who are most likely to get involved in local and state affairs and, therefore, are the group that politicians are most likely to hear from and respond to or contact proactively, especially during campaign season, creating imbalances in local and state public policy.[7] As one set of researchers put it, "California's democracy is neither adequately participatory nor representative."[8]

THE FIVE CALIFORNIAS

The characteristics mentioned in the previous section help predict who is most or least politically active in a community—but it should be kept in mind that these are general tendencies and do not necessarily explain any one individual's behavior. The same can be said of the "Five Californias," or five different groupings of Californians separated by relative levels of well-being and their access to opportunity. After measuring the overall health, income, and education levels of the state's residents, researchers sorted them into five major groups and placed them on a human development scale to indicate their relative differences—disparities that are reflected not only in the everyday challenges and problems that people face but also in the demands they place on the political system.[9] The "good news": all Californians fare slightly better than rest of the nation, and almost 2.5 million more people occupy the upper groups compared to 7 years before. The "bad news": COVID-19 magnified inequalities; those at the top are faring better and better, while almost everyone else is falling behind with diminishing hopes of catching up.

One Percent

Topping the charts with the highest human development scores are "one-percenters" (about 906,000 people) who both propel and benefit from innovation like information technology, and whose standard of living affords privileges unknown to the rest of society. With access to great health care and stable jobs and relationships (84 percent are two-parent households), *One-Percent* Californians are extremely well-educated (one in three holds a graduate or professional degree), and can expect to live long lives. The majority of them are White (57 percent), a quarter are Asian, 8.5 percent are Latinx, and about 4 percent are Black; almost one in three are foreign-born (28.5 percent). Most are highly paid entrepreneurs or have well-paying careers in management, business, science, and the arts, with annual median personal incomes around $82,000. Their children go to preschool, and they can afford expensive private schools, access public schools among the nation's best, and help their children achieve their potential through extracurriculars. One-Percent Californians cluster in six exclusive towns: one in Pacific Palisades (Los Angeles, or L.A.) and the rest in Santa Clara County, such as Palo Alto, where the price of a typical home is over $3.9 million.[10] With the freedom, affluence, and social cohesion to act collectively, their political power is unmatched.

Elite Enclave

Elite Enclave Californians (20.5 percent of the population; about 8 million people) are also well-educated, affluent "knowledge workers" who reside in neighborhoods rich with amenities. Holding careers in business, the arts, and sciences but earning considerably less than One-Percenters (median $65,600 per person a year; that's $21,000 over the state median), they are mostly White (47 percent) and Asian (26 percent); only about 18.5 percent are Latinx, 3.5 percent are Black, and 0.5 percent Pacific Islander or Native American. Almost all have graduated high school and almost six in ten have a college degree; one in four has an advanced degree. Home values in these neighborhoods have skyrocketed recently, and while living costs have as well, generally they can pay their bills every month, can afford age-appropriate childcare, and

MAP 10.2 ■ The Five Californias

	One-Percent California	Elite Enclave California	Main Street California	Struggling California	Disenfranchised California*
Life expectancy at birth (age in years)	86.1	84.8	82.3	79.6	75.3*
At least a B.A. degree	74.5%	58.1%	33.7%	16.5%	7.6%*
Median personal earnings (2019 dollars)	$81,756	$60,577	$39,130	$30,332	$21,764*
Percentage Persons of Color (Non-White)	42.9%	53.1%	61.6%	75.3%	86.5%**
Married-couple family (% of households with children)	87.5%	79.4%	71.7%	62.9%	N/A

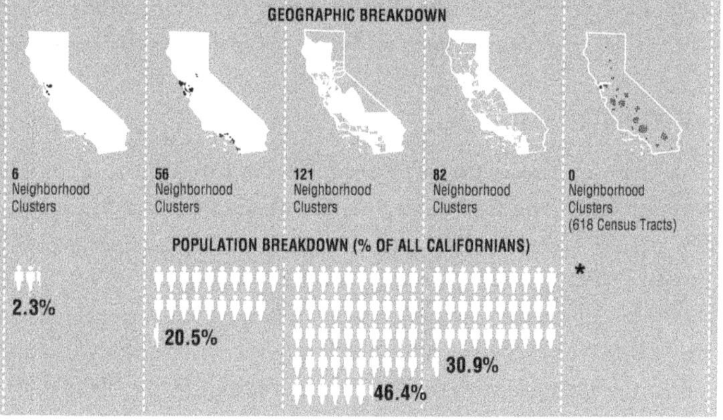

GEOGRAPHIC BREAKDOWN

| 6 Neighborhood Clusters | 56 Neighborhood Clusters | 121 Neighborhood Clusters | 82 Neighborhood Clusters | 0 Neighborhood Clusters (618 Census Tracts) |

POPULATION BREAKDOWN (% OF ALL CALIFORNIANS)

2.3%   20.5%   46.4%   30.9%   *

*The Disenfranchised category is based on 618 small *census tracts*, whereas the other categories are based on 265 *neighborhood clusters* constructed by the researchers. Therefore, the disenfranchised population is not presented as a percentage of the whole. Calculations were based on 2019 ACS estimates, and 2015–19 estimates for census tracts. Each dot on the Disenfranchised map represents roughly 25,000 people in that county. Census tract data were provided by the Measure of America research team led by Kristin Lewis.
**This figure is sourced separately from Burd-Sharps and Lewis, "Portrait of California, 2014–15," the most recent estimate available for neighborhood clusters.

Source: Kristin Lewis, "A Portrait of California, 2021–2022," Measure of America (New York: Social Science Research Council), 2021.

* The Disenfranchised category is based on 611 small *census tracts*, whereas the others are based on 265 *neighborhood clusters* constructed by the researchers. Therefore, the disenfranchised population is not presented as a percentage of the whole. Calculations were based on 2019 ACS estimates, or 2015–19 estimates for U.S. Census tracts. Each dot on the Disenfranchised map represents roughly 25,000 people in that county. Census tract data were provided by the Measure of America research team led by Kristin Lewis.

**This figure is sourced separately from Burd-Sharps and Lewis, "Portrait of California 2014–15," the most recent estimate available.

experience low levels of crime. Located in urban and suburban pockets of L.A., Sacramento, San Diego, San Francisco, and San Jose, most are married (eight out of ten), and about a quarter are foreign-born. Parents in this group are focused on getting their kids into college, and they and their kids largely bypass the hardships of poverty, toxic stress, and crime.

Main Street

Main Street Californians (about 46.5 percent of residents; over 18.3 million people) resemble what many think of as "middle class" America: largely they work in offices as managers and in sales and service occupations, and while over half own their homes, their grip on financial security is weakening as secure retirement and better lives for their children remain out of reach for many. Renters are being priced out of once-affordable markets, and for about a third of them, rent drains away more than half of their income. As in the wider population, *Main Street* includes 38.5 percent Whites, 37 percent Latinxs, 15 percent Asians, and 5.5 percent Blacks, and one of four are foreign born. Almost all have graduated high school (85 percent), whereas 34 percent have a Bachelor's degree, and only 11.5 percent hold a graduate or professional degree. Parents are able to provide afterschool enrichment activities as kids age, but public schools are mostly underperforming. Individual income hovers around $39,100 annually—barely covering housing, health care, and other ever-escalating costs of living. One in three children grows up with a single parent; good childcare is expensive and hard to find. Main Street communities cluster around large cities like Los Angeles and in sprawling inland cities such as Fresno, San Jose, and San Bernardino.

Struggling

The largest number of people (over 12.2 million, or 31 percent) in California struggle to hold it together. Living in suburbs and rural neighborhoods located mostly in parts of L.A., the Inland Empire, the Central Valley, and the north, areas with spotty public transportation options. *Struggling* Californians are largely Latinx (59 percent), White (25 percent), 6 percent Asian American, 7 percent Black, and 1 percent (the largest share) of Pacific Islander/Native Americans; one of four is foreign-born. Mainly high-effort/low-reward/low-paid jobs in sales, office, and service enable them to earn a median personal income of $30,300 a year, about $9,000 short of the state median, and not enough to avoid extreme housing cost burdens or keep one out of four kids out of poverty. Crises such as pandemics affect them disproportionately because of layoffs, crowded homes, and working in high-risk "essential service" jobs. About 40 percent of households are headed by a single parent. Insecure jobs without benefits, more exposure to crime and aggressive policing, little if any access to affordable childcare, extracurriculars, or internet, and caring for a disabled family member take tremendous tolls on health; they live roughly seven years less than the One Percent, and COVID-19 has widened life expectancy gaps further.

Disenfranchised

Disenfranchised persons experience "marginalization, segregation, and social exclusion" along with material scarcity, and lack the skills, networks, and services that enable access to the "normal activities available to the majority."[11] Located in just over 600 small *census tracts* scattered across California (a portion of which may overlap some of the 265 neighborhood clusters from which the other categories are derived, complicating the numerical count in this category), at least a million Californians could be placed at or near the low end of the human development scale, among them many unsheltered or homeless individuals.[12] Isolated from jobs and reliable health care and often living outside the formal economy, about half have at least a high school diploma, and most work in production, transportation and moving, service, sales, and under-the-table jobs that are unreliable. Annual income hovers around $21,700. Daily they experience the toxic stress of deprivation and living in survival mode, which often leads to riskier health behaviors. Mostly persons of color (heavily Latinx), they mostly live in parts of L.A., the

San Joaquin Valley, and the Inland Empire in conditions rivaling those in the worst-performing states of Mississippi and West Virginia.

Although these categories do not map perfectly onto typical patterns of political participation, this human development distribution allows us to better understand the capacity of certain groups to advocate for themselves. Enormous variation in educational background, basic needs, and stressors that Californians experience also creates different kinds of opportunity structures for political participation: whereas some people have plenty of time to stay atop the news and donate to causes that concern them, others may not understand how politics works and feel intimidated by those who do, or only have time to focus on surviving. The issues and goals they consider worth fighting for also differ. One Percenters, for example, have fought for restrictive and exclusionary zoning with historic success.[13]

NEWS AND MEDIA HABITS

Californians know extremely little about state politics unless a crisis develops, a scandal breaks, or an election occurs, and their attitudes, opinions, and beliefs about government are molded by the way they consume news, whether it is through social media, digital media, or traditional media (newspaper, radio, television). Social media networks give people unprecedented access to raw, primary information, which can come straight from the source but often lacks context; social media create more exposure to "fake news" or misinformation that spreads quickly and is not easily retracted, and allow consumers to select only the news that they want to hear, potentially reinforcing their existing views, especially partisan ones. Where digital and traditional media are concerned, even when the facts are indisputable, all news organizations and journalists engage in "framing" stories by highlighting some aspects to reflect particular values, goals, or biases (implicit or explicit) that will shape their message and how their subjects are perceived. For example, protesters might be portrayed as "losers" or out-of-work complainers who expect something for nothing, or contrastingly, be praised as honest justice seekers or as patriots fighting racism. Different frames of reference that tap into viewers' emotional or psychological associations can strongly affect how the subjects of news—citizens, groups, government—are perceived, especially when friends and trusted sources relay the information.

In California, *voters* tend to follow the news, still relying principally on television and internet websites, less so on radio, but also on the in-depth, investigative coverage provided by newspapers (mostly online).[14] The *Los Angeles Times, Mercury News, Sacramento Bee, San Francisco Chronicle, San Diego Union-Tribune,* and several other major city papers struggle to maintain readership as out-of-state corporations continue to buy and consolidate smaller operations. Over time that trend translates into far less original, investigative, local, and state-level reporting of the kind that has been pivotal in uncovering wrongdoing or political corruption in the past. Nevertheless, viewers' ideological biases also drive news consumption; most voters feel good about the news they use, seeing it as fair and comprehensive, but Democrats (about four out of five) and independents (about three out of four) today are more likely to value major news media's role as a watchdog over government, whereas nationally a majority of Republicans view criticism of (Republican) political leaders coming from those media as hindering leaders from doing their jobs.[15] Younger Americans (age 18–29) are far more likely to get their news—including political information—on TikTok and Snapchat as compared to other generations who visit social media sites like Facebook, Reddit, and Twitter (about half of all adults).[16]

Voters of color tend to rely on ethnic media (newspapers written specifically for an ethnic community) for state and local news often or occasionally—outlets that barely survived severe revenue losses during the pandemic.[17] Among the almost 300 ethnic news outlets that serve Californians directly are (print and digital) *Black Voice News, La Opinión*, (Chinese) Sound of Hope radio, and (Korean) KBS America (television), most offering digital spaces designed to facilitate civic participation and community advocacy.[18]

TYPES OF POLITICAL ACTION

In all likelihood, 2020 will be remembered not just for an economy-shredding pandemic but also the extraordinary number of public marches, rallies, demonstrations, and protests stemming from the Black Lives Matter movement and civil rights abuses. Social science research indicates that once activated, people find it easier to branch out into other forms of activity oriented to bring about social or political change, a phenomenon that was documented after millions of Latinxs, mostly students, took to the streets and marched en masse against anti-immigrant proposals in 1994 and 2006, galvanizing new generations of leaders.[19] A less pronounced but steady drumbeat of protests have continued following ground-shifting U.S. Supreme Court decisions, including their overturning of federal abortion rights.

Today, digitally enabled, cause-based activism involves many individuals who have been poorly served by or have been utterly failed by civic institutions.[20] Social networking allows individuals to create, share, and amplify alternative narratives to those advanced by the mainstream press, and to onboard newcomers into politics—people who would otherwise be turned off by the thought of getting involved. From January 2017 through July 2020, an estimated 3 million individuals marched or demonstrated in California.[21] Even more recently, over 2,500 types of public protests were recorded in the first half of 2022 both for and against a wide variety of issues, including reproductive rights, hybrid learning, the war in Ukraine, gun use, animal rights, labor practices, racism, mask mandates, and so on.[22]

Striking patterns emerge from surveys about Californians' political habits. Keeping in mind that Whites are now a minority racial group (about 38 percent), they dominate almost every category of "traditional" political activity except for *attending public meetings* and *protesting*. Pacific Islanders and Black Californians report higher attendance at public meetings (about one out of three people), and Latinxs and Whites attend public meetings at similar rates (about one out of four). Among all adults, Latinxs and Asian Americans generally do not *contact their public officials*, nor do they *make political donations* (totaling less than 25 percent of all those who did these things). Of course there are differences within groups; Indian Americans tend to participate regularly in comparison to Chinese, Hmong, and Korean Americans. In contrast, Whites are responsible for 70 percent of contacts and also donations. Consumer activism, or the act of changing purchasing habits for political reasons such as by *boycotting* (also "buycotting") a business or product, has become more commonplace.[23] Data also show that these same racial/ethnic patterns are replicated by Millennials, but differences fade with protesting and *signing e-petitions*, which they do more frequently compared to older generations.[24]

MAJOR VOTING TRENDS

In a hybrid democracy like California's, the act of voting provides a critical check on office-holders as well as on other voters. Casting a ballot not only offers a constituency the means to reject out-of-touch officeholders and provide cues about what policies they prefer, but it also equalizes power among citizens because the majority of whoever votes wins, and *those who don't participate increase the weight of those who do*. Practically speaking, less than a majority of the state's eligible voting population almost always controls election outcomes. For these reasons, "who votes" in a hybrid democracy such as California's has profound implications for electoral outcomes, policymaking in the common interest, and, ultimately, the quality of representation and governance.

California "has a long way to go before its electorate reflects the size and diversity of the state as a whole, although the state had record voter turnout in November 2020, with 80.7 percent of registered voters casting a ballot."[25] The **electorate**, referring here to the entirety of those who vote, is normally an exclusive, self-selected group, and their choices skew election outcomes. Stated differently, voters neither represent all Californians nor reflect the size, growth, or full-scale diversity of the state's population. Non-Hispanic Whites total 41 percent of California's adult population, but they represent *more than half* of all voters, who also tend to be U.S.-born, older, wealthier, in stable careers, and more centrist or slightly more conservative than nonvoters. At about 35 percent of the adult population but less than a quarter of all likely voters (only 15 percent of them cast ballots in the June 2022 primaries), Latinxs participate at lower rates than their share of eligible voters, although recent changes including universal vote-by-mail and postage-paid ballots helped shrink the turnout difference between them and White voters by almost 3 percentage points.[26] Blacks tend to turn out at rates roughly proportionate to their share of the voting eligible population (7 percent), and the same is true of Asians (15 percent).[27]

Those age 50 and over normally crush the voting rates of younger groups and they dominated the midterm primaries yet again: they were responsible for 75 percent of all ballots returned in June 2022. Voters aged 34 and under have been dismally underrepresented in elections; they were the largest potential segment of voters (one out of four people) but a mere 11 percent of them returned their ballots—a prime target for voter mobilization. The youngest age group gained tremendous ground in the November 2020 presidential election and set new records for voter registration and participation, but hasn't sustained those levels over time.[28]

Excluded from the electorate are approximately 2.3 million legal permanent residents who are eligible to become naturalized citizens (and thus vote); another estimated 2.2 million undocumented immigrant adults who reside and work in the state; and approximately 92,000 imprisoned felons (Californians recently changed the rules through Prop 17 to allow anyone on probation or parole to vote, about 50,000 people).[29] Additionally, almost one of

Protests, such as this one at Los Angeles International Airport, were provoked by Trump administration (federal) immigration policy decisions that banned travel from several countries where Muslims are in the majority. Such policies directly affect residents' legal status, separate families, and stifle the ability to work, among other things.

Source: Amanda Edwards via Getty Images.

five adults who are eligible to vote typically don't register; this equates to roughly 5 million people who are not among what the Public Policy Institute of California calls the state's active and "exclusive electorate." Nonvoters differ from the pool of likely voters in several significant ways: more nonvoters are renters (69 percent of nonvoters), have only a high school diploma or less (only 18 percent graduated college), and are racial or ethnic minorities (79 percent). They make less money overall than those who vote: 76 percent of nonvoting adults are in households earning $60,000 a year or less.[30] A larger share of Latinx and Asian Californians do not register in comparison to Whites.

Lower voter registration barriers in California have helped some groups register at rates relative to their share of the population, and a remarkable 22 million Californians were registered to vote in mid-2022, fully 81.5 percent of eligible adults. The state's robust recruitment efforts include online registration, automatic "motor voter" registration, and all-mail-ballot elections, although mediocre turnout for the June 2022 primary (just 33 percent) suggests that more could be done to encourage turnout among those who are registered. Studies suggest that aggressive mobilization efforts could further accelerate registration and voting rates; in-person contacts and text messages from trusted sources tend to boost turnout.[31]

The nature or *type of election* attracts different groups of voters. Presidential general elections and supercharged ballot issues such as the legalization of marijuana lure many more participants than midterm general elections, special elections, or primaries, which tend to draw more loyal partisans. Turnout is lowest for regular midterm primary elections, averaging just *24.6 percent* of all those *eligible* to vote (in three elections 2012–20), but the turnout rate increases for primaries where there is a presidential nominee to choose, averaging 31.8 percent of eligible voters (or 41.9 percent of those registered, same years). On the other hand, presidential elections can magnetize the electorate, such as in the 2020 match-up of Joe Biden and Donald Trump when 70.9 percent of eligible voters cast a ballot—or 80.7 percent of all registered voters, a record-setting turnout that was also aided by an all-mail ballot election.[32]

Among those who actually vote, bias is also introduced through the phenomenon of "roll-off," which means that many voters cast their ballots only for the "big-ticket" races that appear first, such as president or governor, skipping lower offices and ballot measures located further down the ballot, often because they do not feel informed enough to vote on them or because they view "down-ticket" ballot measures or offices as unimportant. Fewer people actually vote for the officials who are geographically closest to them. Ironically, individual votes are more valuable at this level; candidates frequently win or lose by hundreds, rather than thousands, of votes.

Finally, and significantly, it's important to note that the values and priorities of regular voters sometimes contrast strikingly with those of nonvoters. Those who cast ballots tend to hold distinctly different views about the *proper role of government* than those who don't vote or don't register to vote—patterns that generally hold both at the state and national levels.[33] For instance, economic biases are reflected in voters' views about government: whereas about half of California's likely voters would prefer to "pay higher taxes and have a state government that provides more services," about ten percent more of those who are *not* registered to vote would make the same choice.[34] A stunning 78 percent of Californians who aren't registered to vote think that the government should do more to reduce the gap between the rich and the poor in California, compared to 61 percent of registered voters.[35]

Gaps are also visible in policy preferences or in which issues are viewed as problems. Nonvoters are more likely to trust the federal government to "do what is right when handling environmental issues in the U.S." (43 percent say almost always or most of the time), versus 19 percent of likely voters.[36] Only 55 percent of likely voters say health care is the responsibility of the national government, whereas 72 percent of nonvoters do.[37] Where guns are concerned, 82 percent of unregistered voters think gun laws should be stricter, but far fewer likely voters (58 percent) feel that way.[38] Nonvoters are also more likely to consider limited access to nearby beaches and the coast as somewhat of a problem or a big problem (69 percent) than likely voters (57 percent).[39] Local and low-turnout elections magnify these biases and privilege the policy priorities of narrow electorates, but it's worth noting that on many compelling issues, such as the environment, reproductive rights, and immigration, the overall, state-level aggregate preferences of California's likely voters and nonvoters converge (Figure 10.1).

SPECIAL INTEREST GROUPS: INDIRECTLY CONNECTING CITIZENS TO GOVERNMENT

An organized group that makes its case to the government about its focused concern, or an issue of particular interest to them, is known as a **special interest group**. Such a group might be a well-known institution, such as the Catholic Church, a pro-gun rights organization such as

FIGURE 10.1 ■ **Californians on the State's Role in Reducing Economic Inequality**

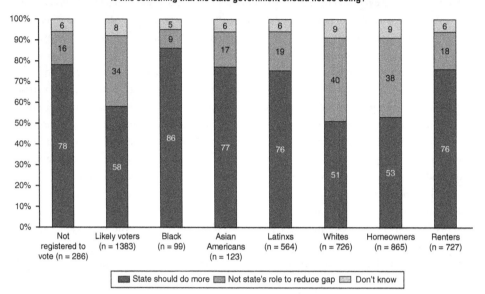

"Should the state government be doing more to reduce the gap between the rich and the poor in California, or is this something that the state government should not be doing?"

■ State should do more   ▨ Not state's role to reduce gap   ▢ Don't know

Source: PPIC Statewide Survey, "Californians and Their Government," May 9–18, 2021.

Notes: Sampling error is +/–3.2 percent at 95 percent confidence level for the unweighted sample of 1,705 adults. Numbers may not add to 100 percent due to rounding. "I don't know" answers were volunteered.

Source: Ava Van Vechten.

the National Rifle Association or the pro-environment Sierra Club, or a grouping of associated businesses, such as the film industry. The term **special interest** can also be a vague reference to any group whose members share the same public policy concerns, such as beachfront property owners who want to protect their homes against erosion or noisy nonlocals. Virtually all politically active special interest groups want to protect their own interests by engaging government in pursuit of legal protections or material benefits, and for this reason, they are often regarded as greedy political creatures that are "not at all interested in the larger societal challenges—they never think about the 'big picture,'" as one state senator put it.[40]

Despite their reputation, many citizens are unaware that they are indirectly linked to government through the interests and goals they share with organized groups. To illustrate: a typical California college student is "represented" in the public sphere by a multitude of interest groups and their lobbyists, among them the university or college itself; sports-related associations; groups based on demographic characteristics, such as economic status, ethnicity, and religion; health-related groups focused on conditions such as depression and anxiety or diabetes; and values-based associations concerned with rights, the environment, and moral issues. Employment provides more links, as would a parent's affiliation with a trade association, such as the 185,000-member California Association of Realtors', which advocates for laws and tax policies that affect real estate agents or their clients, or a labor union, such as the mighty California Correctional Peace Officers Association (CCPOA), which represents more than 30,000 prison guards and parole officers. If that student's family owns a business, then the California Chamber of Commerce, which represents almost 14,000 California businesses both large and small (see Box 10.1), offers a symbiotic political connection.

BOX 10.1
THE POWER OF ORGANIZED INTERESTS

CTA: A Voice for Educators

If education made the news this morning, chances are the powerful California Teachers Association (CTA) had something to do with it. As the state's largest professional employee organization representing approximately 290,000 teachers, school counselors, librarians, and certificated personnel, the CTA is a union that helps bargain for higher salaries and benefits in local districts and provides assistance in contract disputes. An advocacy group affiliated with the National Education Association (NEA), the CTA is committed to "enhance the quality of education" and "advance the cause of free, universal, and quality public education" by influencing state education policy.

Closely aligned with Democratic interests, the CTA participates at all stages of the bill-passage process by writing bills, testifying before committees, shaping legislation by suggesting amendments, and pressuring legislators either to support or to oppose bills. Most of this work is done through lobbyists, but members also are highly active, holding public demonstrations in local districts and loud rallies at the state capitol, contacting lawmakers, and contributing to both initiative and candidates' campaigns. When proposed laws appear to work for or against their interests, the CTA roars to life with ad campaigns and grassroots lobbying, asking teachers to flood legislators' inboxes with emails and phone calls; for ballot measures, they ramp up donations, organize volunteers, and mobilize citizens to vote. They also support local and state school bonds. They advocated for distance learning during the pandemic, more power over charter school expansions, and helped defeat a charter school advocate running for state superintendent of public instruction. The CTA also retains seven lobbyists and spent $11 million on lobbying activities in 2019–20.

When teachers speak, Democratic leaders listen. CTA influences education policy through lobbying, sponsoring ballot initiatives and bonds, and mobilizing voters.

Source: Renée B. Van Vechten.

Sources: California Teachers Association, http://www.cta.org; California Secretary of State, http://cal-access.sos.ca.gov; The 74 Million, https://www.the74million.org.

California Chamber of Commerce: Major Player in Business

Ever heard of a "job killer" bill? The California Chamber of Commerce (or CalChamber) has, and it aims to identify and destroy such bills before they impose new "expensive and unnecessary" regulations on California businesses. What is CalChamber, and why is it so powerful?

Unlike professional associations that represent individuals (such as CTA), the Chamber's members are 14,000 California-based companies, from local shops to Microsoft, enterprises that employ a quarter of the state's private-sector workforce; nearly 40,000 businesses rely on their advocacy. The motto of the state's largest and arguably most important business organization is "Helping California business do business." Aided by seven to nine lobbyists, the Chamber tries to shape laws or administrative rules by educating policymakers about how proposed changes will critically affect California companies, and helps companies comply with complicated labor laws. It also makes campaign donations through its political action committees, supports and opposes ballot measures through independent expenditures and direct donations, and files friend-of-the-court briefs in court cases, among other activities. The Chamber reported lobbying expenditures during 2019–20 of almost $6 million. These figures represent a fraction of what businesses generally spend to protect their interests in California. For example, the Walt Disney Company separately pays hundreds of thousands of dollars a year for ongoing lobbying activities, as do other California businesses.

Calling attention to business-related issues is part of CalChamber's strategy to influence lawmaking and the regulatory environment. Chamber president and CEO Jennifer Barrera's days are regularly filled with media appearances, interviews, meetings with policymakers, and conferences like this one which bring together sympathetic lawmakers and business owners.

Source: Matt Lara for CalChamber.

Sources: California Chamber of Commerce, http://www.calchamber.com; California Secretary of State, http://cal-access. sos.ca.gov.

Special interests are not equal, however, and some in California carry disproportionate political weight because of advantages stemming from their resources, size, and/or perceived importance. In other words, legislators pay more attention to some interests than others. Collectively, (prepandemic) those groups shelled out $300 million in 2019 to make their case, or **lobby**, state government, activities that cost them an average $12 million *per day* between January and September when the legislature was in session (compensation for lobbyists' work soaks up most of that).[41] Among the most prolific and influential special interests in Sacramento are actually *local governments* and *public entities* and *agencies* that work for thousands or millions of Californians: experts and public officials representing cities, counties, and special districts often are in the best positions to judge the impacts of programs or predict how changes would affect the public. Other groups are valued for their important roles in communities, such as company *employers* that provide jobs and subsidize local governments through the taxes they pay and collect from consumers, and *labor groups* that defend workers' rights. Representatives have incentives to satisfy politically active constituencies, so any group or business that has the *ability to mobilize voters* and *influence public opinion* possesses significant advantages. Lawmakers also listen to organizations that *share their issue positions or values,* and they respond to individuals and groups that provide *volunteers* or *financial support for their campaigns.*

The political power of special interests, therefore, is largely derived from what they can provide to decision makers, principally in the form of *information, votes,* or *money.* In lawmaking environments, good information is always in demand, and legislators and their staff members crave answers to questions about the potential impacts of their bills. Groups hire professional **lobbyists** who educate policymakers about the negative or positive effects pending legislation may have—framing a persuasive case that is sympathetic to their clients' interests, of course. So powerful are special interest lobbyists in Sacramento that they are collectively known as the "**third house,**" a satirical reference to the fact that they are vital players in the lawmaking process. Lobbyists can make their clients' cases in face-to-face meetings with legislators or staff, or by testifying in committee hearings where bills are vetted. They also perform research for legislation and actually write client-friendly bills for lawmakers to introduce and sponsor (Table 10.1).

For every one legislator there are almost fourteen registered lobbyists (plus more advocates who do not lobby full-time), and they seek to develop relationships with lawmakers and their staff. Noting that individual lobbyists are barred from making campaign donations, they can boost their access by making sure that the interest groups they represent donate the maximum

TABLE 10.1 ■ Top Ten Spenders on Lobbying in California, 2019–20

Name	Industry	Total Amount Spent
Western States Petroleum Association	Oil and gas	$13,150,706
California Teachers Association	Public sector unions	$10,956,729
Chevron	Oil and gas	$9,330,948
California State Council of Service Employees	Labor unions	$8,371,510
California Hospital Association	Health services	$5,831,749
California Chamber of Commerce	Business	$5,690,283
City of Los Angeles & County of Los Angeles	Government	$5,530,777
Edison International	Electric utilities	$5,095,737
PG&E	Electric utilities	$4,838,925
Davita Kidney Care	Health/business	$4,472,217

Source: Cal-Access, Lobbying Expenditures 2019–20, California Secretary of State.

allowed to lawmakers, and by buying high-priced tickets to fundraising events (happening almost daily around Sacramento when the legislature is in session, or in the districts).[42] Although state law caps the amounts of direct donations that individuals, unions, and corporations can give ($5,500 per candidate in 2023–24; higher limits for executive officials), limits that now apply to city and county candidates if no local limits are in place,[43] special interest groups may spend as much as they want *independently* to influence elections and lobbyists help them decide how best to spread that money. In state politics, organization, information, money, and status amplify voices and provide critical linkages to decision makers. The well-heeled few tip the playing field in their favor with the access their resources can buy. By extension, the unorganized and the disenfranchised are the biggest losers in politics.

CONCLUSION: AN EVOLVING POLITICAL COMMUNITY

Patterns of political activity and the biases that arise from unequal participation among groups do not distinguish California sharply from the rest of the states, but if an even more diverse mix of Californians lived up to their extraordinary potential, local and state policies might reflect different priorities and choices. Regardless, most people scarcely pay any attention to state or local politics, even though their livelihoods are tied more closely to decisions at those levels than at the national level. By creating new challenges (such as longer bus routes, fewer state-run clinics), or breaking them down (such as in-state tuition for undocumented immigrants, tax benefits for housing developers), today's policy decisions shape realities and opportunities for the Five Californias in ways that help determine the state's collective future.

Social media, traditional mass media, and interest groups provide the means for citizens to connect to government affairs, officials, and each other. Being informed helps empower citizens to be politically active, and there is plenty of room for more citizen participation in all types and levels of governments and in politics generally, because even though political scientists disagree about the minimum levels of knowledge, trust, and engagement needed to sustain a governing system for the long term, they generally recognize that "inputs" from civically engaged citizens generally lead to more positive government "outputs." As it stands, better educated, affluent, and Whiter citizens, as well as big corporations, well-heeled unions, and resource-rich organizations are perpetual outsized contributors to California's political system and, consequently, benefit from their investments in politics. As the saying goes, the squeaky wheel gets the grease. And in California as elsewhere, the "haves" are far noisier than the "have-nots."

The most recognizable form of political participation—voting—carries intrinsic value as a democratic exercise and provides a vital link between citizens and their representatives, but so do other actions. Uneven levels of activity among various constituencies contribute to the governing dilemmas of policymakers as they weigh their responsibilities to serve the greater public interest but also respond to those who actually pay attention and care about the results. Until the electorate and the universe of campaign volunteers, social media connectors, public meeting attendees, callers, demonstrators, lobbyists, donors, and petitioners more accurately reflect the entirety of the state's population, elected officials' decisions will continue to reflect the political, cultural, geographic, and demographic biases of those who participate, a dynamic that ultimately constrains how effective government can be. Government will also continue to be viewed as particularly ineffective by those who feel unable to influence it, regardless of its performance. Expanding the electorate and the pool of regular political activists and participants would be surefire ways to make California's government more accountable, representative, and positively exceptional.

KEY TERMS

Electorate: the entirety of those who are eligible to vote; commonly used to refer to all those who actually vote.

Lobby: (verb) to attempt to influence decision makers, usually with information, money, or moral appeals.

Lobbyist: also known as an "advocate," a person who spends most of their time trying to influence decision makers about the merits of their clients' issue position(s), using information and pressure tactics to get policy makers to vote or act in ways that reflect their clients' interests.

Political efficacy: a sense of confidence or feeling that one can personally influence government by participating in public affairs.

Special interest: any group that can be identified by a unique characteristic.

Special interest group: an organized group that tries to influence the government to advance or protect its interests and goals, which are usually related to a narrow set of issues.

Third house: a term referring to lobbyists as a group and—ironically, as if they were on par with the other houses of the legislature—indicating their significant influence in the legislative process.

11 CONCLUDING THOUGHTS
Public Policy and the State of Exceptionalism

California lives in the imagination, but for many who live in the state, paying the bills without accumulating debt and *imagining* owning a home *is* the dream. California's affordability problem has pushed many either to seriously consider relocating or to resettle in a different state.[1] The irony of epic state budget surpluses in recent fiscal years is that the great majority of Californians have not generated them, as prosperity has pooled at the top. Inequality is a widening gulf. Easing hardships has become priority number one for the state's representatives, and state and local political disputes reflect their disagreements about how best to do that.

As a potential nation, California stands apart for its hyperdiverse population that is spread across a giant landmass and generates a world-class economy that outpaces all but four or five countries. Surging housing, gas, and other living costs that have reached previously unthinkable levels accentuate California's singularity. To insiders and outsiders alike, there's no need to question its exceptional nature; the Golden State is clearly an outlier.

Being in a league of its own has entailed policies that aim to protect the environment and thereby raise living standards for all in the long run. The state is committed to building a clean energy economy through a cap-and-trade market for carbon emissions, reductions of pollution from fine particulates and greenhouse gases through greater use of biofuels and zero-emissions vehicles, and solar and wind energy investments. Setting its own course apart from the federal government has meant shielding undocumented families from deportation, treating eligible college-age undocumented youth as citizens by giving them in-state tuition, covering health care for low-income Californians regardless of immigration status, and enabling undocumented people to obtain special driver's licenses that bring them out of the shadow economy. Leadership on privacy rights has brought about the country's first law protecting personal data. Going against the grain has involved enhancing employment benefits: ensuring paid sick leave for part-time workers, minimum wage increases, and an expanded definition of disability that covers paid maternity leave. Trailblazing for equal rights has involved recognizing a third gender option ("X") on legal documents, requiring sexual harassment training for companies with five or more employees, policing reform that restricts deadly use of force, and enshrining reproductive rights in the state constitution. In many ways, California's culture and politics revere individuality.

Other audacious policy experiments are also out of "left" field (figuratively *and* ideologically speaking, especially as compared to conservative states). California's vaccination and mask mandates have been among the most rigorous. Semiautomatic rifles and tobacco products can only be bought by those of age 21 and older; single public restrooms must be all-gender; patients may choose the right to die; and elephants and tigers may not be part of circus productions. California raises the bar for the toughest environmental regulations: single-use food service-ware will be recyclable or compostable by 2032, and composting of organic waste is required of all households and commercial businesses. Taking cues from a Texas law that allows individuals to sue others for aiding and abetting abortion, California law now permits citizens to sue those making, selling, or transporting illegal, untraceable "ghost guns" and assault weapons (pending legal challenges). In contrast to states that have banned abortion, California shields all providers, patients, and their medical information from other states that seek prosecutions for abortion; funding for abortion-related care has expanded; and out-of-pocket costs have been eliminated. Unlike "red" states that have tried to ban race-conscious curricula from schools, California's diversity, equity, and inclusion measures permeate labor law and education; businesses must report pay levels based on gender, race, and ethnicity, and high school students must complete an ethnic studies course for graduation. The state has even established the nation's first task force to explore reparations for direct descendants of slaves.

Reforms that make it easier to vote also distinguish California from those states that have restricted voting through rigid voter identification laws, shorter early voting periods, fewer drop boxes, and the virtual eradication of absentee ballots. California's automatic and online voter registration plus universal vote-by-mail elections combined with vote centers are designed to invite more voter participation while safeguarding the system's integrity. The Top-Two primary further cracks open elections by enabling independents to have a say in primaries, and the Citizens Redistricting Commission empowers citizens to control the redistricting process—innovations that are not California's alone, to be sure.

These reforms scratch the surface of California's deeply rooted political dilemmas, some of which stem from the design of its hybrid government. When the power of direct democracy is spliced with the force of political representation, they coexist in a state of uneasy tension. Voters can change the rules of the game for each other and for representatives in any general election, which can be seen clearly in a 2022 measure (Prop 28) mandating that about $1 billion be spent annually on arts and music education in schools. Ballot-box reforms also promote "one-size-fits-all" policy solutions and hinder comprehensive problem-solving. The initiative process itself is now an overworked policy machine, the gears of which are oiled by oversimplified messages and shifted into overdrive by massive amounts of campaign cash. Special interests parade as public interests, trying to drown out other voices in the political marketplace. Ironically, the initiative process itself remains ripe for reform, despite recent changes.

California politics is riddled with other ironies and paradoxes that help explain the current state of affairs. For example, citizens generally distrust politicians and despise political conflict, so they continue to reach for ways to take politicians—and politics, for that matter—out of politics, such as through term limits and creative initiatives. Public grievance with politics flourishes because political systems are by nature designed to expose conflicting interests in the struggle to reach consensus. The people not only need politicians to govern what is effectively one of the largest countries in the world, but they also need to organize in order to win, and political parties provide that reliable structure. Nevertheless, many independent-minded Californians are unconvinced that institutions like parties matter or that the major parties sincerely promote their interests, and almost one of four register as "No Party Preference" voters. These trends have helped prevent California from becoming a "deep blue" state, despite the superabundance of Democratic representatives at the state and federal levels.

Californians also have a difficult time imagining how state government could possibly need or use as much money as it rakes in, especially compared to other states, and over half of California adults believe that a lot of their tax money was wasted.[2] This partly explains the resentment people feel about higher state fuel taxes, now at 54 cents per gallon.[3] Historically, attitudes like these have led to a gross backlog of infrastructure projects (think roads, water storage, and so forth) and chronic underfunding of services such as education and transportation that local and state governments must provide for all Californians. The irony is that when infrastructure fails because governments have stretched scarce dollars too thinly (the epic $1.1 billion failure of the Oroville Dam spillway is a case in point), citizens are quick to blame politicians for wasting or misspending funds and become even less willing to help government do its work. However, voters do tend to make exceptions for new taxes that have concrete, dedicated purposes, allowing most local governments to meet residents' immediate demands but often to the detriment of long-term critical needs.[4] These tendencies have resulted in a heavy reliance on upper income taxpayers to foot the state's bills, as well as a shift away from paying up-front costs and a pivot to long-term bond debt that costs almost twice as much in the long run because of interest payments.

Quite apart from the paradoxes of governing are socioeconomic issues that determine the political state of affairs—issues that involve nearly 40 million people who live in distinctly different and unequal conditions and who place often incompatible and ever-changing demands on state and local governments. Latinxs constitute the largest ethnic group, and will remain so long into the future.[5] The multiethnic mix of children today signals momentous change: over 55 percent of all schoolchildren in 2020–21 were Latinx/Hispanic, and non-Hispanic Whites were just under 22 percent, yet most kids attend "intensely segregated schools."[6] How will decision makers nurture the inclusive, educated workforce that will be needed to drive the state's service-based economy? Almost a third of all Californians will be 65 years of age or older by 2050 (compared to 23.5 percent in 2023): how will the state provide for a humongous elderly population that places immense demands on health and residential care systems?[7] Although people are leaving California for more affordable states an exodus has not yet occurred,[8] but whether it will reach a tipping point is still an open question: 2021 represented the first year in its history in which lower birthrates and out-migration combined to *decrease* the population. To accommodate those who live here now and the state's future population, the state will need to invest *hundreds of billions* of dollars to repair, upgrade, add to, and expand crumbling transportation, school, water, and other infrastructure; Governor Newsom's five-year plan committing $52 billion to improvements should at least make a dent.[9]

In many ways, political reforms brought California to this point, and political reforms will help transform its future. Yet institutional reforms that reshape rules can go only so far. Rules set guardrails for decision-making, but the choices made within those bounds must be based on realistic understanding about government's capabilities if the state's policies and laws are to work. For instance, many Californians presume that rooting out existing government waste would uncover enough revenues to pay for all the large government programs or infrastructure they want, as if saving millions of dollars could compensate for not raising billions through higher taxes or fees. The larger economy also fashions what's possible and frames debates about what needs reforming: historic budget surpluses have recently created radically different policies than economic recessions have.

Civic engagement can also transform political outcomes, especially at the local level. Social unrest in mid-2020 displayed the power of the people to demand reforms in local policing, and combined with the pandemic, demonstrated the vital importance of counties and cities in shaping daily life. Imagine how involvement by a greater swath of the Five Californias in local problem-solving could reshape their expectations and make real change possible.

California's government faces many of the same challenges as the governments of other states. What helps make California politics exceptional are the scope and scale of the state's public policy issues, which pose enormous challenges as well as opportunities for state elected officials to exercise national and global leadership now and for the foreseeable future:

- *Housing*: At a shocking median (but peak) price of $900,000 in mid-2022 for a home, Californians pay over two-and-a-half-times what the rest of the country pays for a house or in average monthly rents.[10] A chronic shortage of *millions* of housing units which has spiked prices has materialized because of high development impact fees, local zoning requirements, environmental challenges, construction materials expenses, labor shortages, high land prices, and public opposition to low-income and high-density housing near them.[11] An estimated 1.5 million of needed *affordable* housing units for the lowest-income households will *require* government subsidies, as building costs normally far exceed the return on investment. Billions of dollars in subsidies such as help for first-time homebuyers or grants for cities converting motels into affordable housing are tucked into state and local budgets, and fresh laws aim to control annual rent increases, streamline construction for sustainably built projects, and incentivize building such as through SB 9 which wipes away urban single-family zoning by allowing homeowners to build additional dwelling units on their property.[12] The state has spent at least $13.5 billion over five years to shelter more people, but it has not been enough to address all 161,500 people who experience homelessness or those who would like to own a home rather than pay exorbitant rents.[13] Long-term, affordable housing for *all* Californians is sorely needed, a deficit that will take years to remedy.

- *Education*: Only an educated workforce can sustain a sophisticated, diverse, service-oriented modern economy. California spends the most of all states on its K–12 system *overall* and spent more than ever in 2022–23, but it falls short of being a top state in per pupil spending.[14] Free preschool, universal transitional kindergarten (TK) for four-year-olds, and universal school lunch are proactive steps absorbing additional state dollars. Remote learning during the pandemic shutdown exposed digital inequities, exacerbating existing "achievement gaps" between students of color (Latinx, African American, and Native American, who are four out of five K–12 students) on the one hand, and White and Asian American students on the other; and it took traumatic tolls on students' learning, mental health, and wellbeing. An ensuing shortage of teachers and mental health professionals has further stressed the education system. California's master plan for providing tuition-free higher education has been abandoned except at the community college level (where two full-time years are free for residents). Compared to a national average of about $25,500 yearly to attend a public four-year institution and live on campus, the expenses of a state university (roughly $27,200 annually) is slightly higher and substantially higher at a U.C. ($38,500), both translating into serious long-term debt for most.[15] However, education not only boosts earning over a lifetime, but also research suggests that if every Californian could magically jump up to the next higher level of education, about one million fewer people would be in poverty, people would live over a year longer, 1,200 fewer Californians would be murdered every year, and 2.4 million more people would vote.[16]

- *Immigration*: Former Trump administration policies dampened cross-border flows of people, yet California's immigrant population is the still largest in the nation at 10.4 million, equating to 27 percent of residents who were born outside the U.S. For an estimated 2.6 million undocumented immigrants who reside in the state, mostly in the shadows, their fate lies largely in the hands of national policymakers, but California's sanctuary policies grant some a measure of relief (not a guarantee) from surprise deportation. Some safety net benefits have been extended to DREAMers and Deferred Action for Childhood Arrivals (DACA) recipients, a group of undocumented youth, including basic health care coverage and college in-state tuition rates; and health benefits now can be reached by all low-income persons, regardless of immigration status. Overwhelmingly, 87 percent of Californians say that unauthorized immigrants who are living in the U.S. should be allowed to stay, and 82 percent believe they should also be offered the chance to become citizens.[17]

- *Environment*: Long-term climate change threatens California's basic lifelines with "extremes." Bold environmental laws can't fix zig-zagging patterns that yank the state from severe heat and water scarcity to savage storms that replenish snowpack but bring ruinous flooding, coastal storm surges, and destructive soil saturation.[18] Drought raises the risk of wildfires, airborne fine-particle pollution, and public health issues; parched farms, manufacturing plants, and families endure water restrictions. Alternatively, massive rainfall and volatile weather ravage agricultural, recreational, and tourism industries, causing billions in losses. Biodiversity suffers as wildlife cannot quickly adjust to rapid environmental changes. Rising sea levels and less freshwater threaten a densely populated coastline and imperil the Delta agricultural region (the source of drinking water for two-thirds of Californians and irrigation for 750,000 acres of croplands) with rising levels of salinity and irreversible damage to habitats, infrastructure, and private property. Emergencies take huge tolls; a 7.8 earthquake on the San Andreas Fault would cause hundreds of billions in losses in Los Angeles alone; no region is immune.[19] AB 32 has lowered GHG emissions and the more ambitious SB 32 aims to take them

San Diego's oldest Mexican American neighborhood is home to Chicano Park, where the largest outdoor collection of murals in the United States tells an evolving visual story depicting cultural and political history, events, and icons of California's largest ethnic group (about 40 percent of the state's population is Latino or Hispanic).

Source: Renée Van Vechten.

down to 40 percent below 1990 levels by 2030 and 80 percent below by 2050. Planning for a zero-emissions future involves aggressive policies that will replace combustion engine-powered in the transportation sector with zero-emissions vehicles, reaching 100 percent for sale by 2035; following Hawai'i's lead, 100 percent of the state's electricity should come from renewable sources by 2045. Californians largely support these policies.[20] Can the state maintain that support as it continues to build a "green" economy but as related costs continue to rise?

- *Poverty, Health, and Inequality*: The gap between rich and poor, or income inequality among the Five Californias, continues to widen, despite the fact that more people have moved up the scale in the last five years. The pandemic slammed Black, Latinx, and Native American communities most harshly. Today over 12 million residents are Struggling, and many Main Streeters continue to fall behind. Without CalWorks (temporary aid for low-income families), unemployment insurance payouts, refundable tax credits, or CalFresh for food assistance, a much larger number would slip below the federal poverty threshold of $27,750 (for a family of four). When it comes to health care, California boasts the largest insured population of all states but depends heavily on federal funding to deliver health care. Addressing food insecurity, arresting public health crises such as the opioid epidemic that causes close to 7,000 deaths a year,[21] and grappling with human development gaps more broadly will require comprehensive political efforts to address "mutually reinforcing inequalities in health, education, environment, neighborhood conditions, wealth, and political power that have created an opportunity divide" among Californians and which prevent them from leading "a freely chosen life of value."[22]

- *Business and Labor*: Balancing the needs of businesses and employees is often a challenge for political leaders, but majority Democrats' traditional alliances with labor unions have tilted the scales for decades. Scores of employee-friendly regulations—or "antibusiness" mandates, depending on your point of view—have been signed into law in recent years, including more paid time off, a higher minimum wage, job protections for part-time workers, and paid family leave. Agricultural workers became entitled to overtime pay starting in 2022, warehouse workers gained protections from quotas, and hospitality workers gained the right to be rehired first if their jobs became available after they were laid off.[23] As worker rights like these have solidified, the costs of doing business have increased, and California has gained a reputation among the states for a hostile business climate due to its comparatively burdensome regulatory environment and high business taxes.[24] Meanwhile, in spite of snarled global supply chains, the state's post-COVID-shutdown economic reboot has helped produce historic state budget surpluses, eclipsing an economic recession that was expected to materialize earlier. Given the state's overreliance on the continuing good fortunes of a thin tier of financial elites and few industries (technology and agriculture, to name two), the state's economic health remains susceptible to slowdowns.

- *Water*: Southern Californians experiencing mandatory 30 percent water cutbacks in summer 2022 could attest to the state's being stuck in an extended *drought*, a high-severity dry spell characterized by reduced snowpack, lower river flow and lake levels, forest stress, and dry soil, among other effects.[25] Vanishing wetlands had become normal, and so had die-offs of native trees, birds, and fish. Drought prompted the state's first-ever groundwater usage laws that took effect in 2020. Emergency regulations outlawed the watering of decorative grass at businesses and common areas in housing developments. Eleven massive storms or "atmospheric rivers" that slammed California between December 2022 and March 2023 erased some of the hydrologic effects of long-term drought, refilling naked lakebeds and reservoirs all over the state. But the deluges also crippled businesses and residents, causing an estimated $30 billion in damages, including public facilities and systems that need fixing. Between droughts and floods, policymakers have a hard time organizing storage and distribution systems that move water where it's needed, when it's needed, and ensuring quality when water is fouled by agricultural activity, irregular water flows, and urban runoff. Scarcity has exposed the state's fissures over water, involving three separate rights-holders within the state: the *environment* (restoring or sustaining habitat, ensuring water quality, and so forth, which guzzles half of the state's water), *people* (including individual consumers and companies), and *agriculture*. Water availability has pitted urban against agricultural users and farmers against fish as the state has tried to manage water flows through the Delta to sustain an endangered ecosystem, and troubles remain with moving water to thirsty Southern California, which houses about 75 percent of the state's residents who depend on 75 percent of rainfall in the north. Across the Delta region, where millions of people and animals reside and fertile lands are farmed, catastrophic levee failure due to earthquakes or flooding is a palpable risk. A billion-dollar "Delta Conveyance Project" proposal to send water under the Delta through "state-of-the-art" tunnels and pumps is the latest in a raging, longstanding dispute over how to fix these issues.[26] Will leaders be able to craft strategic compromises that comprehensively address the entire state's long-term water-related needs or come up with the money to cover them?

- *Transportation*: The country's highest number of cars (36.2 million registered vehicles) travel almost 400,000 miles of lanes interlacing the state, which are the most congested in the nation, and they cross thousands of bridges and culverts, all of which need continual maintenance or rehabilitation.[27] A stable stream of funds to improve roads, support public transportation, and mitigate climate change impacts are largely supplied through SB 1, the transportation funding bill that raised gas taxes for the first time since 1994 and survived a referendum—taxes that many despise now that California's fuel prices are the highest in the nation. New and cleaner systems are badly needed to move more people faster, including intercity rail projects (to achieve greater "geographic equity"), accommodations for autonomous (self-driving) vehicles, and alternative fueling stations, infrastructure projects that are attracting more state dollars, and attention. Electric high-speed rail connecting San Francisco to Los Angeles could help move people but remains speculative as the projected price tag has escalated from an initial $9 billion to $105 billion, with no construction end-point in sight; still, work on the first 119-mile "bullet train" segment in the Central Valley continues. This will do little to offset the dirty air from millions of gas-powered vehicles, delivery trucks, and farm and construction equipment that contribute to serious respiratory illnesses, but groundbreaking current and proposed Air Resources Board (ARB) regulations aim to reduce pollution and smog. Giant warehouses must offset pollution with solar panels or other measures, and 90 percent of miles driven for app-based ride-sharing services must be in zero-emissions vehicles (by 2030). Planes, ships, and trains pollute the air as well, a consequence of owning the nation's busiest ports that are gateways to Asia and South America and keys to the country's supply chains; the ARB now regulates emissions from ships docked at ports. ARB rules already block registration of any diesel-powered vehicle whose engine lacks a fine particulate matter filter, and the board seeks to phase out diesel-powered vehicles completely. They are developing mandates for governments and companies to transition to zero-emission fleets of shuttle buses, big rigs, and trucks. By 2035 no new gas-powered vehicles will be sold in the state, and ARB has also adopted a ban on sales of new diesel trucks by 2045. These bold efforts are designed to address the externalities from fossil fuels use (such as pollution and GHG-associated climate change).

This composite image compares Lake Oroville (Butte County, northern California) at one-third capacity during severe drought and the lake at capacity (3.5 million acre feet).

Source: Justin Sullivan via Getty Images.

Although California is not a country, state officials have occasionally and wishfully referred to it as a "nation-state," and it often behaves like one—and as home to nearly 40 million people, it has weathered ups and downs and defied accusations that it is either uninhabitable or collapsing.[28] The Golden State has a long history of overcoming pivotal challenges and standing apart, as seen in its unorthodox path to statehood after exploding onto the U.S. stage with the Gold Rush; in Progressive innovations in direct democracy; in measures to confront global climate change; in its robust voter registration and electoral systems; and in its elevation of diversity, equity, and inclusion efforts in law and policy. Sometimes the state is out in front, and sometimes it's just "out there"—its relative placement being a matter of perspective. Politics in the state are indeed exceptional in many ways, but more often than not, California keeps company with at least a few other states in the kindred policy programs, reforms, rules, or rights they advance. On balance, however, the state is a political juggernaut like no other, and as former Assembly Speaker (and former state Senator) Robert Hertzberg phrased it, "There's a magic about California. There's a California brand …. We've got to stay ahead of the game."[29] Whether the state is ahead or behind is an open question, but the title of a book penned by the late Carey McWilliams seventy-five years ago still fits: *California: The Great Exception.*

NOTES

CHAPTER 1

1. See "Gross Domestic Product 2021," World Bank, July 1, 2022, https://databankfiles.worldbank.org/data/download/GDP.pdf; "GDP by State, 2021," Bureau of Economic Analysis, Interactive Tools, updated March 31, 2022, https://apps.bea.gov/itable/iTable.cfm?ReqID=70&step=1.

2. "Slowing State Population Decline Puts Latest Population at 39,105,000," Department of Finance (DOF), State of California, May 2, 2022, https://dof.ca.gov/wp-content/uploads/Forecasting/Demographics/Documents/E-1_2022PressRelease.pdf. The DOF suggests that out-migration, lower birthrates, declining immigration, deaths due to COVID, and a limited international student population contributed to the downward trend. Canada's population was reported to be 38,654,738 between January and March 2022. "Population Estimates, Quarterly," Statistics Canada, Government of Canada, June 22, 2022, https://www150.statcan.gc.ca/n1/pub/91-002-x/91-002-x2022001-eng.htm.

3. Rachel Sandler, "Golden State Billionaires: California Home to the Most Billionaires in the U.S.," *Forbes*, April 5, 2022, https://www.forbes.com/sites/rachelsandler/2022/04/05/golden-state-billionaires-california-home-to-the-most-billionaires-in-the-us/?sh=fd807aa79eef; Richard Chang, "The Countries with the Most Billionaires, 2022," *Forbes*, April 5, 2022.

4. "QuickFacts: Population Estimates," U.S. Census Bureau, July 1, 2021, accessed July 31, 2022, https://www.census.gov/quickfacts/CA; Eric McGhee, "California's AAPI Community," Public Policy Institute of California (PPIC), Blog, May 24, 2022, https://www.ppic.org/blog/californias-aapi-community/.

5. Estimates vary widely. The Migration Policy Institute (MPI) places the figure at 2,739,000 based on their analysis of U.S. Census Bureau data from the pooled 2015–19 American Community Survey (ACS) and the 2008 Survey of Income and Program Participation (SIPP), weighted to 2019 unauthorized immigrant population estimates provided by Jennifer Van Hook of The Pennsylvania State University ("Profile of the Unauthorized Population: California," MPI, accessed August 20, 2022, https://www.migrationpolicy.org/data/unauthorized-immigrant-population/state/CA). The Department of Homeland Security (DHS) estimated the number of undocumented persons to be 2.61 million in 2018 (Bryan Baker, "Estimates of the Unauthorized Immigrant Population Residing in the U.S.: January 2015–January 2018," DHS, April 19, 2021, https://www.dhs.gov/immigration-statistics/population-estimates/unauthorized-resident). Pew Research provided the lowest estimate of 2 million, plus or minus 50,000, based on augmented U.S. Census Bureau data in 2017 (Jeffrey S. Passel and D'Vera Cohn, "Mexicans Decline to Less than Half the Unauthorized Immigrant Population for the First Time," Pew Research Center, June 12, 2019, https://www.pewresearch.org/fact-tank/2019/06/12/us-unauthorized-immigrant-population-2017/).

6. "Report P-1B: Population Projections by Single Year of Age, 2010–2060, California (2019 Baseline)," Demographic Research Unit, Department of Finance, State of California, July 2021, http://www.dof.ca.gov/Forecasting/Demographics.

7. For the 2021 report, only sheltered persons were counted because of COVID-related concerns. California's homelessness count was 136,358 for

2020; the rate was 38 per 10,000 people in 2018. "HUD 202 Continuum of Care Homeless Assistance Programs, Homeless Populations and Subpopulations," U.S. Department of Housing and Urban Development (HUD), December 15, 2020, https://files.hudexchange.info/reports/published/CoC_PopSub_State_CA_2020.pdf. According to HUD in 2018, "California has more than half of all unsheltered homeless people in the country (53 percent or 108,432), with nearly nine times as many unsheltered homeless as the state with the next highest number, Florida (6 percent or 12,476), despite California's population being only twice that of Florida." ("The 2019 Annual Homeless Assessment Report to Congress," HUD Office of Community Planning and Development, January 2020, ii), https://files.hudexchange.info/resources/documents/2019-AHAR-Part-1.pdf. Meghan Henry et al., "The 2021 Annual Homeless Assessment Report to Congress, Part 1: Point in Time," U.S. Department of HUD, February 2022, https://www.huduser.gov/portal/sites/default/files/pdf/2021-AHAR-Part-1.pdf.

8. Note that out-migration has always occurred, but in the past few years those rates have begun to outstrip in-migration rates, and population growth results from natural births. According to the Department of Finance, California added 87,494 residents in 2019, bringing the population total to 39,782,870 on January 1, 2020. California's historically slow growth trend continued at 0.2 percent in 2019, with stronger growth in the inland counties, zero growth on the coasts, and a net loss in Los Angeles County. "California Tops 39.8 Million Residents at New Year," Demographics Research Unit, Department of Finance, State of California, May 1, 2020, http://dof.ca.gov/Forecasting/Demographics/Estimates/E-1/documents/E-1_2020PressRelease.pdf.

9. In the March 2022 PPIC Statewide Survey, 62 percent of all adults surveyed said they paid "much more" or "somewhat more" to state and local governments than they felt they should. Survey conducted with 1,672 adults in California March 16–17, 2022,

+/–4.1 percent margin of error. These results are generally consistent with previous surveys. Mark Baldassare, Dean Bonner, Rachel Lawler, and Deja Thomas, "Californians and Their Government," PPIC, March 2022, https://www.ppic.org/publication/ppic-statewide-survey-californians-and-their-government-march-2022/.

10. Baldassare et al., "Californians and Their Government"; "2020 Election Results by State," 270toWin, updated December 2020, https://www.270towin.com/2020-election-results-live/state/.

11. AB 540 was passed in 2001. In 2022, a total of 38,446 students had applied for aid under the California Dreamer law (through August 17, 2022 with more to come). An estimated 9,500 attended CSU and over 4,000 attended UC institutions; an estimated total of 75,000 undocumented students attended private and public college and university students (2021–22). See California Student Aid Commission, Data and Reports, accessed August 23, 2022; "About the Coalition," The Campaign for College Opportunity, accessed August 22, 2022, https://collegecampaign.org/undoc-coalition/; "California Community College (CCC) Undocumented Students' Resource Snapshot," CCC, October 1, 2020, https://ccleague.org/sites/default/files/pdf/resources/ccc_undocumented_students_-_resource_snapshot.pdf; Joseph Hayes and Laura Hill, "The DACA Ruling and California's Dreamers," PPIC, June 19, 2020.

12. In April 2022, state Assemblyman Kevin Kiley attempted to repeal the California Values Act, the law that prevents state law enforcement from notifying federal agents when an unauthorized immigrant convicted of a felony has been released from jail. It would also have required law enforcement to detain such persons in cooperation with federal authorities. The state also created direct aid for those unable to receive federal relief money during the coronavirus pandemic and sets aside money for immigrants to fight deportation. David Savage, "California

'Sanctuary' Rules Stay in Place after Supreme Court Rejects Trump's Challenge," *Los Angeles Times*, June 15, 2020.

13. Mireya Villareal, "Devastating Wildfires a 'New Normal' for California, Gov. Jerry Brown Says," *CBS News*, August 1, 2018, https://www.cbsnews.com/news/devastating-wildfires-a-new-normal-for-california-gov-brown-says/.

14. Kurtis Alexander, "Drought, Fires, and Beetles—California's Forests Are Dying. Is It Too Late to Save Them?" *San Francisco Chronicle*, February 27, 2022, updated March 4, 2022. See also U.S. Forest Service, "Aerial Detection Survey: 2021 Summary Report," U.S. Department of Agriculture, December 9, 2021, https://www.fs.usda.gov/Internet/FSE_DOCUMENTS/fseprd985397.pdf; Gavin Madakumbura et al., "Recent California Tree Mortality Portends Drought-driven Forest Die-off," *Environmental Research Letters* 15 (2020): 124040, IOP Science, https://iopscience.iop.org/article/10.1088/1748-9326/abc719.

15. Fires have been recorded from 1932 to the present and only two incidents prior to 2003 (in 1934 and 1977) made the "Top 20" List in 2022. "Top 20 Largest California Wildfires," California Department of Forestry and Fire Protection, State of California, January 13, 2022, https://www.fire.ca.gov/media/4jandlhh/top20_acres.pdf.

16. The Oroville Dam spillway failure is a case in point; repair costs eventually soared to over $1.2 billion. The federal government (through the Federal Emergency Management Agency, FEMA) eventually agreed to a partial reimbursement for repairs, and the state expected to receive $630 million in total. See "FEMA Releases Additional Reimbursement Funds for Oroville Spillways Repairs and Reconstruction," California Department of Water Resources, News Release, February 1, 2021.

17. The 2020 plans estimated a $16 billion price tag and do not account for (currently) high inflation or increased construction costs. Rachel Becker, "Tunnel Vision: What's Next for the Governor's Plan to Replumb the Delta?" *Cal Matters*, June 22, 2022, https://calmatters.org/environment/2022/06/california-water-delta-tunnel/.

18. Region Nine of the American Society of Civil Engineers, "2019 Report Card for California's Infrastructure," 2021 Report Card for America's Infrastructure, ASCE, May 2019, https://infrastructurereportcard.org/wp-content/uploads/2021/07/FullReport-CA_051019.pdf.

19. Gavin Newsom, "California Five-Year Infrastructure Plan," Office of the Governor, State of California, 2022–23, https://www.ebudget.ca.gov/2022-Infrastructure-Plan.pdf. Federal funds will be allocated through the Infrastructure Investment and Jobs Act, signed into law by President Joe Biden in 2021. See "The Infrastructure Investment and Jobs Act Will Deliver for California," White House, Press Release, https://www.whitehouse.gov/wp-content/uploads/2021/08/CALIFORNIA_The-Infrastructure-Investment-and-Jobs-Act-State-Fact-Sheet.pdf.

20. Carey McWilliams, *California, the Great Exception* (Berkeley: University of California Press, 1949), 5.

CHAPTER 2

1. Andrew Rolle, *California: A History*, 6th ed. (Wheeling, IL: Harlan Davidson, 2003), 174.

2. Quote is attributed to Robert G. Cleland and Evelyn Hazen, *Cross-Filing in Primary Elections* (Berkeley: University of California, Bureau of Public Administration, 1951), 9.

3. Arthur Samish and Robert Thomas, *The Secret Boss of California* (New York: Crown Books, 1971), 10.

4. See James Gregory, "Upton Sinclair's End Poverty Campaign in California Campaign," Civil Rights and Human Labor Consortium, University of Washington, accessed June 15, 2022, https://depts.washington.edu/epic34/campaign.shtml.

5. *Silver v. Jordan*, 241 Fed. Supp. 576 (1965), and *Reynolds v. Sims*, 377 U.S. 533 (1964), following *Baker v. Carr*, 369 U.S. 186 (1962).

6. T. George Harris, "California's New Politics: Big Daddy's Big Drive," *Look Magazine* 26, no. 20 (September 25, 1962): 78–82.

7. John Burns, *The Sometime Governments: A Critical Study of the 50 American Legislatures* (New York: Bantam Books, 1971), 8.

8. Howard Jarvis and Paul Gann, "Rebuttal to Argument Against Proposition 13," in *Voter Information Guide for 1978*, Office of the Secretary of State, State of California.

9. Proposition 13 limited property tax rates to 1 percent of a property's assessed value in 1975; for properties sold after 1975, the rate would be 1 percent of the property's sale price. These rates would not be allowed to increase more than 2 percent per year.

10. The 2022 general elections included a total of 27 intraparty match-ups. All five U.S. House races and all five state Senate races were between Democrats. Of 17 Assembly intraparty contests, 13 were between Democrats and four were between Republicans. In 2020 (excluding Assembly District 42 in which (former) Republican incumbent Chad Mayes ran with a "No Party Preference" label): two Republican Assemblymen lost their primaries in March 2020, bringing the totals to ten Assembly, six Senate, and four U.S. House open general races, or 20 in all. See the final official election results compiled by the secretary of state (http://www.sos.ca.gov).

11. Proposition 39.

12. Voters approved Proposition 54 in 2016 by a vote of 65.4 percent.

13. Historian James Gregory notes that "It was not until 2010 that the number of native-born Californians surpassed the number who had migrated from somewhere else," either from another country or another state. See: James Gregory, "California's Migration History, 1850–2017," in America's Great Migrations Project, University of Washington, accessed

June 15, 2022, https://depts.washington.edu/moving1/California.shtml.

14. "Table H2: Population and Percent Change by Race (Not Hispanic/Latino) and Hispanic/Latino: 2010 and 2020," Demographic Unit, Department of Finance, State of California, updated August 2021. See also Dan Walters, "California Has by Far Nation's Largest Asian-American Population," *Sacramento Bee*, March 12, 2013, http://blogs.sacbee.com/capitolalertlatest/2012/03/california-has-by-far-nations-largest-asian-american-population.html.

15. "Report P-1D: Total Population Projections by Race/Ethnicity, 2010–2060," Demographic Unit, Department of Finance, State of California, July 19, 2021, https://dof.ca.gov/wp-content/uploads/Forecasting/Demographics/Documents/P1D_State_Race_Ethnicity.xlsx.

16. Benjamin Madley, *An American Genocide* (New Haven, CT: Yale University Press, 2016).

17. Bryan Baker, "Estimates of the Unauthorized Immigration Population Residing in the U.S.: January 2015–January 2018," U.S. Department of Homeland Security, January 2021, https://www.dhs.gov/sites/default/files/publications/immigration-statistics/Pop_Estimate/UnauthImmigrant/unauthorized_immigrant_population_estimates_2015_-_2018.pdf.

18. Approved by 60.9 percent in 1998 as Proposition 227, "English Only Instruction" was replaced in 2016 with Prop 58, which passed with an even higher margin of 73.5 percent.

19. Campaign for College Opportunity, California Undocumented Higher Education Coalition, accessed June 18, 2022, https://collegecampaign.org/undoc-coalition/.

20. "Tuition Benefits for Dreamers," National Conference of State Legislatures, updated March 1, 2021, https://www.ncsl.org/research/immigration/tuition-benefits-for-immigrants.aspx.

21. Heather Tirado Gilligan, "Newsom Proposes Coverage for Last Remaining Group

of Uninsured Californians," California Health Care Foundation, January 24, 2022, https://www.chcf.org/blog/newsom-pr oposes-coverage-last-remaining-unins ured/.

22. "AB 60 Driver's Licenses," California Research Bureau, California State Library, January 2018, https://www.librar y.ca.gov/Content/pdf/crb/reports/AB_60_ Report_2018.pdf.

23. Jens Hainmueller, Duncan Lawrence, and Hans Lueders, "Providing Driver's Licenses to Unauthorized Immigrants Improves Traffic Safety," *Proceedings of the National Academy of Sciences*, March 3, 2017, https://www.pnas.org/content/114/1 6/4111.full.

24. Virginia added this benefit in 2020, and Oregon, New York, and New Jersey added this benefit in 2019, joining Colorado, Connecticut, Delaware, Hawaii, Illinois, New Mexico, Nevada, Utah, Vermont, and Washington ("States Offering Driver's Licenses to Immigrants," National Con- ference of State Legislatures, updated August 9, 2021, https://www.ncsl.org/res earch/immigration/states-offering-driver -s-licenses-to-immigrants.aspx).

25. Kristen Lewis, "A Portrait of California 2021–22," Measure of America, Social Sci- ence Research Council, 2021, https://ssrc -static.s3.amazonaws.com/moa/APortrai tofCalifornia2021-2022.pdf.

26. Edward "Ted" Costa, "Proponent's State- ment of Reasons" and "Proponent's Recall Argument," in *Voter Information Guide for 2003, Special Election*, Office of the Secre- tary of State, State of California, http://rep ository.uchastings.edu/ca_ballot_props /1215.

27. The recall's success is credited to the infusion of cash from Republican U.S. Representative Darrell Issa, who gave more than $1 million to collect signatures. After the measure qualified, hundreds of potential candidates jostled for attention, including actor Arnold Schwarzenegger, who surprised *The Tonight Show* audience by announcing his candidacy during the show. The spectacular election season lasted only 76 days (a normal cycle is about twice as long), during which time the candidates spent $80 million, capti- vated the mainstream media, and partici- pated in televised debates. On October 7, 2003, 55.4 percent of voters selected "yes" on the recall question, and 48.7 percent chose Schwarzenegger from among 135 candidates on the ballot to replace Davis. A total of 61.2 percent of registered voters participated in the election, a high turnout historically speaking.

28. Proposition 23 in 2010 would have disman- tled the law by suspending its implemen- tation until unemployment dipped below 5.5 percent for four consecutive quar- ters, a phenomenon that last occurred in 2006–07. The cap-and-trade system almost collapsed during the COVID shut- down during 2020 and 2021, but the sys- tem has been revived and the partnership with Québec, Canada continues (in 2018 Ontario briefly joined the partnership and then pulled out). The scheduled public auction of carbon credits in May 2022 demonstrated strong demand for allow- ances and generated significant revenues that helped the state reach its projection targets (see Katelyn Roedner Sutter, "May Brings Another Record Auction for the Western Climate Initiative," Environmen- tal Defense Fund, Climate 411 Blog, May 26, 2022, https://blogs.edf.org/climate411 /2022/05/26/may-brings-another-record -auction-for-the-western-climate-initiati ve-as-california-considers-how-to-ramp -up-climate-action/.

29. Brown set a record by serving 16 years as governor, and was one of the youngest governors in California history when he assumed office in 1975 at age thirty-six. He also became the oldest governor with his final reelection at age seventy-six.

30. Justin Worland, "Gov. Jerry Brown Vows to Fight Donald Trump on Climate Change: 'California Will Launch Its Own Damn Sat- ellite,'" *Time*, December 15, 2016, http:// time.com/4603482/jerry - brown-donald-trump-climate-change.

31. Ben Christopher, "Case by Case: Califor- nia's Many Lawsuits against the Trump

Administration," *Cal Matters*, updated June 6, 2020, https://projects.calmatters.org/2017/interactives/trump-lawsuit-2017/index.html.

32. Patrick McGreevy, "With Strong Message Against Creating New Crimes, Gov. Brown Vetoes Drone Bills," *Los Angeles Times*, October 3, 2015, http://www.latimes.com/politics/la-me-pc-gov-brown-vetoes-bills-restricting-hobbyist-drones-at-fires-schools-prisons-20151003-story.html. Brown pardoned 1,189 people and granted 15 commutations in 8 years and 404 in his first term. See Bob Egelko, "Gov. Jerry Brown Sets Record for Pardons, Commutations in California," *San Francisco Chronicle*, December 24, 2018, https://www.sfchronicle.com/politics/article/Gov-Jerry-Brown-sets-record-for-pardons-13487741.php.

33. For an online database of public protests that were documented between January 17, 2017 and January 31, 2021, see http://countlove.org/.

34. Governor Lynn Frazier of North Dakota was removed from office in 1921 through a recall election, and Wisconsin Governor Scott Walker survived a recall in 2012.

35. In what might be referred to as the "French Laundry Affair," in November 2020 after exhorting citizens to avoid gatherings indoors, the governor himself attended a birthday celebration of a close friend at the exclusive French Laundry, a three-star Michelin restaurant in Napa Valley. His gaffe reeked of hypocrisy and elitism and supplied the recall advocates with more ammunition for their cause. See: Taryn Luna and Phil Willon, "Newsom Apologizes for French Laundry Dinner, Says He Will Practice What He Preaches on COVID-19," *Los Angeles Times*, November 16, 2020, https://www.latimes.com/california/story/2020-11-16/gavin-newsom-apology-french-laundry-dinner-covid-19.

36. "Governor Signs Landmark Legislation to Advance Racial Justice and California's Fight against Systemic Racism and Bias in Our Legal System," Office of Governor Gavin Newsom, September 20, 2020, http s://www.gov.ca.gov/2020/09/30/governor-newsom-signs-landmark-legislation-to-advance-racial-justice-and-californias-fight-against-systemic-racism-bias-in-our-legal-system/.

37. "2020 Redistricting Data," California Department of Finance, accessed June 15, 2022, https://dof.ca.gov/forecasting/demographics/redistricting-data/, and Hans Johnson, "Who's Leaving California, and Who's Moving In?" Public Policy Institute of California, Blog Post, March 28, 2022, https://www.ppic.org/blog/whos-leaving-california-and-whos-moving-in/.

CHAPTER 3

1. "Ballot Argument in Favor of California Proposition 7, the Initiative and Referendum Amendment," in *Voter Information Guide for 1911*, Office of the Secretary of State, State of California, October 10, 1911, https://repository.uchastings.edu/cgi/viewcontent.cgi?article=1023&context=ca_ballot_props.

2. The quote is from Secretary of State Alex Padilla as noted in John Myers, "California's Record-Setting 224-page Voter Guide Is Costing Taxpayers Nearly $15 million," *Los Angeles Times*, September 9, 2016, http://www.latimes.com/politics/la-pol-ca-california-voter-guide-november-ballot-20160909-snap-story.html.

3. *Arizona State Legislature v. Arizona Independent Redistricting Commission*, 135 S. Ct. 2652 (2015).

4. The term *hybrid democracy* is attributed to Elizabeth Garrett, "Hybrid Democracy," *George Washington Law Review* 73 (2005): 1096–130.

5. The exact number of proposed initiatives, constitutional amendments, or both is 247 according to the California Legislative Analyst's Office (another nine were proposed from 1974 to 1978). "1974 to Present: Ballot Measures by Type," Legislative Analyst's Office, accessed June 20, 2022, https://lao.ca.gov/BallotAnalysis/BallotByType. See also "Initiative, Referendum,

and Recall," in *Oregon Blue Book* (Salem: Oregon State Archives), https://sos.orego n.gov/blue-book/Documents/elections/i nitiative.pdf. By comparison in 2020, Californians confronted thirteen statewide measures while Oregonians considered four.

6. According to the California Legislative Analyst's Office, from 1979 to 2020, voters considered 240 separate initiatives put forward by citizens (not the legislature), compared to 173 in Oregon (these totals include referenda); 473 state measures were on California's ballots between 1979 and 2020 (the chart begins at 1974; this number also includes bonds). During the same period in Oregon, voters considered 311 measures. See "Oregon Blue Book: Initiative, Recall, and Referendum Intro- duction," in *Oregon Blue Book* (Salem: Oregon State Archives), accessed August 10, 2022, https://sos.oregon.gov/blue-b ook/Documents/elections/initiative.pd f. Colorado has the third-highest ballot measure rates, including 128 propositions and 75 referenda since 1979 (209 in all). These states represent the top three most active users of the initiative process.

7. "Initiative Summary of Data," Office of the Secretary of State, State of California, accessed June 20, 2022, http://elections.c dn.sos.ca.gov/ballot-measures/pdf/sum mary-data.pdf.

8. The precise figure is 74.46 percent, or 1,540 out of 2,068 that were titled and summarized for circulation between 1912 and March 2021 but failed to qualify. "Summary of Data."

9. On rare occasion, an initiative includes language allowing the legislature to amend the law. Proposition 22, which appeared on the November 2020 general election ballot, contained the provision: "After the effective date of this chapter, the Legislature may amend this chapter by a statute passed in each house of the Leg- islature by rollcall vote entered into the journal, seven-eighths of the membership concurring, provided that the statute is consistent with, and furthers the purpose of, this chapter." See "Text of Proposed

Laws: Proposition 22," in *Voter Information Guide for 2020*, Office of the Secretary of State, State of California, accessed June 22, 2022, https://vig.cdn.sos.ca.gov/2020/ general/pdf/topl-prop22.pdf.

10. Ballotpedia calculated that the average cost per required signature ("CPRS") in 2020 for eight qualified initiatives was $7.22. That year, signature gathering for Proposition 22 averaged $10.37 by their measures. See "California Ballot Initiative Petition Signature Costs," Ballotpedia, accessed June 20, 2022, http://ballotpedia .org/wiki/index.php/California_ballot_ini tiative_petition_signature_costs.

11. Elisabeth R. Gerber et al., *Stealing the Ini- tiative: How State Government Responds to Direct Democracy* (Upper Saddle River, NJ: Prentice Hall, 2001), 12.

12. Unadjusted dollars. The rest came from donations averaging over $10,000. The forty-eight big donors include nine labor groups, fifteen businesses (led by PG&E), eight individuals, nine Native American tribes, the major political parties, two of Schwarzenegger's political committees, the League of Cities, one advocacy group, and one political action committee (PAC). See Mike Polyakov, Peter Counts, and Kevin Yin, "California's Initiative System: The Voice of the People Co-opted," Cali- fornia Common Sense, November 6, 2013, cacs.org/pdf/22.pdf.

13. A filing fee of $200 was last set in 1943. Governor Brown agreed with arguments in favor of AB 1100 that the fee should be raised to reflect long-term inflation and to discourage the frivolous filing of initia- tives. The increase took effect January 1, 2016. A public review period was also added in 2014 (AB 1253) to increase trans- parency in the process.

14. State judges agreed to extend those dead- lines during the pandemic.

15. Signature invalidation rates vary by county. Center for Governmental Studies (CGS) reports that Los Angeles and Oak- land have much higher invalidation rates (around 30–35 percent) due to duplicate signatures, signatures of unregistered

voters, or names submitted in counties where they are not registered to vote. CGS estimates the average invalidation rate to be as high as 40 percent. *Democracy by Initiative: Shaping California's Fourth Branch of Government*, 2nd ed. (Los Angeles, CA: Center for Governmental Studies, 2008), http://policyarchive.org/handle/10207/bitstreams/5800.pdf. Interestingly, based on the author's review of 2021 gubernatorial recall petition statistics, the invalidation rates for signatures on the recall petitions were lower than for typical initiative petitions.

16. Ballotpedia calculates the average cost per required signature (CPRS) based on the amounts paid to the signature collection firms (publicly reported information) and the actual numbers of signatures needed. From 2019 to 2022 costs were higher than in the previous 4 years because of higher turnout in 2018. As noted above, the CPRS was $7.22 for eight initiatives in 2020. Costs were slightly lower in 2018, at an average of $6.07 (also for eight initiatives), and the lowest CPRS (for Proposition 6, a proposed gas tax repeal) was $3.58. "California Ballot Initiative Petition Signature Costs," Ballotpedia, accessed June 20, 2022, http://ballotpedia.org/wiki/index.php/California_ballot_initiative_petition_signature_costs.

17. "Power Search," Office of the Secretary of State, State of California, http://powersearch.sos.ca.gov. Figures are periodically updated based on amended filing information.

18. Proponents of Prop 22 reported receiving $205,684,057 in contributions. See "PowerSearch, Campaign Finance, Ballot Measures," California Secretary of State, updated June 21, 2022, http://powersearch.sos.ca.gov/.

19. To clear up ambiguity about the implementation date, voters approved Proposition 72 in 2018, which states that initiatives are no longer effective "the day after the election," but rather take effect five days after the results are officially certified.

20. Governor Brown was aware that many voters only vote for measures appearing at the top of a ballot. The "roll-off," or reduction in number of votes for down-ticket measures, in this case was about 1 percent, meaning that 12,667,751 people cast their votes for Brown's "top of the ticket" Prop 30, whereas 12,331,091 voted for Prop 38, a difference of 336,660 votes (or 0.97 percent). Ultimately, however, Brown's measure won by such a large margin that the roll-off did not matter to the election outcome.

21. *Democracy by Initiative*, 14. See also Polyakov et al., "California's Initiative System."

22. Mark Baldassare et al., "California Statewide Survey: Californians and Education," Public Policy Institute of California (PPIC), April 2022, https://www.ppic.org/publication/ppic-statewide-survey-californians-and-education-april-2022/. Results of polls conducted in 2000, 2006, May and September 2011, and 2013 were also consistent in their finding of strong support for the initiative process.

23. Mark Baldassare, "Reengaging Citizens in the Initiative Process," PPIC Blog, May 11, 2022, https://www.ppic.org/blog/reengaging-citizens-in-the-initiative-process/. Of likely voters surveyed in April 2022, 91 percent agreed that said that the "ballot wording for citizens' initiatives is often too complicated and confusing for voters to understand what happens if the initiative passes": 45 percent strongly agreed and 46 percent somewhat agreed with that statement. The survey was fielded March 30–April 13, 2022; likely voters were a subset (1,059 of 1,591 California residents surveyed); margin of error was +/–3.9 percent.

24. For a complete list of referenda that were circulated or qualified for the ballot, see "Summary of Referendum Data," Office of the Secretary of State, State of California, n.d., https://elections.cdn.sos.ca.gov/ballot-measures/pdf/referenda-data.pdf.

25. From March 2000 to March 2020, voters considered 29 bonds that were either

legislatively referred or put on the ballot by citizens. In all, 86 percent passed (25/29), and two of the four that failed were in recent years (Prop 3 water bond in 2018, which qualified by petition, and Prop 1 in March 2020, a $15 billion education bond).

26. "Bonds," Legislative Analyst's Office, accessed June 20, 2022, https://lao.ca.gov/BallotAnalysis/Bonds.

27. According to the National Conference of State Legislatures (NCSL), 30 states permit recall elections to be held in local jurisdictions, and "some sources place this number at 38" (on "Recall of State Officials" webpage). See "Recall of Local Officials," NCSL, accessed June 22, 2022, https://www.ncsl.org/research/elections-and-campaigns/recall-of-local-officials.aspx.

28. The last person to be impeached and convicted was Judge James Hardy in 1862. Judge Carols Hardy (no relation) was impeached and then acquitted in 1929.

29. The requirement is 30 percent if fewer than 1,000 people are registered, declining to 10 percent if over 100,000 are registered. For more details, see "Procedure for Recalling State and Local Officials," Office of the Secretary of State, State of California, https://elections.cdn.sos.ca.gov/recalls/recall-procedures-guide.pdf.

30. "Recall History in California, 1913–Present," Office of the Secretary of State, State of California, accessed June 21, 2022, http://www.sos.ca.gov/elections/recalls/recall-history-california-1913-present/.

31. Over the past 25 years (1995–2020) at least 373 individuals have been subject to recall. These are counted in: Leonor Ehling et al., "California County, City, and School District Election Outcomes: Candidates and Ballot Measures, 2020 Elections (Trend Table A)," Institute for Social Research, Center for California Studies, CSU Sacramento, 2021, https://csu-csus.esploro.exlibrisgroup.com/esploro/outputs/dataset/California-Elections-Data-Archive-CEDA/99257830890201671.

32. For a more comprehensive but dated report, see Tracy M. Gordon, *The Local Initiative in California* (San Francisco, CA: PPIC, 2004), http://www.ppic.org/content/pubs/report/R_904TGR.pdf.

33. From 2001 to 2020, 69.7 percent of all 8,902 measures introduced to voters at the city, county, or school board level passed (percentage is based on the reported pass rates (rounded) rather than raw numbers of failed measures); pass rates ranged from 62 to 80 percent. In 2020, 63 percent of local ballot measures passed. Note that some cities fail to report by the deadline, but this report is the most accurate available.

34. As noted by the California Tax Foundation, a state Supreme Court decision in *California Cannabis Coalition* v *City of Upland* (2017) "created a loophole that has allowed special taxes to be approved by a simple majority vote if placed on the ballot via an initiative—even when sponsored by elected officials" (p. 2). "Local Tax Trends in California," California Tax Foundation, September 1, 2021, https://www.caltax.org/foundation/reports/2021-Local-Tax-Trends-in-CA.pdf.

35. Cheri Carlson and Kelthleen Wilson, "Multimillion-Dollar Campaign to Defeat Oil Measures Pulls Ahead in Ventura County," *Ventura County Star*, June 14, 2022, https://www.vcstar.com/story/news/politics/elections/2022/06/08/ventura-county-election-results-oil-drilling-measures-a-b-california-ca-primary-results-today/7505935001/.

36. Emily Green, Joaquin Palomino, and Jessica Floum, "Big Bucks Donors Wield Their Influence on SF Ballot Measures," *San Francisco Chronicle*, November 2, 2016, http://www.sfchronicle.com/bayarea/article/Big-bucks-donors-wield-their-influence-on-SF-10535247.

37. These were 2022 thresholds. See: "Guide to Qualifying Initiative Charter Amendments, Ordinances, and Declarations of Policy," San Francisco Department of Elections, https://sfelections.sfgov.org/sites/default/files/110822_InitiativeGuide.

pdf, 7; and San Diego County Clerk, "Current Signature Requirements," accessed June 22, 2022, https://www.sandiego.gov/city-clerk/elections/process/initiative.

38. "County Initiative Procedures 2022," Election Coordination Unit of the Los Angeles County Registrar-Recorder/County Clerk, n.d., https://www.lavote.net/docs/rrcc/documents/county-initiative-procedures.pdf?_v=2.

39. Includes ballot measures at the County, City, and School District levels. Ehling, Williams, Messier, Marfori, and Cambrey, p. 5 (subsection "2020 Election Series Summary: Election Outcomes for County, City, and School District Ballot Measures, and Candidates").

40. The other states that have the direct and/or indirect initiative, popular referendum for statutes and/or constitutional amendments, and the recall are Alaska, Arizona, Colorado, Idaho, Michigan, Montana, Nevada, North Dakota, Oregon, and Washington. "Initiative and Referendum States; Recall of State Officials," NCSL, accessed June 22, 2022.

41. In the May 2022 Statewide Survey (conducted May 12–22, 2022 among 1,179 likely voters with a +/–4.9 percent margin of error), a majority of likely voters (55 percent) reported that they believed this, in line with previous surveys (60 percent in 2013). See also Mark Baldassare, "Most California Voters Say, 'We Know Best,'" PPIC Blog, May 25, 2022, https://www.ppic.org/blog/most-california-voters-say-we-know-best/.

CHAPTER 4

1. California lost a Congressional seat due to reapportionment following the 2020 U.S. Census. According to the Citizens Redistricting Commission, each of the 52 U.S. House districts in California would contain a population of 760,066, ideally. "Report on Final Maps," 2020 Citizens Redistricting Commission, December 26, 2021, 51.

2. The six legislatures that *approach* professionalized status are Alaska, Hawaii, Illinois, Massachusetts, Ohio, and Wisconsin. Most are in "mixed" categories (legislators maintain an outside job to support themselves, meet in longer or shorter sessions, etc.); and four—Montana, North and South Dakota, and Wyoming—operate as purely part-time, "citizen" bodies (very low pay, short sessions, a few institutional staff). "Full- and Part-Time Legislatures," NCSL, updated July 28, 2021, http://www.ncsl.org/research/about-state-legislatures/full-and-part-time-legislatures.aspx.

3. Proposition 140 specified that Assembly members could serve no more than three 2-year terms, and Senators could serve no more than two 4-year terms, for a total of 14 years in office. The original ban was "lifetime." Voters approved Proposition 28 after being reassured that politicians would spend less time in office overall (12 years total instead of 14).

4. The November 2018 elections brought eight new senators, five of whom previously served in the Assembly, and eight new Assembly members. Special elections from June 12, 2019 to May 12, 2020 attracted four new members, bringing the total legislative turnover for 2019–20 to 16.7 percent. It should be noted that although high turnover in 2012 was also prompted by redistricting, term limits have provided the impetus for high turnover in nonredistricting years since 1990.

5. In addition to the fourteen other states with nonlegislative or "independent" commissions and boards, six states have advisory commissions to assist the legislature with state legislative redistricting, and five have backup commissions that will spring into action if the legislature fails to agree. Iowa's process is unique. State legislatures are in charge in thirty-six states. "Creation of Redistricting Commissions," NCSL, updated December 10, 2021, https://www.ncsl.org/research/redistricting/creation-of-redistricting-commissions.aspx.

6. *Arizona State Legislature v. Arizona Independent Redistricting Commission*, 576 U.S. (2015).

7. Proposition 11, Section 2(d).

8. "Outreach Materials: Redistricting Basics Presentation," Citizens Redistricting Commission, accessed June 23, 2022, https://www.wedrawthelinesca.org/final_maps_report. See also Angelo Ancheta, "Redistricting Reform and the California Citizens Redistricting Commission," *Harvard Law and Policy Review* 8, no. 1 (2014).

9. "Citizens Redistricting Commission Defends New Maps—They Represent the Wishes of the People of California," *CBS News Bay Area*, December 27, 2021, https://www.cbsnews.com/sanfrancisco/news/california-citizens-redistricting-commission-defends-new-maps-represent-the-wishes-of-the-people/.

10. "Report on Final Maps," 2020 California Citizens Redistricting Commission, December 26, 2021, https://www.wedrawthelinesca.org/final_maps_report.

11. The 2021 Commission was criticized for spending more than the previous commission, difficulties fielding comments via online platforms, poor timing with posted maps (maps not posted when promised), commissioner absences from meetings, and changes "rushed" near the end of the process (a court challenge alleging secrecy and interest group influence was dismissed by a judge in December 2021). See Sameea Kamal, "Why is California's Redistricting Commission Under Increasing Scrutiny?" *Cal Matters*, December 15, 2021, https://calmatters.org/politics/2021/12/california-redistricting-commission-scrutiny/. Separately, insufficient time passed between the production of maps and this writing for published analyses of the maps to be made available. For a scholarly analysis of the 2011 maps which represented the first mapmaking process conducted outside the California state legislature, see Vladimir Kogan and Eric McGhee, "Redistricting California: An Evaluation of the Citizens Commission Final Plans," *California Journal of Politics &*

Policy 4, no. 1 (2012), https://doi.org/10.5070/P23K5Q. They showed that the commission's state maps did produce more compact and somewhat more competitive districts (initially), and they argue the Democratic tilt that occurred after implementation is likely due to incumbency strength as well as party registration that reflects high concentrations of Democrats in many places and Republicans in relatively few.

12. Unusually high turnover in 2012 yielded to lower turnover in the following four elections; for example, 12 brand new members arrived between November 2018 and May 2020 (special elections included). The turnover in 2022 (at least 26 legislators were retiring prior to the 2022 general election) was higher than in previous years because all seats were reshuffled thanks to redistricting, and some incumbents ran for other offices to avoid running against a colleague.

13. Of the 120 legislators in office in June 2022, 39 were women compared to just 12 in the 2016–17 term. In terms of race and ethnicity, 64 were White, 11 were African American, 31 were Hispanic/Latinx including one Native American, 12 were Asian American or Pacific Islander, and 2 were "Other" (Puerto Rican and Iranian). In all, 56 of 120 (46.5 percent) were persons of color. Author's data. Also see.

14. Quoted in Hannah Pitkin, *The Concept of Representation* (Berkeley: University of California Press, 1967), 60.

15. Budget subcommittees examine specific areas of the state budget, while joint committees and smaller "select" committees on issues ranging from police reform to hydrogen energy advance specific issues through at least one informational hearing per year. Select committees can be instrumental in conducting oversight hearings (to investigate alleged executive branch misdeeds).

16. By tradition and out of courtesy, all bills are given a hearing so that they may be debated in a public forum. However, a 2019 rule change in the Assembly formalized

the authority of committee chairs to ignore or not hold hearings for all bills, meaning they could choose to "kill" bills by not acting on them (i.e., no further action will be taken on it if the bill is not given a hearing). This followed action by Republican member Melissa Melendez who previously had introduced a constitutional amendment, ACA 23, to require that all bills be given a committee hearing. Ironically, it died in 2018 without a hearing.

17. AB 440, authored by Assemblyman. Frank Bigelow, chaptered July 9, 2021.

18. "Frequently Asked Questions About CEQA," Natural Resources Agency, State of California, accessed June 30, 2022, https://files.resources.ca.gov/ceqa/more/faq.html.

19. The Department of Finance cited the May 2022 report of the California Association of Realtors (https://www.car.org/marketdata/data/countysalesactivity) as the source of median single-family home prices, which they peg at $898,980 (Keeley Bosler, "Finance Bulletin," June 2022, State of California Department of Finance, https://dof.ca.gov/wp-content/uploads/Forecasting/Economics/Documents/Jun-22.pdf. Similar conclusions were reached previously by PPIC and the LAO. See "California's High Housing Costs: Causes and Consequences," March 17, 2015, http://www.lao.ca.gov/reports/2015/finance/housing-costs/housing-costs.aspx, and Hans Johnson, Julien LaFortune, and Marisol C. Mejia, "California's Future: Housing," PPIC, January 2020, https://www.ppic.org/wp-content/uploads/californias-future-housing-january-2020.pdf.

20. Arielle Harris and Natalie Kirkish, "2019 Amendments to the CEQA Guidelines: Part—Transportation Impacts," CEQA Chronicles, February 15, 2019, https://www.ceqachronicles.com/2019/02/2019-amendments-to-the-ceqa-guidelines-part-one-transportation-impacts/.

21. SB 886, Authored by Sen. Scott Weiner, https://leginfo.legislature.ca.gov/faces/billTextClient.xhtml?bill_id=202120220SB886.

22. All low-income residents aged 50 or older, regardless of immigration status, became eligible for full-scope coverage beginning May 1, 2022, costs that are paid strictly by the state. Full-scope Medi-Cal coverage is set to extend to all income-eligible (low-income) residents aged 26 and older after January 1, 2024. According to LAO, the governor estimates 714,000 adults immediately would be eligible increasing to 764,000 when fully implemented. See "2022–23 Budget: Health Care Access and Affordability," Legislative Analyst's Office, February 23, 2022, https://lao.ca.gov/Publications/Report/4560; Department of Health Care Services, "Medi-Cal Monthly Eligible Fast Facts, January 2022 as of the MEDS Cut-off for April 2022," California Department of Health Care Services, April 2022, https://www.dhcs.ca.gov/dataandstats/statistics/Documents/FastFacts-January2022.pdf.

23. This statement assumes that trends have held steady since the last NCSL staff survey that was conducted in 2015. See Brian Weberg, "Size of State Legislative Staff," NCSL, May 18, 2021, http://www.ncsl.org/research/about-state-legislatures/staff-change-chart-1979-1988-1996-2003-2009.aspx.

24. The Republican Party achieved supermajority status in both chambers at least a dozen times between 1891 and 1933. Democrats' supermajority status in both the Assembly and Senate was reached in 2012 and then lost and regained from 2012 through mid-2014 because of resignations and special elections. Between 2014 and 2015, only the Assembly briefly reached supermajority status. In 2016 both houses attained the threshold once again; the Senate lost and found it 2016–17. Democrats have had a supermajority lock on both houses since the 2018 general election.

25. James Fallows, "Jerry Brown's Political Reboot," *Atlantic*, May 22, 2013, http://www.theatlantic.com/magazine/archive/2013/06/the-fixer/309324/?single_page=true.

26. Gabriel Petek, "The State Appropriations Limit," Leiglsative Analyst's Office, April 21, 2021, https://lao.ca.gov/Public ations/Report/4416#Constructing_a_ Plan.

27. Author's interview with freshman Assembly member in Sacramento, California, in March 1999.

28. Ibid.

CHAPTER 5

1. "Press Release: At Summit of the Americas, California and Canada to Work Partner to Advance Bold Climate Action," Office of Governor Gavin Newsom, State of California, June 9, 2022, h ttps://www.gov.ca.gov/2022/06/09/at-s ummit-of-the-americas-california-an d-canada-partner-to-advance-bold-cli mate-action/.

2. "Press Release: In Response to Supreme Court Decision, Governor Newsom Signs Legislation to Protect Women and Providers in California from Abortion Bans by Other States," Office of Governor Gavin Newsom, State of California, June 24, 2022, https://www.gov.ca.gov/2022/06/2 4/in-response-to-supreme-court-decisi on-governor-newsom-signs-legislation -to-protect-women-and-providers-in-c alifornia-from-abortion-bans-by-other -states/.

3. "Press Release: Attorney General Bonta Affirms His Support for Commonsense Gun Laws in Response to Supreme Court Decision on New York's Conceal and Carry Laws," Department of Justice, State of California, June 23, 2022, h ttps://oag.ca.gov/news/press-releases /attorney-general-bonta-affirms-his-s upport-commonsense-gun-laws-respo nse-supreme.

4. At last count (numbers provided by the Senate Rules Committee in 2020), appointees to about 100 administrative positions and 80 boards and commissions require Senate approval. Most state workers are members of the powerful union known as the California State Employees Association (CSEA).

5. "How Often Do Governors Say No?" California State Senate Office of Research, October 2022, https://sor.senate.ca.gov/ sites/sor.senate.ca.gov/files/3258%20S OR%20governors%20veto%20report%2 02022.pdf.

6. A series of veto overrides took place in 1979–80, but the last occurred when the Senate overrode a gubernatorial budget line-item veto on September 5, 1979 (Senate Journal, p. 7174). The Assembly overrode this line-item veto on February 4, 1980 (by a vote of 55–12), but a motion to reconsider was noticed. The motion to reconsider lapsed on February 5, 1980, so the override took effect on that day (Assembly Journal, p. 11086).

7. The 2022–23 budget authorized 512 positions. The number was 467 in 2015. Note that in 2020 when the legislature was meeting remotely because of COVID-19 restrictions, they delayed the deadline to pay taxes until June 15. That year, budgeting relied heavily on educated guesswork; the deadline was moved to May 17 in 2021 and restored to April 18 in 2022 (usually April 15, with an exception made for Emancipation Day holiday).

8. Gavin Newsom, "Proclamation of a State of Emergency," March 4, 2020, Executive Department, State of California, https:// www.gov.ca.gov/wp-content/uploads/2 020/03/3.4.20-Coronavirus-SOE-Procl amation.pdf; Maura Dolan, "California's Top Court Lets Stand Ruling That Upheld Gov. Newsom's Emergency Powers," August 11, 2021, https://www.latimes.c om/california/story/2021-08-11/califo rnias-top-court-lets-stand-ruling-tha t-upheld-gov-newsoms-emergency-p owers.

9. Debra Kahn, "Newsom Executive Orders Test Constitutional Bounds—And

Legislative Goodwill," *Politico*, April 22, 2020, https://www.politico.com/states/california/story/2020/04/22/newsom-executive-orders-test-constitutional-bounds-and-legislative-goodwill-1279094.

10. Don Thompson, "California Democrats Shoot Down GOP Bid to End Gavin Newsom's COVID Emergency Powers," *The Sacramento Bee*, March 15, 2022, https://www.sacbee.com/news/politics-government/capitol-alert/article259424559.html.

12. Erich B. Smith, "Partnership Between Cal Guard and Ukraine Shows Benefits of SPP," *Grizzly Magazine, California Army National Guard*, https://grizzly.shorthandstories.com/national-guard-bureau-chief-partnership-between-california-national-guard-and-ukraine-shows-benefits/index.html.

13. In his latter two terms Governor Jerry Brown set a new record: Almost 1,200 pardons plus over 150 commutations for persons who had earned the privilege by demonstrating "exemplary behavior following their conviction" for at least 10 years following their release. Brown typically granted pardons on the eve of Christmas and Easter. For case-by-case explanations of the governor's decisions, see "Executive Report on Pardons, Commutations of Sentence, and Reprieves," issued annually by the governor's office under statutory order (Incidentally, most of those convictions were drug-related offenses.) See also "Governor Newsom Grants Executive Clemency 7.1.22," Office of Governor Gaving Newsom, State of California, July 1, 2022, https://www.gov.ca.gov/2022/07/01/governor-newsom-grants-executive-clemency-7-1-22/; "California Reprieve Power," NYU Center on the Administration of Law, accessed July 2, 2022, https://www.law.nyu.edu/sites/default/files/California%20Reprieve.pdf.

14. In April 2019, survey data showed that 76 percent of Democrats favored life imprisonment without the possibility of parole, compared to 56 percent of independents and 32 percent of Republicans. See Rachel Lawler, "Is Momentum Growing to End California's Death Penalty?" PPIC Blog, April 9, 2019. Note that the recall petitions against Newsom (written in 2020) explicitly noted in the grounds for recall (among other things) that "He unilaterally over-ruled the will of the people regarding the death penalty," a reference to the fact that Proposition 62, a measure to overturn the death penalty in California, was defeated in 2016 (Orrin Heatlie, "Notice of Intent to Circulate Recall Petition," dated February 20, 2020 (received February 21), https://elections.cdn.sos.ca.gov/recalls/newsom-notice-of-intent.pdf).

15. Ricardo Lara, "Strategic Plan 2021–23," Department of Insurance, State of California, n.d., https://www.insurance.ca.gov/0500-about-us/upload/CDI-Strategic-Plan-2021-2023.pdf.

16. According to the secretary of state's final campaign finance filings, the National Institute on Money in State Politics reported that in 2014, $4.4 million was raised in support and $57 million was spent in opposition to Proposition 45, mostly by health insurers (see powersearch.sos.ca.gov/advanced.php).

17. "Initiatives and Programs," Department of Education, State of California, accessed July 2, 2022; https://www.cde.ca.gov/eo/in/; Tony Thurmond, "Charter Schools Task Force Report," Department of Education, State of California, June 6, 2019, https://www.cde.ca.gov/eo/in/documents/charterstaskforcereport.pdf.

18. "Homepage," State Board of Education, State of California, accessed July 3, 2022 https://www.cde.ca.gov/be/.

19. "Government Reorganization Plan," Office of the Governor, State of California, March 30, 2012, http://gov.ca.gov/docs/Cover_Letter_and_Summary.pdf.

20. The total number was 215,169 as of July 2022, including full-time and part-time workers and excluding 22,017 intermittent employees as well as employees of

the California State University system. In June 2009, the comparable state employee workforce numbered 244,061. "State Employee Demographics," State Controller's Office, State of California, accessed July 3, 2022, http://www.sco.ca.gov/ppsd_empinfo_demo.html.

21. P. K. Stockton and E. B. Willis, *Debates and Proceedings of the Constitutional Convention of the State of California: Convened at the City of Sacramento, Saturday, September 28, 1878* (Sacramento, CA: State Office, J.D. Young, 1880–81), 925.

22. Ben Christopher, "California Recall: The 2022 Campaign Starts Now," Associated Press, September 14, 2021 (updated October 22, 2021), https://calmatters.org/politics/2021/09/california-recall-2022-campaign/.

CHAPTER 6

1. Alexandra Yoon-Hendricks, Sacramento Bee, March 2, 2022, "An $80 Ticket Turned into an $800 Debt," https://www.sacbee.com/news/equity-lab/article258899983.html#storylink=cpy.

2. *People v Dueñas* (2019) 30 Cal. App. 5th 1157.

3. This statutory change was enacted through the 2022–23 budget (i.e., trailer bill) and includes a total of $67 million for trial courts to backfill the loss for lower fees and $10 million for waived civil fines. Additionally, the budget enabled a larger pool of people to be eligible for automatic court fee waivers if their income was 200 percent of the federal poverty level (up from 125 percent); an additional $18 million was appropriated for trial courts to fill a potential budget hole created by this new rule.

4. Based on data from California reporting agencies (law enforcement agencies such as California Highway Patrol, as required by law to report data annually), during calendar year 2020, a higher percentage of Black motorists were stopped for reasonable suspicion than any other racial group (p. 7), and Black and Hispanic individuals were more likely to have force used against them compared to Whites (Asians experienced lower rates; see p. 9). When officers stopped motorists and followed with a search, all persons of color had higher search rates "despite having lower rates of discovering contraband compared to individuals perceived as White" (p. 9). See "Annual Report 2022," Racial Identity Profiling Advisory Board, State of California, n.d., https://oag.ca.gov/system/files/media/ripa-board-report-2022.pdf; "Civil Assessments: The Hidden Court Fee that Penalizes Poverty," Lawyers' Committee for Civil Rights of the San Francisco Bay Area, Press Release, March 2, 2022, https://lccrsf.org/pressroom_posts/civil-assessments-the-hidden-court-fee-that-penalizes-poverty/.

5. Tani Cantil-Sakaouye, "Keynote Speech of California Supreme Court Justice Tani Cantil-Sakaouye – Law Day 2022," California State University Monterey Bay, April 29, 2022, Video, https://youtu.be/TEfi1FeBRUU, 4:57–5:40.

6. "2022 Court Statistics Report, Statewide Caseload Trends, 2011–12 through 2020–21," Judicial Council of California, 2022, https://www.courts.ca.gov/documents/2022-Court-Statistics-Report.pdf.

7. According to the 2022 Court Statistics report, in Fiscal Year (FY) 2012, each judicial position was assigned an average of 4,233 cases. In 2021, the average number was 2,227.

8. Mac Taylor, *California's Criminal Justice System: A Primer* (Sacramento: California Legislative Analyst's Office, January 2013), http://www.lao.ca.gov/reports/2013/crim/criminal-justice-primer/criminal-justice-primer-011713.pdf. This is the most recent statewide report.

9. "2022 Court Statistics Report." Includes unlimited, limited, and small claims cases.

10. Enacted throught the 2022–23 budget. Trial and felony sentencing must occur in person, and witnesses for felony trials

must appear in court. Attorneys may also appear remotely when appropriate.

11. SB 1338, the Community Assistance, Recovery, and Empowerment (CARE) Act, goes into effect in one cohort of counties on October 1, 2023, with the second cohort to follow by December 1, 2024. Counties will implement the Department of Health Care Service's plans.

12. Proposition 66 passed by a tiny margin (51.1 percent to 48.9 percent) in November 2016. In *Briggs v. Brown*, S238309, decided August 24, 2017 by a 5–2 margin, the California Supreme Court ruled that the 5-year limit on death penalty cases (i.e., that all cases should be resolved within 5 years) included in the measure was unconstitutional, in that the courts could not be given arbitrary time limits on their work.

13. Newsom signed the executive order on March 13, 2019, effectively sparing (then-) 737 convicted criminals from death, a penalty that Newsom attributed to a system that he said "has been, by all measures, a failure." Citing statistics that show it discriminates against "defendants who are mentally ill, black and brown, or can't afford expensive legal representation," he also noted that convicted people have been exonerated. "Governor Gavin Newsom Orders a Halt to the Death Penalty," Office of the Governor, State of California, March 13, 2019. The number of convicted criminals declined to 672 as of June 9, 2022, in part because of prisoners dying from "natural causes," including COVID-19. "Summary of In-Custody Offender Data Points for Month-end June 2022," Offender Data Points Dashboard, California Department of Corrections and Rehabilitation, accessed July 6, 2022, https://public.tableau.com/app/profile/cdcr.or/viz/OffenderDataPoints/SummaryInCustodyandParole. Assembly Bill 2512, which outlaws the sentencing of anyone who meets the scientific standard for intellectual disability, was passed almost unanimously by both legislative chambers (only one vote short of unanimity).

14. "California Chief Justice Delivers State of the Judiciary Address," California Courts Newsroom, March 10, 2020, https://newsroom.courts.ca.gov/news/california-chief-justice-delivers-state-of-the-judiciary-address.

15. "About California Governor George Deukmejian," National Governors Association, accessed October 30, 2020, https://www.nga.org/governor/george-deukmejian/.

16. By 2021, among 169 appointees: 18.3 percent Asian, 17.8 percent Black, 20.1 percent Hispanic, 1.8 percent Native Hawaiian or Pacific Islander, 4.7 percent unknown, and 37.3 percent White. "Governor Newsom Releases 2021 Judicial Appointment Data," Office of the Governor, State of California, March 1, 2022, https://www.gov.ca.gov/2022/03/01/governor-newsom-releases-2021-judicial-appointment-data/.

17. Douglas Keith and Eric Velasco, "The Politics of Judicial Elections, 2019–20," Brennan Center for Justice at NYU School of Law, January 25, 2022, https://www.brennancenter.org/our-work/research-reports/politics-judicial-elections-2019-20.

18. This is the average for (FY) 2018–20. See "2022 Court Statistics Report," p. 100. The numbers are declining over time; in FY 2015 there were 9,472 trials, and in FY 2012 there were 12,532.

19. In FY 2019–20 (a relatively "normal" year, although this period partially covers the COVID-19 shutdown), the total number of persons who completed service was 4,206,100, and 91.7 percent of them completed their service in one day. A total of 94,084 persons were sworn in and served as a juror. "2019–20 Jury Data Report," Judicial Council of California, 2021, https://www.courts.ca.gov/documents/FY_1920_JDR_Executive_Summary.pdf.

20. According to data compiled by the author, in 2017, thirty-six states paid an average of $23 for the first day of service, plus mileage, and rates are higher for the second day. This figure is replicated on an independent webpage ("Jury Duty Laws by State," juryjuty101.com, accessed July

6, 2022). By comparison, the lowest pay is $5 per day in Mississippi and New Jersey ($6 in South Dakota); four states, including Arkansas, pay $50 (the highest).

21. "Three strikes" was revised through Prop 36 in 2012. Drug offense reclassification, parole expansion, and educational opportunities were made possible by Prop 57 in 2016. That same year, voters decriminalized recreational marijuana use with Prop 64.

22. The *actual* in-custody population was 97,179 and the parole count was 41,047 as of Midnight June 2022 (a point-in-time count) whereas the total institutional population for 2022 was *projected* to be 102,945 and slightly higher (114,968) for 2023, declining thereafter, and are based on prior year trends. See Division of Correctional Policy Research and Oversight, "Monthly Report of Population as of June 30, 2022," Office of Research, Department of Corrections and Rehabilitation (CDCR), State of California, July 1, 2022, and Division of Correctional Policy Research and Oversight, "Spring 2022 Population Projections," Office of Research, CDCR, State of California, May 2022, https://www.cdcr.ca.gov/research/wp-content/uploads/sites/174/2022/05/Spring-2022-Population-Projections.pdf, 3.

23. Mia Bird, Magnus Lofstrom, Brandon Martin, Steven Raphael, and Viet Nguyen, "The Impact of Proposition 47 on Crime and Recidivism," PPIC, June 2018, https://www.ppic.org/publication/the-impact-of-proposition-47-on-crime-and-recidivism/; Magnus Lofstrom, Heather Harris, and Brandon Martin, "California's Future: Criminal Justice," PPIC, January 2020, https://www.ppic.org/wp-content/uploads/californias-future-criminal-justice-january-2020.pdf.

24. All types of crime rates are comparable to those in the 1960s. Because they are low, any uptick will seem great by comparison. Organized retail theft, however, is a new development. See Magnus Lofstrom and Brandon Martin, "Fact Sheet: Crime Trends in California," PPIC, January 2022, https://www.ppic.org/publication/crime-trends-in-california/; Jody Sundt, Emily Salisbury, and Mark Harmon, "Is Downsizing Prisons Dangerous?" *Criminology and Public Policy*, March 9, 2016, https://doi.org/10.1111/1745-9133.12199.

25. The 2022–23 budget provides $110 million to address hate crimes. See also "Anti-Black, Gay, Asian Bias Fuel Hate Crime Surge," Associated Press, June 28, 2022, https://apnews.com/article/covid-health-crime-california-race-and-ethnicity-dfa510a5200e60f1b5f04e191b5414bc.

26. "California State Budget 2022–23: Criminal Justice," 114–15.

27. PPIC reports that 62 percent of adult respondents supported this choice, consistent with previous poll results (Mark Baldassare et al., "Californians and Their Government," PPIC, May 2011). In a March 2022 poll, respondents were asked about four areas of state spending and asked which should have the highest priority (rotated): K–12 public education, higher education, health and human services, and prisons and corrections. Among 1,672 adults (sampling error +/–4.1 percent), 7 percent selected prisons and corrections (Mark Baldassare et al., "Californians and Their Government," PPIC, May 2022).

28. In a January 2015 PPIC poll, 42 percent of adults and 42 percent of likely voters (incorrectly) named prisons and corrections as the largest area for spending in the state budget. See Mark Baldassare et al., "Statewide Survey: Californians and Their Government," PPIC, January 2015. Budget figure is derived from the 2022 Enacted Budget (Summary).

29. Caitlin O'Neil, "Effectively Managing State Prison Infrastructure," Legislative Analyst's Office, February 28, 2020, https://lao.ca.gov/Publications/Report/4186. Note that some of those repairs may be overestimated because the actual cost to partially replace aging materials might be well less than using the best available materials to replace larger areas of

disrepair, which was often assumed in the independent auditor's report (on which the LAO analysis is based).

30. Data provided by the Legislative Analyst's Office, July 2022. Actual per capita expenditures were $92,132 in 2020–21, compared to $51,889 in 2011–12.

31. As of June 30, 2023, counties will be responsible for all juveniles. Department of Finance, "California State Budget 2022–23: Criminal Justice," Enacted Budget Summary, State of California, https://www.ebudget.ca.gov/FullBudgetSummary.pdf, 118.

32. David Billingsley, "Analysis of AB 392 (by Shirley Weber, as amended March 27, 2019)," Assembly Committee on Public Safety, April 9, 2019; Deepak Premkumar et al., "Police Use of Force and Misconduct in California," PPIC, October 2021.

33. "Victims' Bill of Rights," Office of the Attorney General, State of California, 2020, https://oag.ca.gov/victimservices/content/bill_of_rights.

34. For example, see "Law Enforcement Training: What Works for Officers and Communities." Little Hoover Commission, Report #265, November 2021, http://lhc.ca.gov.

CHAPTER 7

1. "2017 Census of Governments: Table 1, Government Units by State," U.S. Census Bureau, 2017, https://www.census.gov/data/tables/2017/econ/gus/2017-governments.html.

2. A local measure to direct the county's board of supervisors to explore seceding from California to form a new state was placed on the November 2022 ballot, following Siskiyou County in northern California that voted "yes" on a similar measure in 2013. A few local mayors backed it, saying they were "fed up with the way they treat our local public safety" and the state's mandating of local changes; board chairman Kurt Hagman

noted that "It's about losing the ability to govern on a local level." Christian Martinez, "'Empire' State? San Bernardino County Developer Pushes Seceding from California," *Los Angeles Times*, July 28, 2022, https://www.latimes.com/california/story/2022-07-28/san-bernardino-county-developer-pushes-idea-of-seceding-from-california.

3. The phrase "cookie cutter" was suggested by Jeffrey Epp, City Manager of the City of Escondido, October 2020.

4. The city manager alone was making $800,000 a year in salary plus exorbitant benefits. The *Los Angeles Times* broke the story in 2010 (for which they won two Pulitzer Prizes). Archives of their investigative stories can be found on their website at http://www.latimes.com/local/bell.

5. "Government Compensation in California, California Cities 2021," State Controller's Office, State of California, http://publicpay.ca.gov/Reports/Cities/Cities.aspx. The posting includes reported information for 464 cities. The highest paid city manager worked for the City of Artesia (population 16,200) received wages totaling $650,167. Excluding the three highest paid city managers who were paid over $650,000 each, the average city manager's pay is closer to $218,000, plus $44,000 in health and retirement benefits.

6. These numbers are based on 2015 reports when the total was $1,826 per homeowner, and since then, San Diego has added many new Mello-Roos districts with generally higher fees. See Leonardo Castañeda, "Special Property Taxes Lack Robust Oversight, Accountability," *KPBS News*, June 20, 2017, https://inewsource.org/2017/06/20/mello-roos-tax-lacks-oversight/, and Ernest Dronenburg, Jr., "Active Mello-Roos Districts (CFD) FY 2021–22," Office of the Assessor/Recorder/County Clerk, County of San Diego, n.d., https://www.sandiegocounty.gov/content/dam/sdc/auditor/pdf/cfd.pdf.

7. Mac Taylor, "Common Claims about Prop 13," Legislative Analyst's Office,

September 19, 2016, http://www.lao.ca. gov/Publications/Report/3497#Introdu ction.

8. California State Treasurer's Office, http: //debtwatch.treasurer.ca.gov, accessed July 14, 2022. This figure only includes principal amounts sold through June 2022 and excludes interest payments and projected bond sales. Cities carried $284 billion in bond debt (total sold); counties carried $247 billion; K–14 school districts had sold a reported $324 billion in bonds.

9. Public workers in twelve other states are now similarly guarded. The Califor- nia Supreme Court left the "California Rule" rule intact in March 2019 and July 2020 when it decided that pensions are a right protected by the state constitu- tional contracts clause, but add-ons such as benefits may not be protected and local governments may have the right to renegotiate or cancel those benefits, or exclude certain types of pay (e.g., over- time) from pension payouts. The cases are *Cal Fire Local 2881 v. California Public Employees' Retirement System and Alam- eda County Deputy Sheriff's Association v. Alameda County Employees' Retirement Association.*

10. These statistics are for the 2020–21 school year (the most recent at this writ- ing), published by the California Depart- ment of Education on their data website. See "Fingertip Facts on Education in Cali- fornia— CalEdFacts," http://www.cde.ca. gov/ds/sd/cb/ceffingertipfacts.asp.

11. CalEdFacts (2020–21 school year). That term, 690,245 students were enrolled in 1,293 California public charter schools.

12. These amounts were proposed in the gov- ernor's January 2022 initial budget but are in line with previous levels. "K-12 Funding by Source," Legislative Analyst's Office January 2022, https://lao.ca.gov/Educatio n/EdBudget/Details/588.

13. Funding levels were supplied by the LAO in August 2022. These numbers are dif- ficult to compare to other composite mea- sures often used to rank states due to the types of items included. These figures are

intended to be "all-inclusive" of funding provided under Proposition 98, plus fed- eral, state, and local funds related to K–12 education in California. The prior year was anomalous because the state used more than $30 billion in federal Coronavirus relief funding: 2021–22 levels reached $24,656 per student, compared to $22,876 the year before, and $17,014 in 2019–20.

14. According to Bill Higgins at CalCOG, a COG might be formed to deal with only one or some combination functions, and there are at least five types (including those covered in the text). The two others are a *regional transportation planning authority* which must meet state requirements for managing traffic congestion, and a *transit agency* that operates buses or metros, such as BART. See Bill Higgins, "Regions 101," California Association of Councils of Government, August 29, 2020; Bill Hig- gins and Caia Pedroncelli, "Ring of Fiber Brings Affordable, High-Speed Broadband to LA's South Bay," CalCOG, November 2, 2020, https://calcog.org/ring-of-fiber-to-i mprove-connectivity-in-south-bay-la/.

15. "About ABAG" and "History," Association of Bay Area Governments, San Francisco, accessed July 16, 2022, https://abag.ca.g ov; "RHNA: Regional Housing Needs Allo- cation," ABAG, accessed July 16, 2022, htt ps://abag.ca.gov/our-work/housing/rhna -regional-housing-needs-allocation.

16. In 2022–23 total federal funds are an esti- mated $135.8 billion out of $422.267 bil- lion (all sources). See "Chart B, Historical Data, Budget Expenditures," Department of Finance, State of California, January 2022, https://dof.ca.gov/wp-content/uplo ads/budget/summary-schedules-charts/ January-2022/CHART-B.pdf.

17. This total includes funds directly given to the state for emergency response, testing, health care, and vaccinations; funds sent to families and individuals through the federal Child Tax Credit, Earned Income Tax Credit, partial tax exemptions on unemployment benefits, and expanded financial assistance for health care; and direct payments given to hospitals and medical providers, businesses, higher

education institutions, and college students, local housing authorities, airports, farmers, and local government. "COVID-19 Federal Stimulus," Department of Finance, State of California, accessed July 13, 2022, https://dof.ca.gov/budget/covid-19-information/covid-19-federal-stimulus/.

18. Local government agencies, including cities and counties, received 2020 Coronavirus Relief Act funds that were passed through the state, and also from the 2021 American Rescue Plan Act which provided funds directly. "COVID-19 Federal Stimulus," accessed July 13, 2022.

19. "BART Advocates for Emergency Funds in Response to COVID-19," Bay Area Rapid Transit, San Francisco, updated March 3, 2022, https://www.bart.gov/news/articles/2020/news20200317; "BART Facts 2022," BART, San Francisco, n.d., https://www.bart.gov/sites/default/files/docs/BARTFacts2022.pdf.

20. "How Much Money Does the Federal Government Spend in California?" Legislative Analyst's Office, January 18, 2017, http://lao.ca.gov/Publications/Report/3531/1.

21. "COVID-19 Federal Stimulus," Accessed July 13, 2022.

22. In March 2020, the EPA reversed itself and finalized new rules for California, rescinding the tailpipe emission and mileage waivers while defending its own ability to set (lower) national standards. Leading a coalition of twenty-four states plus D.C., California Attorney General Xavier Becerra sued the Donald Trump administration over these "attacks on state authority," accusing them of "flouting Congress' intent" under the Clean Air Act. Ultimately California resecured its regulatory ability when President Biden's administration reversed course. See Damien Newton, "California's Power to Regulate Tailpipe Emissions Will Be Restored," Streetsblog California, Open Plans, February 16, 2022, https://cal.streetsblog.org/2022/02/16/californias-power-to-regulate-tailpipe-emissions-will-be-restored/; "Protecting our Environment—Defending National Clean Car Standards," Office of the Attorney General, State of California, accessed June 27, 2020, https://oag.ca.gov/cleancars; "NHTSA and EPA Establish One National Program for Fuel Economy Regulation," National Highway Traffic Safety Administration, September 19, 2019, https://www.nhtsa.gov/sites/nhtsa.dot.gov/files/documents/safe_vehicles_rule_part1_09192019_v2.pdf.

23. A few smaller, more remotely located tribes have recently angled into the gaming business through this route, thus enabling them to erect casinos in higher trafficked areas. Voters rejected a proposed compact in 2014 that would have allowed the North Fork Rancheria of Mono Indians and Wiyot Tribe to build a casino on new land they acquired for that purpose in Madera County some thirty-eight miles from the North Fork reservation. Recent rule changes adopted by the federal government's Bureau of Indian Affairs make it more likely that casinos will crop up in urban areas such as Orange County or San Francisco as state tribes petition for federal recognition or additional lands are obtained.

24. "Overview of Gambling in California," Legislative Analyst's Office, February 26, 2019, https://lao.ca.gov/handouts/crimjust/2019/Gambling-Overview-022619.pdf.

25. Several tribal compacts were renegotiated in 2022 with new provisions, including enforcement of environmental and labor laws (e.g., anti-discrimination) and spousal and child support. "Ratified Tribal-State Gaming Compacts (New and Amended)," California Gambling Control Commission, State of California, http://www.cgcc.ca.gov/?pageID=compacts.

26. Author's calculations based on lobbying reports from the California secretary of state's campaign finance database, http://cal-access.sos.ca.gov. For a running tally of campaign contributions, see "Indian Gaming," OpenSecrets.org, https://www.opensecrets.org/industries/indus.php?ind=G6550.

27. The case is *Oklahoma v. Castro-Huerta*, 21-429. See Lawrence Hurley, "U.S. Supreme Court Expands State Power over Native American Tribes," *Reuters*, June 29, 2022; Matthew Fletcher, "In 5-4 Ruling, Court Dramatically Expands the Power of States to Prosecute Crimes on Reservations," SCOTUSblog, June 29, 2022, https://www.scotusblog.com/2022/06/in-5-4-ruling-court-dramatically-expands-the-power-of-states-to-prosecute-crimes-on-reservations/.

28. AB 923 was authored by Assemblyman Ramos. Elise Gyore, "Assembly Floor Analysis of AB 923," Assembly Rules Committee, State of California, August 22, 2022.

29. "Governor Gavin Newsom Issues Apology to Native Americans for State's Historical Wrongdoings, Establishes Truth and Healing Council," Office of the Governor, State of California, Press Release, June 18, 2019. See the Governor's Gallery for governors' references to the "war of extermination": Peter Burnett, "State of the State Address," January 6, 1851, and John McDougal, "State of the State Address," January 7, 1852, California State Library, "The Governor's Gallery," 2019, https://governors.library.ca.gov/. See also Theresa Gregor, "Decolonizing San Diego's History," *Journal of San Diego History* 65, no. 2 (Summer 2019), https://sandiegohistory.org/journal/2019/july/decolonizing-san-diegos-history-an-iipay-reflection-on-the-context-and-impact-of-1769/. For a general overview of the history of genocide, see Chris Clarke, "Untold History: The Survival of California's Indians," KCET, September 26, 2016, https://www.kcet.org/shows/tending-the-wild/untold-history-the-survival-of-californias-indians; Benjamin Madley, *An American Genocide* (New Haven, CT: Yale University Press, 2016).

CHAPTER 8

1. The surplus represents a moving target and can be estimated using various measures. If the fund balances in every special fund plus the general fund are summed and totaled before nondiscretionary (mandatory) spending items are included (such as payments to the Budget Stabilization Account), the top number of $98.5 billion could apply. Alternatively, the Legislative Analyst estimated that $54 billion in discretionary funds (i.e., surplus funds) were available. Also, the State Appropriations Limit (SAL) was made possible by voter-approved Proposition 4 in 1979.

2. Usually budget conference committees include three members of the Assembly and three from the Senate, including budget committee chairs and vice chairs. In some years the rules have been suspended to include five members from each chamber. In 2020 due to COVID-19 restrictions on meeting in person and the chambers' ability to align their preferences, no conference committees were convened.

3. Betty Yee, "Schedule of General Fund Cash Receipts and Disbursements, July 2022," State Controller's Office, State of California, August 10, 2022, A-1, https://www.sco.ca.gov/Files-ARD/CASH/July2022StatementofGeneralFundCashReceiptsandDisbursements.pdf.

4. In the enacted budget for 2022–23, the total amount projected from taxes and fees was $222.7 billion, plus another $66 billion in special funds (including excise taxes and motor vehicle fees), bringing the total revenues to $288.697 billion. See the full budget summary at https://www.ebudget.ca.gov/2022-23/pdf/Enacted/BudgetSummary/SummaryCharts.pdf. Charts are subject to updates.

5. For tax rates (2021 is the most recent year at this writing), see "2021 Tax Rate Schedules," Franchise Tax Board, State of California, revised July 2022, https://www.ftb.ca.gov/forms/2021/2021-540-bookl

et.html#2021-California-Tax-Rate-Sche
dules.

6.   "Table B-9.1, Personal Income Tax: Statistics for Resident Tax Returns, High Income
Returns, Tax Year 2019," in *PIT 2020 Annual
Report*, Franchise Tax Board, State of California, updated January 3, 2022, https://da
ta.ftb.ca.gov/California-Personal-Income
-Tax/PIT-Annual-Report-2020/s2q7-rtsh.

7.   "Table B-3, Personal Income Tax Statistics
for Resident Tax Returns, Tax Year 2019,"
2020 PIT Annual Report, 2022.

8.   Calculations for California are based on
"California City & County Sales & Use Tax
Rates, Current Tax Rates, Tax Rates Effective April 1, 2022," Department of Tax and
Fee Administration, State of California, htt
ps://www.cdtfa.ca.gov/taxes-and-fees/sa
les-use-tax-rates.htm.

9.   The state expected to received
$143,613,500,000 from the federal gov-
ernment in 2022–23. "Chart B, Historical
Data, Budget Expenditures," Department
of Finance, State of California, July 2022, h
ttps://dof.ca.gov/wp-content/uploads/bu
dget/summary-schedules-charts/CHAR
T-B.pdf.

10. Numbers provided by the Legislative Analyst's Office, July 2022 (figures are estimates, subject to change over the fiscal
year). See also "Budget Summary, K–12
Education 2022–23," California Office of
the Governor, https://www.ebudget.ca.go
v/2022-23/pdf/Enacted/BudgetSummary
/K-12Education.pdf. Following historically
low per-pupil spending amounts, California's ranking on the U.S. Census Bureau's
national list climbed to nineteenth for
K–12 spending in 2019, above the national
average for the first time in decades, with
the expectation of jumping further ahead
in 2021 and after (those rankings have not
been released at this writing).

11. "Entire Education Budget," Department of
Finance, accessed August 10, 2022, https
://www.ebudget.ca.gov/2022-23/pdf/En
acted/GovernorsBudget/6000.pdf; "California Community Colleges Funding by
Source," Legislative Analyst's Office, State

of California, July 2022, https://lao.ca.gov
/Education/EdBudget/Details/627.

12. Senate Rules Committee, Floor Analysis
of SB-1 (April 5, 2017). Cost estimates
vary; legislative analyses are based on
CalTrans projections.

13. The total amount varies with market
conditions, such as the rates at which different bonds were (and are) sold or are
renegotiated.

14. "Introduction: Climate Change," DOF,
State of California, https://www.ebudget.c
a.gov/FullBudgetSummary.pdf, 57.

15. Shane Goldmacher and Anthony York,
"Governor Vetoes 'Unbalanced' State Budget," *Los Angeles Times*, June 17, 2011, http
://articles.latimes.com/2011/jun/17/local
/la-me-0617-state-budget-20110617.

16. Gavin Newsom, "California Five-Year
Infrastructure Plan," Office of the Governor, State of California, 2022–23, https://w
ww.ebudget.ca.gov/2022-Infrastructure
-Plan.pdf.

17. "General Obligation and Revenue Bonds,
Summary of Debt Service Requirements,"
Office of the Treasurer, State of California,
July 1, 2022, https://www.buycaliforniabo
nds.com/state-of-california-ca/documen
ts/view-file/i27?mediaId=639222.

18. In the 2019 and 2020 debt reports, Treasurer Fiona Ma noted that through refi-
nancing she saved taxpayers $4 billion in
total over the life of those bonds; in 2021,
restructuring saved approximately $804
billion in the long run. "2021 Debt Affordability Report," Office of the State Treasurer, State of California, October 2021, ht
tps://www.treasurer.ca.gov/publications/
dar/2021.pdf, 5.

19. Under Prop 4, annually the state must set
aside funds for unanticipated economic
hardships or emergency spending. As of
2022–23, the Rainy Day Fund (Budget Stabilization Account) had reached its constitutional maximum, which is 10 percent
of General Fund revenues. See "Introduction," ebudget, State of California, https://
www.ebudget.ca.gov/FullBudgetSumma
ry.pdf, 9.

20. "Table B-3, Personal Income Tax Statistics for Resident Tax Returns, Tax Year 2019," in *2020 PIT Annual Report*, 2022, https://data.ftb.ca.gov/stories/s/Personal-Income-Tax/2it8-edzu/#annual-report.

21. The only exception involves the risky move of including one or more fee hikes in the budget itself, which requires just a simple majority vote for approval, such as when the majority Democrats raised vehicle license fees an additional $12 through the 2011–12 budget without the approval of Republicans.

22. Erica York and Jared Walczak, "State and Local Tax Burdens, Calendar Year 2022," Tax Foundation, April 7, 2022, https://taxfoundation.org/tax-burden-by-state-2022/. Note that methodology will yield different rankings. For a different calculation and chart that displays total tax as a share of family income (on p. 40), see Meg Wiehe, Aidan Davis, Carl Davis, Matt Gardner, Lisa Christensen Gee, and Dylan Grundman, "Who Pays? A Distributional Analysis of the Tax Systems in All 50 States," 6th ed., Institute on Taxation and Economic Policy, 2018, https://itep.org/wp-content/uploads/whopays-ITEP-2018.pdf.

23. It should be noted that such estimates are typically based on lagged data; analyses of current-year data are almost impossible to obtain. Kitson (2022) reports that Kayla Kitson, "California's Tax and Revenue System Isn't Fair for All," California Budget and Policy Center, March 2022, https://calbudgetcenter.org/resources/californias-tax-revenue-system-isnt-fair-for-all/.

24. A reported 62 percent of all adults feel this way, according to the Public Policy Institute of California (PPIC); 35 percent of adults say they pay "much more" and 27 percent say "somewhat more" than they feel they should; 32 percent say it's about the right amount. These perceptions vary by partisanship: 52 percent of Democrats say they pay somewhat or much more, compared to 82 percent of Republicans. Survey conducted March 6–17, 2022 with 1,672 adults, sampling error +/–4.1 percent. Mark Baldassare et al., "Californians and Their Government," PPIC, March 2022, https://www.ppic.org/publication/ppic-statewide-survey-californians-and-their-government-march-2022/.

25. Calculations based on "California City & County Sales & Use Tax Rates, Current Tax Rates, Tax Rates Effective April 1, 2022." All municipalities that charge a 10 percent or higher sales tax rate are located in Los Angeles or Alameda County (the only place where consumers pay 10.75 percent). For a nationwide comparison, see Janelle Fritts, "State and Local Sales Tax Rates, 2022," Tax Foundation, February 3, 2022, https://taxfoundation.org/2022-sales-taxes/.

26. At least seven other states raised fuel taxes in summer 2022. As of July 2021 (before taxes were raised in California and potentially elsewhere to current rates), the American Petroleum Institute pegged California's total state taxes on motor vehicle fuel at 68.15 cents per gallon, compared to 59.6 cents in Illinois, 58.7 cents in Pennsylvania, and 51.69 cents in Hawaii; the lowest was Alaska at 15.13 cents and the U.S. average was 38.69 cents per gallon. "Gasoline Taxes," American Petroleum Institute, January 1, 2022, https://www.api.org/-/media/Files/Statistics/State-Motor-Fuel-Notes-Summary-january-2022.pdf?la=en&hash=F649022BA19339184C9ED8DAEFD26ABE8DEE2377.

27. "Table B-3, Personal Income Tax Statistics for Resident Tax Returns, Tax Year 2019," 2022.

28. "Range of State Corporate Income Tax Rates," Federation of Tax Administrators, as of January 1, 2022, https://www.taxadmin.org/current-tax-rates.

29. According to the Institute on Taxation and Economic Policy, California ranks last on the regressive tax scale (fifty-first, including D.C.). Other progressive tax code features include a requirement of the use of combined reporting for the corporate income tax, and provisions for a refundable Earned Income Tax Credit (EITC). Regressive measures within the state's code include failing to provide a

property tax "circuit breaker" credit for low-income, nonelderly taxpayers, and a lack of state inheritance or estate taxes. See Wiehe et al., "Who Pays?"

30. Sarah Bohn and Tess Thorman, "Income Inequality in California," PPIC, January 2020, https://www.ppic.org/publication/income-inequality-in-california/.

31. Among all adults (1,695 adults interviewed; sampling error is +/–3.9 percent), 33 percent chose the "increase services" option over: paying down debt and building up the reserve (13 percent); one-time spending for transportation, water, infrastructure (22 percent); refunding some of the money (27 percent); "other" was 2 percent and don't know was 3 percent (volunteered). Among Republicans, 16 percent would increase funding and 36 percent would refund money, compared to 42 percent of Democrats who would increase funding and 21 percent who would refund. Mark Baldassare et al., "Californians and Their Government," PPIC, May 2022, https://www.ppic.org/publication/ppic-statewide-survey-californians-and-their-government-may-2022/. Survey included 1,702 adults and was conducted May 12–22, 2022 with a sampling error of +/–3.9.

32. When asked which of four areas should have the highest priority when it comes to state spending, only 6 percent of adults selected "prisons and corrections"; see "Californians and Their Government," March 2022. In response to a January 2014 survey by PPIC, 72 percent of California adults opposed increasing spending on "prisons and corrections" (23 percent favored, 5 percent didn't know in response to the question, "Next, please tell me if you favor or oppose increasing state spending in the following areas. [rotate questions 20–23] How about increasing state spending on prisons and corrections?"). Survey samples generally include a minimum of 1,700 adults, yielding results that are reliable within +/–3.3 percentage points. See Mark Baldassare, Dean Bonner, Sonja Petek, and Jui Shrestha, "Californians and Their Government," PPIC, January 2014.

CHAPTER 9

1. Mark Baldassare et al., "Californians and Their Government," Public Policy Institute of California (PPIC), February 2020, https://www.ppic.org/wp-content/uploads/ppic-statewide-survey-californians-and-their-government-february-2020.pdf. The survey included 1,702 California adult residents, took place from February 7 to 17, 2020, and had a sampling error of +/–3.4 percent.

2. The PPIC reports that about two out of three Republicans and independents (65 percent each) and 47 percent of Democrats (55 percent of all respondents) say the decisions made through the citizens' initiative process are probably better than those made by the governor and legislature (Mark Baldassare, "Most California Voters Say 'We Know Best,'" PPIC, Blog Post, May 25, 2022, https://www.ppic.org/blog/most-california-voters-say-we-know-best/); 77 percent of adults and 78 percent of likely voters prefer that voters make some decisions about spending and taxes at the ballot box, and only one in five (19 percent of all adults, 18 percent of likely voters) prefer that the governor and legislature make all those decisions. See "California Statewide Survey," PPIC, January 2019, https://www.ppic.org/wp-content/uploads/ppic-statewide-survey-californians-and-their-government-january-2019.pdf. A 2010 PPIC survey found that 44 percent have little trust in their fellow initiative voters. See "Californians and Their Government," PPIC, December 2010, http://www.ppic.org/content/pubs/survey/S_1210MBS.pdf.

3. Elmer Eric Schattschneider, *Party Government: American Government in Action* (New York: Holt, Rinehart & Winston, 1942), 1.

4. Eli J. Finkel et al., "Political Sectarianism in America," *Science* 370, no. 6516 (October 30, 2020).

5. Megan Cassidy, "Chesa Boudin Recall: What to Know About S.F.'s June 7 Election," *San Francisco Chronicle*, May 5, 2022,

https://www.sfchronicle.com/politics/article/chesa-boudin-recall-17151778.php; "June 7, 2022 Election Results—Summary," Department of Elections, San Francisco, accessed July 21, 2022, https://sfelections.sfgov.org/june-7-2022-election-results-summary.

6. Since 2014, a majority have responded affirmatively to the question, "In your view, do the Republican and Democratic Parties do an adequate job representing the American people, or do they do such a poor job that a third major party is needed?" Results for "third party is needed" were: 57 percent (October 2020). 54 percent (November 2019), 55 percent (October 2018), 60 percent (November 2017), and 58 percent (October 2016). See "Survey Tools: California Statewide Survey," PPIC, accessed June 15, 2020, https://www.ppic.org/survey/survey-tools/. Note that on average, over 1,700 adults were surveyed with an average sampling error of +/−3.4 percent.

7. Mark Baldassare et al., "Just the Facts: California Voter and Party Profiles," PPIC, August 2022; Mark Baldassare et al., "Just the Facts: California's Independent Voters," PPIC, August 2018, https://www.ppic.org/publication/californias-independent-voters/.

8. Baldassare et al., "Californians and Their Government."

9. Rounded figures. As of June 7, 2022, out of 21,941,212 total registered voters, Democrats were 46.8 percent, Republicans 23.9 percent, Other parties 6.59 percent, and 22.7 percent No Party Preference. "Historical Voter Registration and Participation in Statewide Primary Elections 1914–2022," "Primary Election Statement of the Vote," June 7, 2022, Secretary of State, State of California, n.d., https://www.sos.ca.gov/elections/prior-elections/statewide-election-results/primary-election-june-7-2022/statement-vote.

10. Baldassare et al., "California Voter and Party Profiles," August 2022; Mark Baldassare et al., "California's Likely Voters"

and "Voter and Party Profiles," PPIC, September 2021; Baldassare et al., "California's Independent Voters," August 2018.

11. Baldassare et al., "Voter and Party Profiles"; "Presidential Results," *CNN*, http://www.cnn.com/election/results/states/california; "Exit Poll for Governor Race," *CBS News*, June 19, 2020, http://www.cbsnews.com/elections/2014/governor/california/exit. Exit polls with reliable figures from the 2018 gubernatorial race are limited; NBC News exit polls reported 53 percent of independent women, and 54 percent of independent men voted for Newsom; see "California Results," *NBC News*, updated November 13, 2018, https://www.nbcnews.com/politics/2018-election/midterms/ca.

12. Baldassare et al., "California Voter and Party Profiles," August 2022; Baldassare et al., "California's Independent Voters," September 2021.

13. "Fifteen-day Report of Registration," Secretary of State, State of California, May 23, 2022. Registered No Party Preference has been dipping for several years. In February 2020, the highest rates were above 30 percent in Santa Clara (30.99 percent); San Francisco was a close second (28.88 percent). In 2022, the highest rate was Santa Clara (28 percent) and San Francisco (25.4 percent).

14. The total is 47 percent White. Baldassare et al., "California Voter and Party Profiles," August 2022.

15. Baldassare et al., "California Voter and Party Profiles," August 2022.

16. Baldassare et al., "California Voter and Party Profiles," August 2022.

17. Mark Baldassare et al., "California Voter and Party Profiles," August 2019, https://www.ppic.org/publication/california-voter-and-party-profiles/.

18. Baldassare et al., "California Statewide Survey," March 2022.

19. Baldassare et al., "California Voter and Party Profiles," September 2021;

"California Statewide Survey" (January 2021; the number of respondents saying that immigrants were a benefit was closer to 31 percent in April 2019, consistent with responses in September 2019, October 2018, and May 2017); 64 percent of Republicans and 18 percent of Democrats said government "goes too far" in restricting gun rights in 2017.

20. Baldassare et al., "Californians and Their Government," May 2017 and January 2017. On abortion, 60 percent of Republicans favor restrictions, whereas 87 percent of Democrats say the government should not interfere with a woman's right to access abortion.

21. "California Statewide Survey," PPIC, March 2022, November 2021, May 2020, and November 2019 for health care questions; April 2022 for *Roe v. Wade* question (87 percent opposed overturning it); May 2021 for gun rights.

22. Baldassare et al., "California's Independent Voters"; "California Voter and Party Profiles"; "California Statewide Survey," October 2018 for government responsibility question and November 2021 for government health insurance option question.

23. "California Statewide Survey," April 2022 for *Roe v. Wade* question; Mark Baldassare et al., "Californians and the Environment," PPIC, July 2021.

24. See Seth E. Masket, *No Middle Ground: How Informal Party Organizations Control Nominations and Polarize Legislatures* (Ann Arbor: University of Michigan Press, 2009).

25. A precedent was set for high numbers of voluntary retirements in 2012 when six Democrats, nine Republicans, and one independent decided not to run for reelection. In the end, 39 first-time legislators were elected, two seats switched parties, and two Assembly incumbents were defeated. In 2022, many of the 26 legislators from both houses ran for Congress and county boards of supervisors. See Ben Christopher, "What's Behind the 'Great Resignation' of California lawmakers?"

CalMatters, January 10, 2022, updated March 12, 2022, https://calmatters.org/politics/2022/01/california-legislature-great-resignation/.

26. Eric McGhee analyzed the effects of reforms on the 2022 primaries in "California's Election Reforms at the Dawn of a New Decade," PPIC, July 18, 2022, https://www.ppic.org/blog/californias-election-reforms-at-the-dawn-of-a-new-decade/. The 2020 count of intraparty match-ups was 23, excluding Assembly District 42 in which Chad Mayes, the incumbent and former Republican Assembly minority leader, ran with a "No Party Preference" label. Two Republican Assembly members lost their primaries in March 2020, bringing the total to ten Assembly, six Senate, and four U.S. House open general races. The incumbent was expected to cruise to victory in most, and only five among the nineteen open seats for the U.S. House or state legislature were competitive, intraparty contests.

27. Thad Kousser, Justin Phillips, and Boris Shor, "Reform and Representation: A New Method Applied to Recent Electoral Changes," *Political Science Research and Methods* 6, no. 4 (2018): 809–27.

28. McGhee, "California's Election Reforms at the Dawn of a New Decade," 2022.

29. Steven Sparks, "Quality Challenger Emergence under the Top-Two Primary: Comparing One-Party and Two-Party Election Contests," *Electoral Studies* 65 (June 2020), https://doi.org/10.1016/j.electstud.2020.102136.

30. Finkel et al., "Political Sectarianism in America," 2020. Several pieces of scholarship are devoted to analyzing the outcomes of these reforms, including: McGhee, "California's Election Reforms at the Dawn of a New Decade," 2022; Douglas Ahler, Jack Citrin, and Gabriel Lenz, "Do Open Primaries Improve Representation?" *Legislative Studies Quarterly* 41, no. 2 (2016): 237–68; see the special journal devoted to research on the topic, beginning with Betsy Sinclair, "The California Top-Two Primary," *California Journal of*

Politics and Policy 7, no. 1 (2015), http://esc holarship.org/uc/item/4qk24589; Masket, *No Middle Ground*; Seth Masket, "Polarization Interrupted? California's Experiment with the Top-Two Primary," in *Governing California: Politics, Government, and Public Policy in the Golden State*, 3rd ed., ed. Ethan Rarick (Berkeley, CA: Berkeley Public Policy Press, 2013); Eric McGhee, "The Top-Two System and Election 2016," PPIC, November 10, 2016, http://www.ppic.org /blog/the-top-two-system-and-election -2016.

31. In eleven (one Senate and ten Assembly special primary and general elections) held between March 2, 2021 and April 5, 2022, turnout was 19.15 percent overall. In *all* special elections that were not consolidated with a statewide election from 2011 (after the reform was adopted) until April 2022, the total was 17 percent, the same percentage (16.9) for elections held before the COVID-19 shutdown and prior to all-mail elections.

32. The total price tag included $174,059,031.11 in county costs (personnel, renting space for vote centers, postage, ballot printing) and $26,182,649.08 in Secretary of State costs (for printing and mailing voter information guides, providing hotline support, security, voter education, and communications outreach), about $43 million lower than initially estimated. Shirley Weber, Secretary of State, Letter to the Legislature Regarding Recall Election Costs, February 1, 2022, https://e lections.cdn.sos.ca.gov/statewide-electio ns/2021-recall/report-to-legislature.pdf.

33. "Los Angeles County VSAP," Office of the Secretary of State, State of California, accessed July 1, 2020, https://www.sos.ca .gov/elections/ovsta/voting-technology-v endors/los-angeles-county-vsap/.

34. Daniel Thompson et al., "The Neutral Partisan Effects of Vote-by-Mail: Evidence from County-Level Roll-Outs," Stanford Institute for Economic Policy Research, April 2020, Working Paper 20-015. Using a differences-in-differences research design, the authors analyzed county-level data from California, Utah, and Washington, 1996–2018.

35. Eric McGhee, Jennifer Paluch, and Mindy Romero, "Equity in Voter Turnout after Pandemic Election Policy Changes," PPIC, March 2022, https://www.ppic.org/public ation/equity-in-voter-turnout-after-pand emic-election-policy-changes/.

36. "New Report of California Voter Registration: Highest Percentage of Eligible Voters Registered in 67 Years (AP19:087)," Office of the Secretary of State, State of California, November 6, 2019, https://www.sos. ca.gov/administration/news-releases-a nd-advisories/2019-news-releases-and -advisories/new-report-california-voter -registration-highest-percentage-eligibl e-voters-registered-67-years/. However, note that this bump has occurred during the 2020 presidential election year, and it is not clear whether these higher numbers are due to election excitement or are sustainable. This is one conclusion reached by a recent study of the motor voter law: Eric McGhee, Radhika Mehlotra, and Mindy Romero, "Implementing Automated Voter Registration in California," PPIC, March 2020.

37. Quoted in Lou Cannon, *Ronnie and Jesse: A Political Odyssey* (New York: Doubleday, 1969), 99.

38. Author's calculations for 2020 general election winners' expenditures based on data gathered from Cal-Access. In 2020, Senate candidates won after spending $1,312,261 on average, with a low of $221,709 by (safe) Republican Brian Dahle, and a high of $4,121,735 by Democrat Josh Newman. Among all winning Assembly members, the average expenditure was $870,727. Republican Randy Voepel (in a safe seat) spent as "little" as $174,214, compared to Democrat Cottie Petrie-Norris's $3,380,805, the biggest spender. Twenty-three Assembly races ranged between $1 million and $3.3 million. Costs have not increased much over the past decade; for 2010 races, the winning Senate candidates spent over $1 million, and Assembly races cost an average of $750,000.

39. Figures reported in Cal-Access, accessed August 19, 2022.

40. Dave Jones served as state Insurance Commissioner from 2010 to 2019 and Assembly member between 2004 and 2010. As of this writing, only campaign finance reports through June 30, 2022 was were available on Cal-Access (general election figures forthcoming). Jones expended $980,756 while Ashby spent $794,669 (figures rounded in the text).

CHAPTER 10

1. Close tracking of protests published by CountLove.org and the *New York Times* point to historically unprecedented numbers of protests and protesters after Donald Trump became U.S. president. From January 20, 2017 through January 31, 2021, CountLove had documented upward of 2,994,366 attendees at 2,967 different protests "for a kinder world" in California, accessed July 25, 2022. See also: Larry Buchanan, Quoctrung Bui, and Jugal Patel, "Black Lives Matter May Be the Largest Movement in U.S. History," *New York Times*, July 3, 2020, https://www.nytimes.com/interactive/2020/07/03/us/george-floyd-protests-crowd-size.html.

2. John Dobard et al., "Unequal Voices: Who Speaks for California? Part II," American Majority Project Research Institute, University of California Riverside, February 2017.

3. Raymond E. Wolfinger and Steven J. Rosenstone, *Who Votes?* (New Haven, CT: Yale University Press, 1980).

4. California Statewide Surveys, 2020 aggregate file, Public Policy Institute of California (PPIC), January, February, April, and May, 2020.

5. "California's 2020 Primary Election: Turnout Analysis," California Civic Engagement Project, June 2020, https://cid.usc.edu/fact-sheets; Mark Baldassare et al., "California's Exclusive Electorate: A New Look at Who Votes and Why it Matters," PPIC, September 2019, https://www.ppic.org/publication/californias-exclusive-electorate-a-new-look-at-who-votes-and-why-it-matters/; Dobard et al., "Unequal Voices."

6. Taylor Carlson, Lisa García Bedolla, and Marisa Abrejano, "Political Discussion Networks and Political Engagement Amongst Voters of Color," *Political Research Quarterly* 73, no. 1 (2019); Dobard et al., "Unequal Voices," 27.

7. Baldassare et al., "California's Exclusive Electorate"; Dobard et al., "Unequal Voices."

8. Dobard et al., "Unequal Voices," 3.

9. Kristin Lewis, "A Portrait of California, 2021–2022," Measure of America (New York: Social Science Research Council, 2021). As described in the first version of the report, "A Portrait of California brings together data, innovative analysis, and the American HD Index methodology to enable 'apples-to-apples' comparisons of California's counties, major cities, 265 Census Bureau–defined areas, women and men, and racial and ethnic groups. It provides a gauge of how different groups of Californians are doing in comparison to one another and a benchmark for tracking progress over time" (Kristin Lewis and Sarah Burd-Sharps, "A Portrait of California, 2014–15," Measure of America (New York: Social Science Research Council, 2014), 7).

10. Whereas the figures in these synopses are derived from the original report, this updated figure is based on the median home's selling price in July 2022, according to Zillow, https://www.zillow.com/palo-alto-ca/home-values/.

11. Lewis and Burd-Sharps, "A Portrait of California," 66.

12. In a bit of good news, by Lewis's measures (Lewis, "A Portrait of California 2021–22"), today none of the 265 examined neighborhood clusters fall into the "disenfranchised" category partly because the fortunes of all Californians have risen over the years. However, the condition of being "disenfranchised" still applies to

individuals who experience deprivation regularly. In 2014–15, the largest majority of the 1,195,623 people in neighborhood clusters examined were Latinx (71 percent), 13.5 percent were White, 8.6 percent were Black, and 5 percent were Asian. Based on the most recent U.S. Census figures, if counted as members of California's 8,057 census tracts, then 618 tracts contain 2,910,462 individuals who score 3.0 or below on the Measure of America's 10-point human development index scale. Because this category is based on a different measure than the others, the total population is not presented as a percentage of the whole.

13. Lewis, 72.

14. Among voters, 71 percent rely on television, 58 percent on internet news, and 30 percent on radio. "California Voter Consumption of Media on Government and Politics," Fairbank, Maslin, Maullin, Metz, and Associates (FM3), and Mercury Public Affairs, August 2013, https://www.ca-ilg.o rg/sites/main/files/file-attachments/cam ediaconsumptionsurvey_fullreport.pdf.

15. "California Voter Consumption of Media on Government and Politics," 4; Michael Barthel and Amy Mitchell, "Views of the Watchdog Role of the Media" (infographic), May 9, 2017, http://www.jou rnalism.org/2017/05/10/americans - attitudes-about-the-news-media- deeply-divided-along-partisan-lines/ pj_2017-05-10_media-attitudes_a-06/.

16. Mason Walker and Katerina Eva Matsa, "News Consumption Across Social Media in 2021," Pew Research Center, September 20, 2021.

17. "California Voter Consumption of Media on Government and Politics," 3.

18. In 2022, a proposed bill to shore up small ethnic news operations would turn many into nonprofits dependent on government funding and oversight, but that model would prohibit them from endorsing candidates. See "SB 911 Would Drive a Stake in the Heart of California's Ethnic Media," Ethnic Media Services, July 14, 2022.

Sources for ethnic media statistics: "California Ethnic and Community Media Directory," Ethnic Media Services, Spring 2020; Sherry S. Yu and Matthew D. Matsaganis, *Ethnic Media in the Digital Age* (New York: Routledge, 2019).

19. Marisa Abrajano and Lisa García Bedolla, "Latino Political Participation 25 Years After the Passage of Proposition 187: Opportunities and Continuing Challenges," *UC Davis Law Review* 55 (2020): 1831; Adrian Pantoja, Cecelia Menjívar, and Lisa Magaña, "The Spring Marches of 2006," *American Behavioral Scientist* 52, no. 5 (2008): 499–506.

20. Deen Freelon, Charleton McIlwain, and Meredith D. Clark, "Beyond the Hashtag: #Ferguson, #Blacklivesmatter, and the Online Struggle for Offline Justice," Center for Media and Social Impact, February 2016.

21. "Statistics," CountLove.org, accessed July 25, 2022, https://countlove.org/statistics. html.

22. Crowd Counting Consortium, accessed August 1, 2022, https://sites.google.com/v iew/crowdcountingconsortium/home?au thuser=0.

23. Research based on the 2016 American National Election Study finds no significant effect of race with respect to this activity. See Kyle Endres and Costas Panagopoulos, "Boycotts, Buycotts, and Political Consumerism in America," *Research and Politics* (October–December 2017): 1–9.

24. Dobard et al., "Unequal Voices"; James Prieger and Kelly Faltis, "Non-Electoral Civic Engagement in California," *California Journal of Politics and Policy* 5, no. 4 (2013): 671–710 (Note that their data were collected in 2009.). See also Luis Fraga and Ann Frost, "Democratic Institutions, Public Engagement, and Latinos in American Public Schools," in *Public Engagement for Public Education*, eds. Marion Orr and John Rogers (Palo Alto, CA: Stanford University Press, 2010), 117–38.

25. Mark Baldassare et al., "California's Exclusive Electorate," PPIC, September 2019.

26. Eric McGhee, Jennifer Paluch, and Mindy Romero, "Equity in Voter Turnout after Pandemic Policy Changes," PPIC, March 2022, https://www.ppic.org/publication/equity-in-voter-turnout-after-pandemic-election-policy-changes/.

27. Mark Baldassare et al., "Race and Voting in California," PPIC, September 2020; California's 2020 Primary Election: Turnout Analysis"; Mindy Romero et al., "The Experience of Black Voters in California: 2020 Election and Beyond" (Los Angeles, CA: Center for Inclusive Democracy, June 2021).

28. "2022 Primary Ballot Tracker, State of California (May 9, 2022–June 13, 2022)," Political Data Inc., accessed July 30, 2022, https://politicaldata.com/2022-primary-ballots-returned-tracker/.

29. The number of undocumented immigrants is estimated to be between 2.35 and 2.6 million in California. The Migration Policy Institute places the estimate at 2.5 million adults ("Profile of the Unauthorized Population: California," Migration Policy Institute, accessed July 29, 2022, https://www.migrationpolicy.org/data/unauthorized-immigrant-population/state/CA) whereas Pew places the number at 2.2 million in total based on 2016 estimates ("U.S. Unauthorized Immigrant Population Estimates by State, 2016," Pew Research Center, updated February 5, 2019, https://www.pewresearch.org/hispanic/interactives/u-s-unauthorized-immigrants-by-state/; Joseph Hayes and Laura Hill, "Undocumented Immigrants in California," PPIC, March 2017, http://www.ppic.org/content/pubs/jtf/JTF_UndocumentedImmigrantsJTF.pdf; Bryan Baker, "Estimates of the Lawful Permanent Resident Population in the United States and the Subpopulation Eligible to Naturalize: 2019–2021," U.S. Department of Homeland Security, April 2022; "Weekly Report of Population as of July 27, 2022," Department of Corrections, State of California, Office of Research; the exact number was 92,423.

30. Baldassare et al., "California's Exclusive Electorate."

31. Abrajano and García Bedolla, "Latino Political Participation"; Eric McGhee, "California's Missing Voters," PPIC, June 2017.

32. California Secretary of State, "Historical Voter Registration and Participation in Statewide Primary Elections 1914–2022," and "Historical Voter Registration and Participation in Statewide General and Special Elections 1910–2021," State of California, n.d.

33. See Jan E. Leighley and Jonathan Nagler, *Who Votes Now? Demographics, Issues, Inequality, and Turnout in the United States* (Princeton and Oxford: Princeton University Press, 2014).

34. Mark Baldassare et al., "Californians and Their Government," PPIC, March 2022, https://www.ppic.org/wp-content/uploads/crosstabs-all-adults-0322.pdf. Respondents included 1,672 California residents, with a sampling error of +/–4.1 percent (at the 95 percent confidence level) for the unweighted sample.

35. Baldassare et al., "Californians and Their Government," PPIC, May 2021, https://www.ppic.org/publication/ppic-statewide-survey-californians-and-their-government-may-2021/; sampling error is +/–3.2 percent for the unweighted sample of 1,705 adults.

36. Mark Baldassare et al., "PPIC Statewide Survey: Californians and the Environment," PPIC, July 2021.

37. Dean Bonner and Rachel Lawler, "Voting Matters to Most Californians, but Many Don't Show Up," PPIC Blog, March 3, 2020, https://www.ppic.org/blog/voting-matters-to-most-californians-but-many-dont-show-up.

38. Mark Baldassare, Dean Bonner, Rachel Lawler, and Deja Thomas, "PPIC Statewide Survey: Californians and their Government," PPIC, May 2021.

39. Baldassare et al., "Californians and the Environment."

40. "California Legislature's 2016 Session Accomplishments Assessed by State Senator Hertzberg," Planning Report, September 2016, http://www.planningrep ort.com/2016/09/22/california-legislatur e-s-2016-session-accomplishments-ass essed-state-senator-hertzberg.

41. The reported number was $296.4 million. John Myers, "Newsletter: California Interest Groups Near the $300-Million Mark in Sacramento Lobbying," *Los Angeles Times, November 4, 2019.*

42. Patrick McGreevy, "Spending on Lobbying in California Tops $309 Million, the Second-Highest Amount Ever Recorded in the State," *Los Angeles Times, February 1, 2017.*

43. Per AB 571, beginning January 1, 2021, state contribution limits apply by default to city and county candidates if those governments have not adopted their own limits for such candidates. Limits are adjusted biennially for inflation. See the Fair Political Practices Commission's "Regulations" webpage for more information, https://w ww.fppc.ca.gov/the-law/fppc-regulations /regulations-index.html.

CHAPTER 11

1. In March 2022, PPIC reported that 37 percent of all Californians said that the cost of housing makes them and their family "seriously consider moving away from the part of California" they live in now, compared to 33 percent a year earlier (numbers were similar in 2019, at 35 percent); these are considerably higher percentages than in November 2004 when 15 percent gave that answer. The March 2022 results are based on 1,672 adult respondents, and the sampling error is +/–4.1 percent for the unweighted sample. See time trends for all adults: Mark Baldassare et al., "Californians and their Government," PPIC, March 2022, https://www.ppi c.org/wp-content/uploads/time-trends-a ll-adults-0322.pdf.

2. Mark Baldassare et al., "Californians and Their Government," Public Policy Institute of California (PPIC), May 2015. A total of 1,706 adults were surveyed; Sampling error was +/–3.6 percent.

3. The vehicle fuel tax rose to 53.9 cents per gallon on July 1, 2022.

4. For a study of these tendencies among Californians, see Kevin Wallsten and Gene Park, "Confidence, Perception, and Politics in California: The Determinants of Attitudes Toward Taxes by Level of Government," *California Journal of Politics and Policy* 7, no. 2 (2015).

5. Demographic Research Unit, "P-1D: Total Population by Total Hispanic and Non-Hispanic Race, 2010–2060 (2019 Baseline)," Department of Finance, State of California, accessed on July 17, 2022, https://dof. ca.gov/forecasting/demographics/proje ctions/.

6. Erica Frankenberg et al., "Harming Our Common Future: America's Segregated Schools 65 Years After *Brown*," The Civil Rights Project and the Center for Education and Civil Rights, May 10, 2019, https:// www.civilrightsproject.ucla.edu/researc h/k-12-education/integration-and-diversi ty/harming-our-common-future-america s-segregated-schools-65-years-after-br own/Brown-65-050919v4-final.pdf.

7. Demographic Research Unit, "P-1B Total Population by Individual Year of Age (2010– 2060)," Department of Finance, State of California, July 19, 2021, https://dof.ca.gov /forecasting/demographics/projections/.

8. Thad Kousser and Cassidy Reller, "Do Californians Still See Their State Moving in the Right Direction, or Do They See Themselves Moving out of California?" UC San Diego, Working Paper, July 2021, https://w ww.universityofcalifornia.edu/sites/defa ult/files/uc-san-diego-california-exodus -report.pdf.

9. Gavin Newsom, "California Five-Year Infrastructure Plan," Office of the Governor, State of California, 2022–23, https://w ww.ebudget.ca.gov/2022-Infrastructure -Plan.pdf. For overall infrastructure estimates (now dated), refer to Ellen Hanak, "Paying for Infrastructure: California's Choices," PPIC, January 2009, http://ww

w.ppic.org/content/pubs/atissue/AI_109
EHAI.pdf.

10. The median price of an existing single-family home sold in California in May 2022 hit an all-time high of $898,980 (Keeley Bosler, "Finance Bulletin," Department of Finance, State of California, June 2022) and decreased to $863,790 in June 2022, according to the California Association of Realtors®, "California Housing Market Snapshot," California Association of Realtors®, June 2022, https://www.car.org/market data/data/countysalesactivity.

11. Estimates vary, but in 2017 one report placed the shortfall at 3.5 million units by 2025, a number generally accepted by Governor Newsom (cited in his 2019–20 budget analysis) and the Legislative Analyst's Office. See "A Toolkit to Close California's Housing Gap," McKinsey and Company, 2016, https://www.mckinsey.c om/featured-insights/urbanization/closi ng-californias-housing-gap. For a different estimate, see "California's 3.5 Million Housing Shortage Raises Questions," The Embarcadero Institute, July 2019, https:// embarcaderoinstitute.com/portfolio-item s/3-5-million-california-housing-shortag e-number-is-wrong-fueling-poor-policy/.

12. According to the state Senate, Senate Bill 9 "streamlines the process for a homeowner to create a duplex or subdivide an existing lot," allowing no more than four units on a parcel; new dwellings must be "in keeping with the look of a neighborhood" and abide by local zoning requirements. See "SB 9, the California H.O.M.E. Act," California State Senate, accessed August 5, 2022, https://focus.senate.ca.go v/sb9.

13. Gabriel Petek, "The 2022–23 Budget: The Governor's Homelessness Plan," Legislative Analyst's Office, State of California, February 2022; Meghan Henry, Tanya de Sousa, Colette Tano, Nathaniel Dick, Rhaia Hull, Meghan Shea, Toni Morris, and Sean Morris, "The 2021 Annual Homeless Assessment Report to Congress, Part 1:

Point in Time," U.S. Department of Housing and Urban Development, February 2022, https://www.huduser.gov/portal/sit es/default/files/pdf/2021-AHAR-Part-1 .pdf.

14. A per-pupil figure of $22,893 is an estimate supplied by the Legislative Analyst's Office in August 2022 and could change based on final appropriations and spending. It includes funding provided under Prop 98 as well as all federal and local funds related to K–12 education in California. The ranking of California for per pupil spending against other states can be calculated using a variety of costs; for a discussion of how different formulas produce different rankings, see John Fensterwald, "How Does California Rank in per Pupil Spending? It All Depends," EdSource, February 20, 2017, https://edsource.org/2017/ how-does-california-rank-in-per-pupil-s pending-it-all-depends/577405.

15. These are annual estimated costs for 2022–23 for in-state tuition and fees and living expenses. Melanie Hanson, "Average Cost of College and Tuition," Education Data Initiative, updated June 12, 2022, https://ed ucationdata.org/average-cost-of-college ; "2022–23 Estimated Undergraduate Cost of Attendance," The California State University, accessed August 5, 2022, https://www .calstate.edu/attend/paying-for-college/D ocuments/cost-of-attendance.pdf; "Tuition and Cost of Attendance," Office of Admissions, University of California, accessed August 5, 2022, https://admission.university ofcalifornia.edu/tuition-financial-aid/tuition -cost-of-attendance/.

16. Kristin Lewis and Sarah Burd-Sharps, "A Portrait of California, 2014–2015," California Human Development Report, Measure of America, December 9, 2014, http://www .measureofamerica.org/california2014 -15.

17. Mark Baldassare et al., "Statewide Survey: Californians and their Government," PPIC, January 2021 and May 2022. The January 2021 survey included 1,703 adults and the sampling error was +/–3.3

percent; the May 2022 findings were based on 1,702 adults surveyed, margin of error +/−3.9 percent.

18. Ian James, "Western Drought is Worst in 1,200 Years, Intensified by Climate Change, Study Finds," *Los Angeles Times*, February 14, 2022, https://www.latimes.com/environment/story/2022-02-14/western-megadrought-driest-in-1200-years.

19. "The ShakeOut Scenario," California Geological Survey (CGS) Preliminary Report 25; U.S. Geological Survey Open File Report 2008, 1150 Version 1, 2008: 11, http://pubs.usgs.gov/of/2008/1150; Rui Chen and Chris Willis, "Update of HAZUS Annualized Earthquake Loss Estimates for California, 2016 Analysis," Department of Conservation, September 2016, https://www.conservation.ca.gov/cgs/Pages/Program-SHP/2016_Analysis.aspx.

20. Mark Baldassare et al., "Californians and the Environment," PPIC, July 2019; Mark Baldassare et al., "Californians and the Environment," PPIC, July 2022. In July 2020, 1,706 adult Californians were interviewed and the sampling error was +/−3.4 percent; in July 2022 the sample size was 1,648 and the sampling error was +/−3.4 percent.

21. In 2021, a reported 6,843 Californians died of opioid-related overdoses. See California Overdose Surveillance Dashboard, California Department of Public Health, accessed August 6, 2022, https://skylab.cdph.ca.gov/ODdash/?tab=Home.

22. Lewis and Burd-Sharps, "A Portrait of California," 7, and Kristen Lewis, "A Portrait of California, 2021–22," Measure of America (New York: Social Science Research Council, 2021), 12.

23. "Recall" rights for some service sector employees were enshrined in SB 93. AB 1066 was passed in 2016 and, starting January 1, 2022, gave agricultural workers the right to receive overtime pay after 8 hours per day or 40 hours per week if employed by a company with 26 or more employees; those working for employers with 25 or fewer employees must be paid overtime after 9.5 hours of work or 55 hours per week.

24. Bureau of Labor Statistics, "State Employment and Unemployment Summary," U.S. Department of Labor, July 22, 2022, https://www.bls.gov/news.release/laus.nr0.htm; "Best States for Business: California (2019 Ranking)," *Forbes.com*, November 2019, https://www.forbes.com/places/ca/#13abe113fefc. The ranking has not been updated as of this writing.

25. A. Park Williams et al., "Large Contribution from Anthropogenic Warming to an Emerging North American Megadrought," *Science* 368, no. 6488 (April 17, 2020), https://www.science.org/doi/10.1126/science.aaz9600.

26. Maven's Notebook, "Delta Conveyance Project," updated February 7, 2021, https://mavensnotebook.com/delta-conveyance-project/?doing_wp_cron=1660103826.3143339157104492187500; "Delta Conveyance," Department of Water Resources, State of California, accessed August 7, 2022, https://water.ca.gov/deltaconveyance.

27. Local roadways include more than 183,067 lane miles of city streets and 146,594 lane miles of county roads; plus there are 15,606 lane miles managed by federal agencies and 1,839 miles managed by state parks and other agencies: 399,145 lane miles in all. Reported mileage fluctuates year over year because different systems to measure roadway miles (national Highway Performance Monitoring System and state Linear Referencing System) are continually being realigned. See Table 1 in "California 2020 Public Road Data," Department of Transportation, State of California, December 2021, https://dot.ca.gov/-/media/dot-media/programs/research-innovation-system-information/documents/california-public-road-data/prd-2020-a11y.pdf.

28. Dan Kammen noted that "California is not a nation, but it's behaving as one" in an article on climate change. Rachel Uranga, "California Governor's Green Swing through China," *Long Beach Press Telegram*, June 10, 2017.

29. "California Legislature's 2016 Session Accomplishments Assessed by State Senator Hertzberg," The Planning Report, September 2016, http://www.planningreport.com/2016/09/22/california-legislatures-2016-session-accomplishments-assessed-state-senator-hertzberg.

INDEX